Un-American Activities: Countercultural Themes In Christianity

A modern father and a postmodern daughter reflect on their pilgrimages of life and faith

Tom Wilkens
Kim Wilkens

Fairway Press
Lima, Ohio

FIRST EDITION
Copyright © 2009 by
Tom Wilkens and Kim Wilkens

Scripture quotations are from:
The New Revised Standard Version of the Bible, copyright 1989 by the Division of Christian Education of the National Council of the Churches of Christ in the USA. Used by permission.

The King James Version of the Bible, in the public domain.

The Contemporary English Version of the Bible, copyright 1995 by the American Bible Society. Used by permission.

The Holy Bible, New International Version. Copyright © 1973, 1978, 1984 International Bible Society. Used by permission of Zondervan Bible Publishers. All rights reserved.

The Revised Standard Version of the Bible, copyrighted 1946, 1952 ©, 1971, 1973, by the Division of Christian Education of the National Council of the Churches of Christ in the USA. Used by permission.

Library Of Congress Control Number. 2009930516

ISBN-13: 978-0-7880-2230-2
ISBN-10: 0-7880-2230-X

PRINTED IN USA

Soli Deo gloria

TABLE OF CONTENTS

ACKNOWLEDGMENTS

We wish to acknowledge the contributions of many people to our writing project. First, thanks to Karen Hett, Dr. Allene Booth-Judson, Professor Norman A. Beck, the Reverend Dan Biles, the Reverend Dr. Darrel Gilbertson, Julie Thorsheim, Dr. Adam Blatner, Virginia Wilcox, Gerri Giddings, and the Reverend John Herman for their feedback on shared portions of our draft manuscript.

Our thanks also to Tom's siblings/Kim's aunt and uncles — Sue Bishop, Dr. Jim Wilkens, and Frank Wilkens — for their validation of many of the memories shared in this book. And we appreciate son/brother Dr. Nick Wilkens for his responses to our work and wife/mother Betty for her Foreword and Afterword, and for the encouragement we received from both of them.

Kim is thankful for the support of her husband, Tom Herrick, and son, Xander, of this writing project and grateful for the encouragement she received from her community of faith at Peace Lutheran Church, especially her discipleship group of Jenny Cudahy, Lore Amlinger, and Carey Hess.

Finally, we offer our special gratitude to Professor Mark Allan Powell, Bishop Emeritus Paul J. Blom, and Pastor Jim Taylor for their endorsements of our work that appear on the back cover of the book.

This list of acknowledgments could be much longer, for both of us have learned so much from so many people on our pilgrimages of life and faith. We have thought of them often as we remembered and reflected and wrote. We will never forget their service to us.

Tom Wilkens
Kim Wilkens

FOREWORD

We live in a time of fractured relationships and division among people. There is need for dialogue in our families, churches, our nation, and the world at large that requires us to be intentional in how we bridge differences of opinions and beliefs in the communities in which we live, particularly our families. In every encounter there is an opportunity to learn from one another and have respect for differing people and perspectives. There can be richness in embracing diversity that expands our horizons in how we think and relate to others.

In our country we speak a common language, yet the words we use take on different meaning depending on our personal history. What can be more dismaying is that judgments are made of other people with respect to color, creed, and the community in which they live. The first challenge for those of you who read this book is to allow my husband, Tom, and our daughter, Kim, to tell their stories and observations. Even though you may not agree with them, hear them out. There will be many of you who are searching as Kim is and others who have had life experiences that resonate with Tom's journey.

Over the years, I have heard most of the homilies that Tom has included in this book. In the classroom, he was good at presenting different sides of controversial subjects and giving his students the challenge of forming their own conclusions that they then had to defend. In his homilies, Tom offers perspectives, conclusions, and challenges to the listeners. When giving a sermon, he has always spoken from a manuscript that is developed from much research, fine tuning of language, and practice in delivery to give the right emphasis to the words to make them carry the desired impact. Use of language is very important to him.

Sometimes he would ask that I read what he had written before he would deliver it to an intended audience. I am quite sensitive to controversial subjects and ways of saying them; there usually was something in most of his homilies that made me uncomfortable. My reaction was noted and sometimes Tom did soften the language by using words that still communicated what he wanted to convey but in a less shocking way. Now when I reread the homilies I find they were prophetic for those times, and still are. Many people have recognized this and have appreciated someone who could say what could be difficult to verbalize and open opportunity for further discussion and dialogue.

The title of this book is long and loaded with meaning. Tom has asked that I write a foreword to this book, not a disclaimer. However, if it were the latter I could say I do not much like the title of the book, not just that it is too long but it contains the words "un-American activities." The phrase bothers me and probably has kept a number of people from even getting past the cover. It is an example of how words carry weight as interpreted from the reader's perspective. There are many subtle ways one conforms to the culture in which one lives. Yet when one reads the following chapters that point to this recurring theme, one can appreciate and evaluate how pervasive one's own culture is and how it affects the way in which scripture is interpreted, judgments are made, and beliefs are formulated. In the introductory remarks to each chapter, Tom shares the way in which his background shaped him and then he elaborates on discerning faith because of it, apart from it, or in spite of it, followed by the homilies that he wrote and presented some years earlier.

It was quite amazing to us that our daughter, Kim, wanted to take on reacting formally to what her father has written. She is currently going through a time in her life where she is giving voice to her search for ways to express and to grow in faith and service. Kim's responses are to the point and easily understood; they are of a new reality of an Emerging Church that defies definition. Her ongoing transformation is easier to observe. Both father and daughter are learning from one another as they clearly have their own perspectives. They are gifted in seeing new insights or ways of defining elements of faith as they communicate from their perspectives.

There can indeed be tension created when dealing with different perspectives and world-views on a personal level. Even though I like order and tradition, I appreciate new ways of seeing and understanding. I am excited by the possibilities where inclusion of people of diverse backgrounds is promoted even when it requires a humbling personal admission of lack of empathy or involvement. The books that I have read on the Emerging Church movement help to peel away layers of theology that have accumulated over the centuries in order to cut to the core of what Jesus' ministry was and how it can be meaningful and life-changing in today's world.

There is clarity in the Emerging Church's message, especially for those who are outside of a traditional church background, that offers language and ideas for ways of being the church that are more easily understood than the traditional religious terminology that goes with liturgy, hymns, prayers, and even the way we talk about our faith. It is refreshing to have something that can be experienced as mundane or routine take on new life by the way it is verbalized. I have experienced this in conversation with international friends and while working on service-mission projects outside of our country. When I don't have the crutch of familiar settings and ways of doing things, I am more open to new insights as I am exposed to a different reality. Small group discussions, whether reviewing a book or in Bible study, can also have this stimulating effect of taking one to places and people outside of one's own environment. Young children can provoke us to think in new ways when expressing thoughts that are not biased by their environment. Students involved in global studies in the classroom or on an international study program have opportunities for transforming experiences.

These are some of the ways I personally have found helpful in breaking down the barriers to communication, to overcome preconceptions, prejudices, or to deal with controversial issues that transcend the confines of where we are perhaps too comfortable. I want to grow in ways that open me up to the needs of others. Along with this are the questions and uncertainties of how to do this. I believe the Spirit of God can be most active in our lives when we are willing to listen to voices with different perspectives.

For those who read what a father and a daughter have written, the hope is that you will enter into the dialogue as well and that you will wrestle with the core beliefs that give life to your faith journey.

Betty Wilkens

PREFACE

This book emerges from a collaborative effort by me; my wife, Betty; our daughter, Kim; and our son, Nick. It did not begin that way. It began with encouragement from the family that I do some writing in my retirement. My initial idea was to build something around a selection of sermons, papers, and articles that I had given or written over the last half of my tenure as professor of theology at Texas Lutheran University and the subsequent years of my retirement. I thought that it might be an interesting exercise to provide background essays detailing the historical contexts, both personal and public, out of which each of them came. This could accomplish two purposes. First, it might render the original material more understandable and relevant to the general reader. Second, it might be of some special interest to those who deliver homilies and make other theological presentations to see explicit deliberations about the effect of context on my work as occasions for thinking about the interaction of context and content in their own.

It then occurred to me that it would make the project more interesting and helpful to involve our son, Nick. He holds degrees in English (BA), theology (MA), and marriage and family therapy (PhD). He is rostered as a Diaconal Minister by the ELCA (Evangelical Lutheran Church in America). Nick currently directs an ecumenical clinic that provides counseling services in a region of south central Texas east of San Antonio. Initially I asked him to write some essays responding to the material I had written. He declined due to demands on his time that included a writing project — a book — of his own. I then pointed out that he was uniquely qualified to provide some editorial assistance in the initial writing stage, giving us valuable feedback from his multi-disciplinary background. He did agree to this task.

Next, our daughter, Kim, began sharing with us a journal about her spiritual pilgrimage. Many of her insights had points of contact with my reflections — not at all, I think, rooted directly in my writing but which nonetheless took issue with or went further than some of my thoughts. Kim writes out of her experience as a computer consultant and teacher, wife and mother, a thoughtful, probing woman, and — in recent years — a social justice advocate. I asked for her participation in this project and she quickly agreed. She would write the responsive essays to my homilies, papers, and accompanying background essays.

Finally, Betty's role would be to provide a Foreword and an Afterword. She thus gets the first and last words, sharing reflections as the wife and mother of the book's co-authors. Betty writes on a rich tapestry of life woven from many years of active participation and leadership in the church (ranging from Sunday school teacher to church council member to chair of a Synod committee), from a diverse career as nurse and childbirth educator, from long participation in book club discussions and continuing education programs, and from several decades of providing the human and humane ground zero base for our family.

The first part of the title of this collection of reflections, *Un-American Activities*, comes from a US House of Representatives Committee (1938-1975) with the same name. That Committee's charter required it to investigate and rein in activities that it viewed as being counter to the interests of America. It did so, often with excessive, embarrassing, and destructive zeal.

I mean something quite different. I hold that there are some counter-cultural motifs in Christianity that imply — indeed oblige — resistance to certain ideas, values, and practices widely approved in our society. As I reviewed my work of the past quarter of a century, it became evident that this was one of the most recurrent thoughts. Kim concurs that this notion is central to her own emerging understanding of Christian life and faith. It is not, it should be noted, the only issue. But it is pervasive enough to add *Countercultural Themes in Christianity* to the title of our book. Our list of conflicts with culture, you will discover, differs markedly from lists utilized by many American Christians in recent decades.

The book's subtitle, *A modern father and a postmodern daughter reflect on their pilgrimages of life and faith*, assumes two truths about parents and adult children of today. First, often there is a profound difference in point of view between them that must be taken into account if significant communication is to take place. This entails more than the perennial generation gap. It involves a sea change in perspective from post-enlightenment modernism to postmodernism. Another *Weltanshauung*, or worldview, is sweeping western culture. I grieve a loss; my daughter celebrates a gain (see her essay in chapter 1).

Second, the chasm between modernism and postmodernism can be bridged. It does take time, honesty, and the desire to build the bridge. Both Kim and I discover that we have the desire. I have her at an advantage with respect to time spent, though surely not time left. She has a long lead with respect to honesty: her essays speak of her personal odyssey in life and faith with a tone, depth, and intimacy that induce a troubled silence in me, the silence of a father's pain at a daughter's anguish.

But silence, uninterrupted silence, is not sufficient. Many adult family members find it difficult to initiate conversation about things that matter deeply, things such as faith and hope and love. We have discovered, in sharing segments of the draft manuscript with our friends and extended family and then receiving requests to use the material as discussion-starters in their own families, that this book has potential to serve as the basis — or at least a point of departure — for meaningful dialogue between adult children and their parents. We would be most pleased if it can serve that function for you.

Kim offers responses to my material, both to the recently written background essays and to the earlier homilies, papers, and articles. In general, she finds the optimism of enlightenment-generated modernism about our ability to sort things out in coherent, consistent, and encompassing rational and moral systems unwarranted and irrelevant at best, arrogant and counter-productive at worst. She shares the postmodern pessimism about such endeavors. She also clearly shares a pessimism about the growing irrelevance of much of mainstream Protestantism, which has led her to participate with passion and creativity in a contemporary protest phenomenon sometimes identified as the Emerging Church (see especially chapters 7, 12, 21, 24, and 30). What we share together is the view that there are pressing intellectual, theological, and moral issues confronting us that require responses, both theoretical and practical. This collection of writings is a montage of our efforts to meet those challenges.

You are invited to engage in these deliberations. You should know that while both Kim and Betty have had opportunities to react to my work, I have not responded to theirs. I have modified the content of neither the original homilies and papers nor the subsequent background essays as they have reacted to both. Our intent is not that we engage simply in an in-house and thereby somewhat circular dialogue, with our differences resolved and loose ends tied together. Rather, the hope is that lines of thought will lead out of our "house" — that is, outside of our small family sphere — from me to them and then to you. While Betty has the last word in our book, you should have the last word in the reflective enterprise that the book is intended to encourage.

Each chapter of the book follows the same format. First, I provide a background essay to a particular homily, paper, or article, detailing in an autobiographical fashion its personal and public contexts. Second, I share that homily, paper or article. These appear, chapter by chapter in chronological order, dating from 1983 to 2007. Third, Kim presents a response.

Let me make some general observations about my contributions to this volume. For Christian pastors and theologians, communication with an audience or a readership involves constant interaction between content and context. The messages to be proclaimed or taught (content) have often been embedded in cultures distant in both space and time (context). Those messages must be understood in their originating contexts and then retrieved. Biblical scholars call this work *exegesis*, which means leading or reading *out of* texts the meanings in their originating contexts. The opposite of exegesis, and much more easily done, is called *eisegesis*: reading *into* biblical or other historical texts the messages that we want to find there. Even assuming, however, that proper exegesis has been done, to stop at this point would render sermons (in this book more typically called homilies) little more than exercises in data-sharing about matters of historical interest.

Therefore, the messages must be recontextualized into present-day times and places. We call this hermeneutics, or interpretation. The preacher serves much the same function as Hermes, messenger from the gods to humans in Greek mythology, but without the advantage that Hermes had of being one of the gods himself. The whole procedure, exegesis and hermeneutics, is complicated by the fact that the exegete/interpreter operates out of a context not only remote from the originating cultures of the biblical material but also at least somewhat different than the micro- or personal cultures of the people in the target audience. It is thus difficult and at times daunting work.

There are, to be sure, different methods for accomplishing these goals. I begin with the approach of modern critical biblical and historical scholarship. I have engaged in this type of analytical study for half a century. Modern critical scholars assume that both the author (including the input of oral storytellers, writers, and editors in the case of much of the biblical literature) and the reader play key roles in determining a text's meaning and purpose, with the author's function at least as important if not even more significant than that of the reader. The contributions of historical criticism come mainly in the area of exegesis — that is, in the attempt to understand texts as they developed in their originating contexts. In my hermeneutics — that is, my efforts to render the messages retrieved by exegesis relevant in the contemporary world — I have been especially influenced by two relatively recent phenomena called liberation theology (with its focus on this world, not the next) and process theology (with its emphasis on change, not permanence), influences that will become more evident as this book unfolds.

There are many variations of the modern critical approach to the Bible, but there are also many other approaches. I will mention just two: postmodernism and fundamentalism. Starting from quite different premises, postmodern scholars claim that, because language is so inherently unstable and shifting, the reader rather than the author plays the central role in determining a text's significance. Postmodernism's way of analyzing literature is commonly called *deconstruction*: breaking down texts into component parts. Those parts — when shorn of their traditional biases, assumptions, and ideologies — are not perceived to be sources for timeless truths or universal values. Rather, the smaller components are understood to convey individual chunks of human experience. The primary or even the sole concern of the deconstructionist is to determine the current relevance of those text-borne experiences. The focus is thus on interpretation, on discerning the sense and practical implications of literature within contemporary contexts, and not on exegesis.

There is also the approach of fundamentalism, specifically biblical fundamentalism. Biblical fundamentalists subscribe to a theory of verbal inspiration of the biblical literature, to a corollary of verbal inerrancy of the Bible, and thereby to the importance of not going beyond a literal understanding of the divinely inspired biblical texts. They hold that the original writers did not leave their own imprints on the literature; nor, they argue, should contemporary readers.

Different assumptions lead not only to different approaches but also to different constraints. Fundamentalists, in embracing literalism, admit to little if any subjectivity in working with texts (see comments on my past link with biblical fundamentalism in chapter 7). Postmodernists, in embracing deconstructionism, consider little if any objectivity to be possible (see Kim's remarks about the interpretation of scripture in her essay in chapter 24). Modernists, in embracing historical criticism, bring as much objectivity as they can muster to the task of exegesis, yet all the while acknowledging that they also bring a subjectivity conditioned by history to every text. Modernists then exercise a less restrained subjectivity in the task of interpretation, in applying the messages discovered through exegesis to current personal and social realities. They do, however, seek some objectivity in analyzing and understanding those realities — using in particular the social sciences toward those ends.

I belong to that group of modernists who believe that the breath of God, that is, the Holy Spirit, infuses the whole process — authoring and editing the literature originally, canonizing certain texts as authoritative for the life and faith of the community, transmitting those texts over the centuries, and reading them today — yet without destroying the human marks on that process. As a Christian modernist, I have more latitude in dealing with biblical material than Christian fundamentalists but less than Christian postmodernists.

I make no claim to have mastered the modern approach to texts. The results in this volume will make that abundantly clear. What I hope to do is to make the preacher's and scholar's history and experience — that is, their historically-conditioned subjectivity — more transparent as factors in the final outcome of such an approach. Each of the largely autobiographical background essays attempts to give context helpful for understanding references, perceptions, and perspectives in the homily, paper, or article that follows it. Perhaps the reader will find it a useful exercise in self-understanding as he or she follows my attempt to sort out the process by which an author produces a theological product, not in an abstract theoretical manner but in a concrete autobiographical way.

It turns out that modern theologians and scientists share a common operational effort: approximation. Modern scientists seek to approximate truth about the world by a method called experimental. The method of modern biblical scholars and historical theologians, briefly depicted above, differs but the goal is similar: an approximation of truth, in this case the truth of formative and normative documents for the Christian community such as the Bible, creeds, and confessions of faith. The pastor is the most significant practitioner of approximating and then sharing this truth when engaged in the activities called *homiletics* (preaching) and *catechetics* (teaching).

My own output of homilies, papers, and articles is far less than that of most pastors and professors. I stand in considerable awe of those preachers who, week in and week out, fulfill their obligation of "speaking the truth in love" (Ephesians 4:15). And I have enormous admiration for those teaching colleagues who, over the years, found the time and energy to write far more articles and give far more papers than I did. On the other hand, my paucity of product will make this book a shorter and less expensive read.

We offer it to pastors, teachers, seminarians, and other students as an encouragement for practical self-awareness. Socrates once observed that the unexamined life is not worth living. This pertains as well to faith, to the tasks of faithful proclamation and pedagogy, and to the ways of expressing love and justice in the world: they should be subject to recurring scrutiny. We also offer the book to those who neither preach nor teach as an opportunity to catch a glimpse of the challenging work of articulating the Word in the contemporary world.

At another level, this book documents some exterior and interior aspects of two different pilgrimages of life and faith. Mine has been longer in time and much longer in physical distance. It has included a series of experiences that began in Latin America in the 1980s and has continued around the globe to the present day. Kim's consciousness of pilgrimage has emerged more recently and the odyssey itself has been much more inward, triggered by the circumstances of her life in North America — though it has taken increasingly outward expression in the past several years. We offer this record of our pilgrimages both as a foil for those who are taking and reflecting on their own journeys and as an encouragement for others to begin or, in many cases, to become more fully aware of pilgrimages they are already on.

Our writing styles are dissimilar and, although we lived in the same household for eighteen years, in many ways our lifestyles and points of view have been unalike. Yet it appears that, a quarter of a century later, we are now on the same page — though we still read it with quite different eyes.

Tom Wilkens
Georgetown, Texas
Epiphany 2009

CHAPTER 1

RISKY BUSINESS

Background essay

Tom Wilkens

The piece that follows, titled "Risky business," did not originate as an article published to popularize important developments in the global church, although this later became one of its purposes. It began rather as an exercise in liturgical desperation. Late one Saturday evening in January of 1983, I received a phone call from our campus pastor. He was ill, he said, and could not lead the campus congregation's worship in the morning. He asked me to fill in for him and I agreed to do so. But I had no sermon or homily prepared and no real "barrel" or file from which to draw an older homily that could be revised and reused.

Consequently I based my homily the next morning on something that I, as a professor, could quite quickly prepare: an exam. I was at the time teaching a course on liberation theology. So I wrote a test, made copies, and distributed them at the beginning of the homily period. After giving the congregants time to take and score the exam, I then elaborated the meaning of their answers in light of themes and developments in liberation theology. It seemed to work: in addition to gracious compliments, I got some expressions of consternation at the end of the service. Perhaps the old adage that preaching should comfort the afflicted and afflict the comfortable applied in this instance.

Certain expressions of liberation theology, especially those arising out of Latin American environments, hold not only that there are intimate connections among liturgy, theology, and life but also that these connections are essential to the integrity of Christianity. Theology that is not

1

rooted in liturgy and liturgy that is not rooted in life — the whole of life — are fraudulent. The older I get, the more I agree. Most of the occasions in which my theological perspective has come into sharper and more relevant focus have been times when I was preparing to preach; that is, when I was attempting to connect liturgy, theology, and life. Such occasions were not that frequent, yet this factor in itself gave me the opportunity each time to listen, to see, and to hone the message and interpret the mission in some detail and with some precision. It was at those points that my own theological formation received its most definitive expression.

It had become evident to me by this time that while I had some insight into the phenomenon of liberation theology — or, more accurately, the phenomena of liberation theologies — I was not in a position to understand or appreciate them in much more than a superficial, theoretical way. I needed to become a part of the actual life settings out of which these movements were arising. I was particularly interested in Latin American liberation theology. I had already set in motion a process to learn Spanish and to experience firsthand those communities in which liberation theology was taking shape. I would go to Cuernavaca, Mexico, in the summer of 1983 to do language study and there, through the good offices of the Augsburg House that was affiliated with the Center for Global Education program of Augsburg College in Minneapolis, gain some access to base Christian communities so central to Latin American liberation theology. This was for me the first of several transforming experiences over the next 25 years.

Prior to all of this, I had begun to organize a symposium dedicated to highlighting key voices of liberation theology: voices from black theology, feminist theology, Mexican-American liberation theology, and Latin American liberation theology. I titled the symposium "Liberation: Common Hope in a Complex Hemisphere." All of the people mentioned in the following article — James Cone, Rosemary Radford Ruether, Virgilio Elizondo, Gustavo Gutiérrez, and Jon Sobrino — agreed to participate, though Gutiérrez was at the last moment prevented from leaving his home country of Peru. Sponsored by Texas Lutheran, the three-day event in February of 1984 drew a large audience of people from across the state and nation as well as from the ranks of the student body, faculty, and administration. On campus, at any rate, I became identified with the voices of liberation. I was not averse to that identification.

2

Liberation theology is celebrating its fortieth birthday. It continues to change, to evolve, and to precipitate controversy. In the meantime, there is this new kid on the block: another way of understanding the faith, of living as disciples, of dealing with Christian tradition, of functioning as church. As a movement in the world, it is called postmodernism. As a movement in the community of Christ, it is often called the Emerging Church. Kim and I will comment on these developments as we continue to elaborate our postmodern and modern pilgrimages and perspectives.

It turns out that one of the North American expressions of liberation theology, black theology, was freshly relevant in the recent US presidential primary season. James Cone, mentioned in the article that follows and one of the key founders of the black theology movement, has had a significant influence on many black Christian communities and people — including the Reverend Jeremiah Wright, former pastor to Barack Obama.

Cone's theology contains intense anger: anger with the history of injustice that whites have visited upon blacks, and anger with modern black collusion with that injustice. His message was, and still is, a strong countercultural call to confront the injustice and to find a course for black participation in American life in more just, less destructive ways. Cone's rhetoric is filled with hyperbole: he often overstates his social and political diagnoses and prescriptions. Such exaggeration is not uncommon among prophets and reformers, including Martin Luther, the founder of the Christian stream in which I currently swim.

Pastor Wright reads the works of James Cone and is thereby mentored by Cone. Wright clearly does not want to be counted among the blacks who collude with white racism. Obama had been mentored by Pastor Wright, but found himself in disagreement with Wright's more contentious and divisive views.

I understand Obama's dilemma. I have a similar relationship with Luther. For the most part I agree with his perspective, but I find that I must distance myself from certain of his excesses — such as his inflammatory and ultimately deadly condemnation of the hurting, rebellious peasants in the south of Germany in 1525 and the increasingly vitriolic anti-Semitism of his later years. Still, the things Luther got wrong do not invalidate the larger number of things he got right and do not set him beyond the pale of either the Christian or the human community. It may not be possible to

3

be countercultural, at least not countercultural in a manner that actually awakens and energizes people, without occasionally going "over the top" in ways that are inappropriate and at times harmful. If we require perfect mentors, we will have no mentors. At their imperfect best, mentors help to create critical people, not uncritical protégés.

Risky business[1]

Tom Wilkens

It's test time. You've had no warning, but that's okay. Your answers will not depend on study. For each question you must choose between two alternatives — even if you agree or disagree with both — by circling either 1 or 2. This is not a scientifically designed exam. If you answer honestly, though, you may learn something about yourself and your faith.

A. Which title for Jesus is more important to understanding his identity and mission?
   1. Servant of God
   2. Savior of humankind
B. Which description of the Christian message is more basic to comprehending its primary function and effect?
   1. Subvert what is negative, destructive, and dehumanizing in life
   2. Affirm what is positive, true, good, and beautiful in life
C. Which phrase is more fundamental to what it means to be a Christian?
   1. Following Jesus as a disciple
   2. Knowing Jesus as the Redeemer
D. Which practice is more necessary for becoming and remaining faithful children of God?
   1. Solidarity with the poor through sacrificial living in the world
   2. Solidarity with the saints through sacramental worship in the church
E. Which way of helping others is more in tune with an authentic expression of Christian love?

4

Question	Secular	Soft-secular	Christian
How should your enemies be treated?	I'll retaliate and get even	I'll forgive if...	I'll forgive and pray
On whom should you rely?	I am self-reliant	I believe in God, but trust myself	I'll trust God
How do you follow Jesus?	Why follow— religion is a crutch	I'll fit Jesus into my agenda	I'll be shaped by Jesus' agenda
How should you serve others?	It's all about me	I'll decide where, when, how, and whom to serve	I'll be a servant
What is life all about?	Being successful	Doing good deeds and feeling good about myself	Making a difference

Chapter Endnotes

1. "Risky business," *The Lutheran Standard* (August 10, 1984), 8-10. Published subsequently as "The risk of loving boldly," *The Lutheran* (October 3, 1984), 12-14. This article was used as background reading for participants in travel seminars sponsored by the Center for Global Education (see ch. 3).
2. Mike Slaughter, *The great requirement*, 2004 Ginghamsburg Change Conference, October 7, 2004.
3. Pastor John Herman, based on a message delivered at Peace Lutheran Church, Charlottesville, VA, November 20, 2004.

CHAPTER 2

LUTHERAN DISDAIN FOR THE EPISTLE OF JAMES

Background essay

Tom Wilkens

The first word about context for the homily that follows has to do with my position at Texas Lutheran, a college when I came in 1968 and a university when I left in 1999.[1] It has a current enrollment of 1,300 to 1,400 students; during my tenure there enrollment hovered between 900 and 1,100. Students and faculty could thus become well acquainted. Texas Lutheran is a liberal arts institution — some prefer the expression arts and sciences as a more accurate label — affiliated with the Evangelical Lutheran Church in America.

Throughout my time at Texas Lutheran, the chapel schedule remained the same: Monday, Wednesday, and Friday mornings from 10:00 until 10:20. Students, staff, and faculty all had opportunities to lead chapel services, under the gentle guidance of the campus pastor. At this particular time John Bade, mentioned in the following homily, held that position. Attendance was voluntary and in light of that fact, I must say, amazingly good.

I would typically lead a chapel service once or twice during the academic year. It was a challenge in a number of ways, not the least of which was the tight time frame. The homily could take no more than twelve minutes. This required good discipline and preparation. In my own case, I met the time constraint by becoming a manuscript preacher: I wrote, and rewrote again and again, each homily out completely. I would then practice it enough so that, though I was reading, it would not seem that I was doing so.

The second word about context deals with a series of experiences in Latin America. I prepared and delivered the homily titled "Lutheran disdain for the epistle of James" after three personally significant journeys to Latin America. I have already mentioned the summer of 1983 in Cuernavaca, Mexico, for language study. It was there that I had my first experience with *comunidades de base*, base communities — more typically referred to as base Christian communities in the English-speaking world. Probably the best introduction that I can give to a base Christian community is to share an afternoon with Ireneo and Alicia on a return visit to their Cuernavaca neighborhood in 1986. I had lived with them during the Spanish-language study program in the summer of 1983 and had gone back to see them again in 1984.

Alicia ran the *casa*, the house; Irineo ran the *tienda*, a small and sparsely stocked grocery shop located in the street-side front room of the house. They lived in a poor neighborhood and they shared the poverty. They also shared something else: themselves. Irineo and Alicia had become participants in a neighborhood base Christian community many years earlier. Base communities are groups that gather for singing, sharing, Bible study, prayer, and social action.[2] In time Irineo and Alicia became missionaries, forming new groups all over Cuernavaca. These two were marginalized people, people on the cutting edge of poverty. And yet several days each month they closed their shop early and went out to share the Word.

One afternoon they invited me along to a large *colonia* (neighborhood) on the edge of the city. In Mexico, the poorest of the poor live in the suburbs. We had to take a taxi. Irineo was crippled; he could scarcely walk the last few hundred yards over the dirt and stone "street." He was nine years younger than I; he looked a decade older. Poverty sucks, literally, the lifeline of the poor.

The meeting began with a song and four people. It ended with a prayer and fourteen people. In between, Irineo led a Bible study based on the epistle and gospel lessons to be read in the parish church the next Sunday. His own observations about the texts were augmented by comments that he coaxed out of the others. They were not used to this: the

14

group had been meeting for only three or four months. But they obviously treasured the opportunity to express an opinion and have it valued, especially the women. Irineo also invited comments from me, and I made a few. However, mostly I was listening and marveling: marveling at Irineo's leadership skills (Irineo had only learned to read and write after he had been elected as his base community's secretary); at the readiness with which these people related to the texts; and at the insights that emerged.

Later we rejoined Alicia, who had been leading a different group in a nearby part of the *colonia*. And then it was back to their home/shop, where we said our goodbyes for the third time in three years. Why did I keep returning? Why did I have such enormous respect and affection for these folks? And why did I not feel at all uncomfortable in their milieu, so different from my own? I still have not sorted it all out.

That day ended in tranquility; the next with anger and frustration. In the following days I became somewhat depressed about my own diminished humanity. I recorded my impressions of that time in a journal. Stoics, it turns out, probably should not write journals. Journals amplify both pleasure and pain. Stoics, and I have often tried to be one, are averse to such disturbances of their equanimity.

The home base group to which Irineo and Alicia belonged had a project to which the participants contributed: medicine for Nicaraguans. What a pitiful world: the poor of Cuernavaca trying to stave off the misdirected wealth of the US, which was being used to support a violent insurgency. Those poor had already won. The prize? A level of humanity and wholeness most of us have either never seen or, having seen, do not recognize.

I once heard a Boy Scout leader observe that each year when the scouts went out to retrieve bags for donations they had left on doorsteps the previous weekend, they might as well not have canvassed the wealthy neighborhoods. Almost none of the bags were filled and set out. The rate of return was better in the middle class neighborhoods, but best of all in the neighborhoods of the poor. The poor know about need: the need for food and clothing and shelter and, above all, the need for the hope that expressions of care can give. The poor of Cuernavaca, I should like to note, contributed three semi-truckloads of medicine plus food and clothing to the even poorer Nicaraguans who had fled from the *Contra* war of terror and were housed in UN-monitored refugee camps in southern Mexico.

I must make a remark on the irony of insurgency. The US was funding the enormously destructive and deadly *Contra* insurgence in Nicaragua at the time of this visit. We have a quite different attitude toward and policy with respect to insurgency today, now that we are on the receiving and not just the sponsoring end.

I may have at least a partial answer to the question about my absence of discomfort with the poor: the seed was planted in my childhood. My family, though thoroughly middle class, nonetheless affiliated with the congregation in our hometown that — more than the others — served and attracted the poor of the community. My mother, through both the congregation where she worshipped and the county home extension office where she volunteered, made it a point to assist youth from poor families, especially the girls, by providing instruction in domestic skills and encouragement to pursue post-high school education. She did both tasks successfully.

But Mother did not just model solidarity with the poor. She gently prompted me to participate. One way that I did was to attend church-sponsored youth meetings, sometimes held in the homes of the poor. One of those homes was a converted chicken coop. What was problematic about my attendance was that occasionally my hair would become infested with lice. What became evident was that this was a price I had to pay to continue my friendship with my poor peers. I still remember the noxious-smelling liquid that my mother would use on my scalp each time it happened and her infectious good humor and positive spirit about it all.

That seed took a long time to germinate. The poor of the earth went off my radar screen for several decades before I rediscovered them and their reality. The experiences in Latin America proved to be occasions for the reexamination of my life and faith. They triggered small changes that cumulatively led to a larger transformation of my perspective and practice. A journal entry may help the reader to understand what was taking place:

> Can we, the non-marginalized — the people who are on the edge of nothing, who crave security instead of faith — can we be Christian? I have been confronted with that question for several years. I do not have a fully satisfactory resolution. Either answer, yes or no, is accompanied by a gnawing remainder of doubt. For me, an affirmative response to that question is more a matter of hope than of confidence. One source

of hope is the Lukan gospel. The editor of that gospel was, quite obviously, not marginalized. And yet he was, also quite obviously, challenged and informed and shaped by the poor — by their grasp of Jesus with strength that neither the Lukan editor nor we, unconditioned by the fitness program of poverty, could possibly possess. Good news for the poor. And, hopefully, good news through the poor for us. The Lukan editor listened and heard. Do we?

Gustavo Gutiérrez, the Peruvian priest, social scientist, and theologian, speaks of solidarity with the poor. That solidarity, that connectedness, that community links us with a paradox of vulnerability and endurance. The poor suffer profusely; they die profligately; they are nonetheless with us persistently. Bonhoeffer, the German theologian/martyr of a generation ago, wrote about costly grace. If, as seems likely, the poor are a means by which God's grace flows — perhaps for us, the non-marginalized, the *sine qua non*[3] of our salvation — then that is costly grace indeed. And for us, as for the non-marginalized of the ancient Mediterranean world, an offense and a stumbling block.

Such impressions and reflections describe as well and efficiently as I can a new, changing, and unsettling portion of the context out of which my teaching and preaching had begun to emerge. In particular, they convey some of the experiential background that has led to my changing relation with the epistle of James — and a whole lot more of the biblical literature, the Christian tradition, and the contemporary world with its incredibly diverse people.

Lutheran disdain for the epistle of James[4]

Tom Wilkens

The text

My brothers and sisters, do you with your acts of favoritism really believe in our glorious Lord Jesus Christ? For if a person with gold rings and in fine clothes comes into your assembly, and if a poor person in dirty clothes also comes in, and if you take notice of the one wearing the fine clothes and say, "Have a seat here, please," while to the one who is poor you say, "Stand there," or, "Sit at my feet," have you not made distinctions among yourselves, and become judges with evil thoughts? Listen, my beloved brothers and sisters. Has not God chosen the poor in the world to be rich in faith and to be heirs of the kingdom that he has promised to those who love him?

You do well if you really fulfill the royal law according to the scripture, "You shall love your neighbor as yourself." But if you show partiality, you commit sin and are convicted by the law as transgressors. For whoever keeps the whole law but fails in one point has become accountable for all of it.

What good is it, my brothers and sisters, if you say you have faith but do not have works? Can faith save you? If a brother or sister is naked and lacks daily food, and one of you says to them, "Go in peace; keep warm and eat your fill," and yet you do not supply their bodily needs, what is the good of that? So faith by itself, if it has no works, is dead. But someone will say, "You have faith and I have works." Show me your faith apart from your works, and I by my works will show you "my faith" (James 2:1-5, 8-10, 14-18).[5]

Introduction

The lesson that Pastor Bade just read is the second of four selections from the epistle of James in Series B of the three-year Lutheran lection-ary, heard on four consecutive Sundays during the Pentecost season of the church year. The only other time Lutherans read from James is one Sunday in Advent during Series A. James is entirely absent from the third year of the cycle.

That we hear so seldom from James would likely please Martin Luther. Luther held the epistle of James in great disdain. He called it "the epistle of straw." Luther viewed James as a serious distortion of Saint Paul's gospel, the good news that we are saved by grace through faith and not by works of the law. Luther wanted James dropped from the New Testament — though he did not, of course, get his way.

My changing relation with James

My own relation with James has undergone a number of changes. As a student from a somewhat fundamentalist and legalist non-Lutheran church background, enrolled at Luther College, I began to share Luther's discomfort with James. I found Luther's proclamation of the good news of God's boundless grace to be refreshing, exhilarating, liberating. I con-cluded that the epistle of James represented a compromise of that gospel. James had too much emphasis and insistence on law and works for my newly acquired Lutheran tastes.

Later, as a pastor and young professor, I began to have discomfort with Luther. I began to see that Luther had very likely misinterpreted James. Luther didn't often do that with biblical literature, but in this case I thought that he probably did. James was written much later than the Pauline letters. The author faced a very different situation. By that time even the definitions of terms had changed, including the definition of faith.

For example, it would never have occurred to Saint Paul that faith could be unaccompanied by works. Faith, as Paul used that term, would always issue forth in works of love. But the people to whom the epistle of James was written no longer defined faith as a living relationship with a living God through the living Christ. For them, faith meant creed, belief, doctrine. Faith as relationship is always alive, fruitful, and productive. Faith as doctrine or confession may not be. It may, indeed, be dead. Such faith is dead if the vital signs of loving works are absent. Luther in the 16th century didn't see this. Lutheran scholars in the 20th century have. We have become uncomfortable with Luther, not with James.

More recently, as an older teacher, I have once again become uncomfortable with James — though now for a very different reason and after some very different life experiences. My life experience this past decade has included some generous helpings of the Third World, particularly Latin America. My Christian sisters and brothers there have taught me a great deal about the Bible and its message. They have given me a different perspective. They call it "the view from below."

What does the Bible look like to those on the bottom of the human heap — those for whom, quite frankly, much of scripture was written? The Bible looks and sounds very different "from below" than it does from my privileged First-World perch. When the Bible speaks — as it does so often — of real, concrete, public, nameable sins of injustice, discrimination, exploitation and the like, I would prefer to spiritualize, privatize, and interiorize the text. But I no longer can. My Salvadoran, Honduran, Nicaraguan, and Costa Rican sisters and brothers in the faith no longer permit me to do that.

And so I am once more uncomfortable with the message of James. I invite you to share my discomfort. Luther would have called this an invitation to reflect on a theology of the cross. You may recall, for instance, this passage from an earlier pericope from James:

If any think they are religious, and do not bridle their tongues but deceive their hearts, their religion is worthless. Religion that is pure and undefiled before God, the Father, is this: to care for orphans and widows in their distress, and to keep oneself unstained by the world (1:26-27).

We still have orphans and widows. They still need our care. But we can't stop there. Orphans and widows were among the most vulnerable people in the ancient world. Today, in addition to orphans and widows, we have the hungry and the homeless: the hungry in North Africa — where nature and human nature seem to conspire against the poor; the homeless in Latin America — where economic gains, such as those in today's Mexico, seldom seem to trickle down to the peasants.

But the hungry and the homeless are not just in distant places. They are here: in my hometown of Seguin and in your hometown, wherever it is. James unnerves me by insisting that the truly redeemed embrace their responsibilities as keepers of the earth and its inhabitants, by caring for orphans and widows, and for hungry and homeless people. If you doubt that insistence, listen again to a portion of today's reading:

> What good is it, my brothers and sisters, if you say you have faith but do not have works? Can faith save you? If a brother or sister is naked and lacks daily food, and one of you says to them, "Go in peace; keep warm and eat your fill," and yet you do not supply their bodily needs, what is the good of that? So faith by itself, if it has no works, is dead (2:14-17).

James doesn't pull any punches. Let me reread another portion of today's text:

> My brothers and sisters, do you with your acts of favoritism really believe in our glorious Lord Jesus Christ? For if a person with gold rings and in fine clothes comes into your assembly, and if a poor person in dirty clothes also comes in, and if you take notice of the one wearing the fine clothes and say, "Have a seat here, please," while to the one who is poor you say, "Stand there," or, "Sit at my feet," have you not made distinctions among yourselves, and become judges with evil thoughts? Listen, my beloved brothers and sisters. Has not God chosen the poor in the world to be rich in faith and to be heirs of the kingdom that he has promised to those who love him? (2:1-5).

Many of us belong to a national Lutheran church that seems to me is seriously trying to come to grips with this text and its clear condemnation of discrimination. Our church has raised to a very high priority the practice of inclusivity: gender inclusivity, ethnic inclusivity, racial inclusivity, and class inclusivity.

Yet there is strong vocal opposition and enormous lethargy in the ranks about inclusivity. And we at the local and synodical levels seem to be so critical, on the one hand, or so indifferent, on the other, toward the national church that we appear to be starving it into submission. Again and again, the national church cuts budgets and releases staff. And soon it may lose the means, if not its will, to challenge our bad old discriminatory ways.

Perhaps the most jarring text from James isn't even in the lectionary. We won't ordinarily hear it read. It's from chapter 5:

> Come now, you rich people, weep and wail for the miseries that are coming to you. Your riches have rotted, and your clothes are moth-eaten. Your gold and silver have rusted, and their rust will be evidence against you, and it will eat your flesh like fire. You have laid up treasure for the last days. Listen! The wages of the laborers who mowed your fields, which you kept back by fraud, cry out, and the cries of the harvesters have reached the ears of the Lord of hosts. You have lived on the earth in luxury and in pleasure; you have fattened your hearts in a day of slaughter. You have condemned and murdered the righteous one, who does not resist you (5:1-6).

Can't we deflect this angry diatribe against the rich? After all, we're not rich: we're middle class. We've got anxieties about jobs and paying our education bills and our medical costs and coverage. Yet in the global village, we are the rich. Do we exploit? Maybe not knowingly. But perhaps we exploit through pension funds invested in a company with a bad environmental track record or endowment funds invested in a company with a history of unfair labor practices, here or abroad.

Yes, it's a more complex world today than when the book of James was written. However, do not be deceived: we are not thereby off the hook. If we fail to examine the exploitative dimensions of our lives in a world of integrated economies and multinational businesses, if we fail to think through the human implications of our personal and institutional financial decisions, we do so at our own grave peril.

21

Conclusion

Perhaps some day I'll be comfortable again with the epistle of James. Perhaps. But not now. James gives me an uneasy conscience. It is a word from the Lord, prompted by the Spirit of God. It cuts. It hurts. It kills. It forcefully reminds me of my desperate need for resurrection — each day, every day.

The same Spirit who brings disquietude also brings comfort. The Spirit calms us with truly great news: Jesus, the servant and the sovereign, remains faithful even in the face of our unfaithfulness, loving in the face of our indifference, hopeful in the face of our despair at the world and at our inadequacies in dealing with it.

Luther may have gotten James wrong, but he got the gospel right: Jesus loves us, this we know. We are loved sisters and brothers of Jesus the Christ, beloved children of God. We are not asked to do what we cannot or to be what we are not. Our vocation is simply to be what we are: women and men made and remade — again and again and again — in the image of a God we call love.

Response: The fear factor

Kim Wilkens

> You know I have the Lutheran curse. Conviction without action has no meaning for me. Yet what is conviction? How do we identify it? Is it to be found in the heart, or in the intellect? And what if it is only to be found in the one and not the other? ... I had no conscious faith, but if I acted, then the faith would surely follow... Perhaps that is how faith is born, I thought: by action and not by contemplation.
>
> — John le Carré[6]

Have you ever read a book or watched a movie that gets your mind so worked up that it literally feels like it is buzzing? This doesn't happen to me often, but when it does I either get obsessed with the ideas bouncing around my head and I try to understand them or I am at a loss as to how to move beyond these thoughts and I try to turn them off. For some reason, that happened after I read the background for this homily and my mind went into shutdown mode. Oh, I had plenty of excuses for not responding right away, my son was ill and then we went on a ski trip. But even once I was back and settled, I still found excuses to avoid working on this response.

I know in my heart and mind that James is right — that faith without works is dead. In fact, I find that my faith grows stronger out of my works. I also know in my heart and mind that my works are not currently measuring up to the potential God has given me. But I struggle with how to get beyond where I am now. I am reminded of how far I have to go when my son sees a homeless person begging on a street corner; he wants to know how we can help that person right now. Neither of us is satisfied with my rationale that we give to charities that can eventually help that person. The path seems overwhelming when I read from my dad's journal about his experiences in Latin America. There are so many people in this world who are homeless and hungry — where do you even begin?

It is at this point in my thoughts that my mind overloads and I attempt to shut it down, unable to get beyond the feeling of hopelessness and helplessness. I get so wrapped up in this feeling that the problems of this world are just too overwhelming to deal with on my own that it paralyzes me.

Fortunately, I got an opportunity to learn about and try to move beyond the fear. This lesson came from an ELCA Global Mission Event session titled "In Your Face: Teaching and Learning About Poverty." It was led by Bob Sitze, a dynamic leader who was definitely in your face. In this way, he helped the group come to the following conclusions about poverty:

1. When we try to educate about poverty, we face the fear factor — the brain's natural defense mechanism to tag unpleasant information as fearsome or dangerous and our natural instinct of flight, fight or freeze in face of that danger.
2. If we are honest with ourselves, there is hunger because of us. We need to stop thinking of hunger as a problem out there. It is a by-product we cause by our consumption and waste patterns. We need to change.
3. Change doesn't happen until faced with "death."

That sounds pretty drastic, but I've heard that change most often occurs after experiencing one of the four D's: death, divorce, disease, or destruction. As Tracy Chapman alludes to in her song "Change"[7] — why wait?

If you want to go looking for change, I can recommend the annual ELCA Global Mission Events. This conference brings together an amazing collection of human beings from all over the globe to share their experiences about living and working in places where the realities of death, disease, and destruction are ever present.

- From an African theologian, I learned a good definition of sharing. Sharing is not "I don't need it, you can have it." Sharing is "I need it, but I see you need it, too — let's share."
- From the Director of ELCA Global Mission, I learned that mission is about restoring community. It's not about us vs. them. It's about taking a good look at your community and realizing that it is wanting, needing, missing, and broken. A broken community realizes it can only be made whole again by going out and restoring.
- From a couple of young adult missionaries who went to Argentina for a year, I learned that being away from everything that makes your life comfortable means you understand more than ever that God is in control, you must live on your faith alone, you will learn and receive more than you can give, and it is the journey with others that is important.
- From an ELCA Mission Director, I learned that "If God wants you to do something, God has already given you what you need to get started."

Chapter Endnotes

1. Texas Lutheran was established in 1891; it is located in Seguin, about 35 miles east of San Antonio.
2. The *comunidades de base* in Latin America bear a great resemblance to the earlier *collegia pietatis* (schools or communities of piety) of the seventeenth and eighteenth century pietists in Europe. Both movements have/had sensitive social consciences, though Pietism sometimes lost that edge in later generations. See chs. 8 and 12 for more on Lutheran Pietism.
3. *Sine qua non* means without which not, or a necessary condition for a consequence to occur.
4. A homily presented in the Chapel of the Abiding Presence at Texas Lutheran College during the fall term, 1986. For a later elaboration of some of the points made in this homily, see Elsa Támaz' *The Scandalous Message of James: Faith Without Works Is Dead* (Crossroad Publishing Company, 1990).
5. All biblical quotations are from the New Revised Standard Version (NRSV), unless otherwise noted.
6. John le Carré, *Absolute Friends* New York: (Back Bay, 2004), 216.
7. Tracy Chapman, performer, "Change: Where You Live" (Atlantic Records, 2005).

can be in solidarity with the poor and can do something that might make a difference. Often it has simply been a ministry of presence — of just being there in the developing world — and then, back in my developed world, a ministry of consciousness-raising about the plight of the poor and oppressed. My career in academia afforded many opportunities for these ministries.

On my pilgrimage I have discovered that guilt and the resultant bad conscience are, on the one hand, regularly recurring realities of my life and, on the other, exceedingly poor motivators for positive change or effective action. Hope for a better future and excitement about participating in it are, for me at any rate, much more powerful stimuli.

I have also discovered that I cannot shed my developed-world skin, nor should I try. I still use the critical tools of biblical exegesis that I learned early on in seminary, practiced in the parish and in graduate school, and continued to hone under the able tutelage of Dr. Norman Beck — friend, biblical scholar, author, teaching colleague, and frequent team-teaching classroom partner at Texas Lutheran. Nor can I shed my skin as a teacher when I preach. My sermons often begin with the kind of pedagogy that you will find in the homily that follows. But I do try to add a layer of insight that arises from my exposure to the life and faith of sisters and brothers in Christ in the developing world. This, too, you will find in many of the homilies and papers that follow.

A final note: toward the end of the next homily I encourage the development of a global perspective. My encouragement had a specificity for the student audience there that may elude the general reader. Texas Lutheran offered an elective course, called Global Perspectives, that I often team-taught with colleagues from several other disciplines. It was, in my view, one of the best opportunities our students had, short of overseas semesters or less lengthy service-learning projects, for gaining new and broader points-of-view about the planet on which we all live and the global village in which we all interconnect.

The case of the missing punch line[4]

Tom Wilkens

Introduction

The text to be investigated, Exodus 6:2-8, is called a pericope. Pericopes are prescribed portions of scripture read during the service on Sundays and on other special occasions throughout the church year. Normally four texts are appointed for each Sunday or special occasion: an Old Testament lesson, a Psalm, an Epistle lesson, and a Gospel reading. Our Exodus text is the appointed Old Testament lesson for this week, at least in American Lutheran congregations.

The practice of prescribing readings roots all the way back to the fourth century. It became quite widespread and eventually one-, two-, and three-year cycles of these texts were collected and bound into books called lectionaries.

There are some very real advantages to this custom of assigning weekly texts. For instance, if the texts are chosen wisely, a congregation of the faithful can hear — throughout a three-year cycle — virtually all of the substantive biblical material. Thus even if their pastor or priest has some pet topics or themes, the congregation will nonetheless have the opportunity to respond to a wider sampling of their religious heritage through the hearing of the varied pericopes.

There are also some problems, however. What happens if the choice of texts is not wise? What happens, for example, if troubling texts with unpopular motifs are systematically avoided? Or what happens when, as with today's text from Exodus, the punch line is left off? Thereby hangs our tale: "The case of the missing punch line."

The text

Let's begin with what we have, verses two through eight of chapter six in the book of Exodus:

> And God said to Moses, "I am the Lord. I appeared to Abraham, to Isaac, and to Jacob, as God Almighty, but by my name the Lord I did not make myself known to them. I also established my covenant with them, to give them the land of Canaan, the land in which they dwelt as sojourners. Moreover I have heard the groaning of the people of Israel

whom the Egyptians hold in bondage and I have remembered my covenant. Say therefore to the people of Israel, 'I am the Lord, and I will bring you out from under the burdens of the Egyptians, and I will deliver you from their bondage, and I will redeem you with an outstretched arm and with great acts of judgment, and I will take you for my people, and I will be your God; and you shall know that I am the Lord your God, who has brought you out from under the burdens of the Egyptians. And I will bring you into the land which I swore to give to Abraham, to Isaac, and to Jacob; and I will give it to you for a possession. I am the Lord.' "

Exodus is the second book of that section of the Hebrew scriptures that Jews call Torah and Christian scholars commonly refer to as the Pentateuch. Many of you have learned that the sacred writings likely went through several stages of development. You have become aware, for instance, that there are two creation stories in Genesis, skillfully and subtly spliced together by priestly editors.[5]

It turns out that there are also two accounts of the call of Moses in the book of Exodus. Our text is a portion of the second and more recent account, once again edited with some finesse with an older telling of the "burning bush" episode. This priestly version of the call of Moses by God seems to be a stirring summons to a manifest destiny for the people of God. It is, as my learned colleague, Dr. Norman Beck, points out in one of his publications, an excellent example of Israelite religion well on its way to becoming a civil religion.[6]

The punch line

But is that all there is? Is there no more here than footnote fodder for a doctoral thesis on the development of civil religions? Are we reduced to antiquarian interests? I think not, but I do think that we need the punch line, that verse which the pericope committee decided to omit. Here it is, in verse 9:

Moses spoke thus to the people of Israel; but they did not listen to Moses, because of their broken spirit and their cruel bondage.

This punch line — a shocking commentary on the human condition that the vast majority of humanity in every age, including our own, must face — this punch line pulls the inspiring portrait of God's call of Moses to leadership from the remote corners of history and heaven to an earthy present reality. Today's human community still trades in the currency of exploitation and enslavement. You and I, willing or unwilling, are players in the market. We watch — at times with genuine bewilderment, at times with condescension or impatience — as the wretched of the earth ignore our lordly advice, our tutorials on how to run their lives, their governments, and their economies. They ignore our insistence that our gospel — of economic development or population control — our gospel is their only sure salvation.

Yet the poor, the inarticulate, and the unheeding poor, do not listen. They do not listen even to a Moses: neither an upwardly mobile Moses acculturated into the ways of their slave masters nor a downwardly mobile Moses who was fugitive from the long arm of Egyptian law. They do not listen: not to Moses; not to God. They cannot listen "because of their broken spirit and their cruel bondage." Still, they are not condemned; they are exonerated.

Implications

Why is the punch line missing from this pericope? Is there some dark conspiracy to keep things from us in the church pews? I doubt that, although I confess a personal weakness for conspiracy theories. I think it more probable that the punch line was lopped off this text because of inexperience and resultant insensitivity.

We in the First World have little experience of dehumanizing poverty and pain. Surely the deafness of an enslaved people could not be noteworthy, much less the punch line of an otherwise uplifting discourse. We don't notice. Moses remains a wooden actor in the children's theater of our memories and God remains a director of special effects who was challenged by Cecil B. DeMille and likely has at last met his match in Steven Spielberg.

How can we avoid missing the punch lines of our religious heritage? I can only tell you what has begun, at least, to be helpful for me: gaining experience, perspective, and sensitivity from the poor, the oppressed, the ostracized, the contemptible people of the world. Firsthand experience is best, and I have been most fortunate in the opportunities that have presented themselves to me for travel and study in the Third World. It has assisted me in reexamining my cultural and religious heritage, in noticing dimensions of the biblical message that did not — perhaps could not

— register before. I am not poor but I notice pain, and thus reality, more frequently these days.

Firsthand experience is best, but secondhand will do. Make connections with those people who have connections with the larger world: with its chaos and order, its traumas and celebrations, its fears and hopes. Gain a global perspective. That's not an advertisement; it's an admonition. Learn to understand the deafness of the world's poor. And learn, finally, how to be tutored by those poor whose ears have been unstopped and who — when they finally can listen to the gospel — grasp it more fully and forcefully and fearlessly than all the rest of us.

Response:
Pushing the needle

Kim Wilkens

Moses spoke this to the people of Israel, but they did not listen to Moses, because of their broken spirit and their cruel bondage (Exodus 6:9).

I don't have experience with the poor. My experience is with middle-class America and I think this punch line reflects my culture as well. Turn on the TV, listen to the radio, read the news, and you will find examples of broken spirits and self-inflicted bondage everywhere. I've been there. I can confirm that when I've been in that state of mind, I don't listen — not to well-intentioned advice from friends, not to the worried voices of loved ones, not to preachers, not to prophets and certainly not to God.

For me brokenness felt like anxiety attacks that brought me to the hospital. My self-inflicted bondage felt like a high pressure, fast-track job that I thought defined who I was. Turns out I was really just a stressed-out, workaholic, soon-to-be divorced woman.

While in marriage counseling I began to realize that I needed a serious attitude adjustment. I didn't have any plan or twelve-step program to follow. I wasn't going to church and I didn't feel God's call. What I did discover was some kind of internal compass trying to guide me. When I really paid attention to it — it felt like serenity. When I didn't, my competitive nature took over and I'd try to work harder, be better; handle more pressure until I boiled over again.

As this road trip progressed, I found that my internal compass was pointing to God. This was an unexpected turn that I tried to ignore. I would try pushing the needle and turning another direction, but if I let go, it would return to God. When I finally started following this path, I was reminded that being a Christian "felt" right. As I explored my faith, I unearthed different ways to view Christianity from those I had grown up with.

My dad writes in his article about some real suffering, brokenness, and cruel bondage brought about by the circumstances of poverty, corruption, and living in a third-world country. So, how can we, who are so well off, be so screwed up? As the Indigo Girls suggest in their song, maybe we're "Pushing the Needle Too Far."[7]

"Life is difficult," writes M. Scott Peck in *The Road Less Traveled.*[8] But in America, we think we have the resources to try to fix it. We get extreme makeovers and trade spaces. We try to boost it, civilize it, correct it, cultivate it, edit it, enhance it, promote it, recover it, or revise it. In 2004, the United Church of Christ (UCC) started a new and controversial campaign called "God is still speaking." Listening to God doesn't require these resources and, in fact, is probably more difficult because of the layers of material goods we've put between God and ourselves. I believe listening to God is the only way to heal our broken spirits and ease our cruel bondage.

I heard a message recently that gave me some clues on how to listen to God. It was about King Solomon's last reigning years and his son's succession. King Solomon starts off his reign with his heart in the right place — with God. But by the end of his reign he has been tempted by idols and was cruel to his people. His son followed in his footsteps and picks up where he left off. His son's reign lasted only three days. Reverend Pete Hartwig[9] reminded the congregation that "our children will follow our example." He goes on to describe modeling behavior that will help keep our needle pointing to God:

- **Start each day humbly asking for God's help**
  In my corporate culture days, I certainly didn't ask for God's help. I wasn't very humble. My desire was to be self-sufficient and in control. Now I understand that the idea of being in control in this

36

I flew instead from Nicaragua to Honduras. At the airport in Tegucigalpa, the capital city of Honduras, I was stripped of my documents and made to stand in a corner of the customs and immigration section for over two hours — with no communication at all from the officials. Finally, they returned my documents and let me through. Fortunately, my host from an ecumenical relief and development agency had waited for me.

It was in Honduras, on a journey to the southern province of Choluteca, that I heard one of the worst horror stories about the *Contras*. As we drove to visit some development projects in a rural region of the province, a young Oxfam publicist told me of an interview she had had the night before with a Honduran teen who had just been raped and physically brutalized by a *Contra* officer on "R and R" in Tegucigalpa. During this period the US government was referring to the *Contra* insurgency as a "low intensity conflict" and the *Contras* themselves as "freedom fighters." Tell that to this teenager. We supported the *Contras* because their insurgency prevented the Sandinista government, which we held to be on the wrong side of the East-West cold war instead of on the weak side of the more historic North-South tensions, from using their resources to improve life for the Nicaraguan people. Some of the favorite *Contra* targets were school buildings, teachers, clinics, and medical workers.

It was a lesson in *realpolitik*, where policy is based on perceived national interests with little if any regard for ethical considerations. The chief State Department administrator of the policy, Elliott Abrams, continued in government with a senior position in the George W. Bush White House.[1] He was part of the fabric of the cloak of righteousness worn by extreme conservatives in contemporary American politics. Not that the extreme left has fewer tendencies toward deadly violence or smug self-righteousness. They simply have not had their hands on as many levers of power in the past few years.

The third trip, in the summer of 1988, was another travel seminar, focused this time on higher education in Central America. The itinerary included El Salvador, Nicaragua, and — for my first time — Costa Rica. I had by then developed a modest fluency in Spanish. Even though my fluency was on the low side of moderate, it nevertheless had enabled me to participate in academic conferences in Mexico, in both Monterrey and Merida, and to travel on my own in Latin America during the '80s and early '90s. It is rather ironic, therefore, that I was to feign total ignorance of Spanish during our stay in El Salvador.

The most unforgettable experience on this visit to El Salvador was being placed under arrest. One morning our group — typically called a *delegación* in Latin America — was rounded up at our hotel, taken to the Treasury Police headquarters, and held *incommunicado*. The police told us that our embassies (US, Canadian, and Swedish) had been informed. We learned later that they had not. Not that it would have done much good for the US citizens in our delegation. The Salvadoran government had us arrested to intimidate us and thereby, they hoped, to stem the flow of church-related visitors coming to El Salvador to see the violent, oppressive reality there. The US government also wanted to stem that flow: it was supporting their government and the terror both of the marauding insurgency into Nicaragua and, at least by default, of the roving death squads within El Salvador itself. It is not likely that they would have intervened on our behalf.

The police said that they suspected us of aiding the rebels in rural El Salvador. They then placed some Spanish-language forms in front of us and told us to fill them out. The heading at the top of the first page made it clear that they already regarded us as criminals. One of the initial questions had to do with identifying the subversive organizations to which we belonged. I was tempted to write *la iglesia* (the church), but that might have put many progressive, publicly protesting Salvadoran Christians in even more jeopardy than they already were. Instead, I summoned up a glazed look in my eyes, the kind intended to communicate that I did not understand a word of what I was looking at. It worked. None of us filled out the forms (most on our team truly did not know Spanish) and by noon the *commandante*, all smiles and regrets, apologized for the "bureaucratic error" that had resulted in our arrest. We were free to go, he said. We went — quickly.

Later that day we met a reporter affiliated with the *Christian Science Monitor*. He confirmed that the Salvadoran government had recently been ratcheting up their harassment of church-related delegations from the US in an effort to dissuade future delegations from coming. However, the harassment had not worked on us and it would not deter future groups coming from the US and Europe.

US officials regularly told US citizens considering travel to Nicaragua in the '80s that it was unsafe, that the Sandinista government there would harass and intimidate them, and that — at best — their time in Nicaragua would be thoroughly miserable. My experience was just the opposite: I always breathed a sigh of relief when I got to Nicaragua from other Central American nations. It was there in the capital city of Managua that I got to interview Ernesto Cardenal: priest, poet, and Minister of Culture. And it was there in the countryside that I heard from a North American agricultural expert, "Wheels" Robinson, engaged in small, efficient, and effective rural development projects. For all the problems faced by the Nicaraguan people, there nonetheless was always a glimmer of hope, a refusal to despair at their desperate circumstances. It was always inspiring; it always contributed to my ongoing transformation.

Civil disobedience was a growing phenomenon in Costa Rica at that time, especially in the rural areas. The farmers were angry about government policies, ranging from lower subsidies for the small farmer to generous incentives for farm mechanization. High tech farming requires less labor, thus contributing to unemployment, and larger farms, thus driving many peasant farmers off the land. Civil disobedience is not unchristian. In Ephesians 4:26 it says: "Be angry but do not sin." In other words, anger is not the same as sin; anger is okay. This is not the peevish anger of the egocentric, but the righteous indignation of the eccentric — the prophets and social protesters who hear a different drummer.

Most people are reluctant to speak out, and why not? After all, whistle-blowers often get fired; faultfinding generals are scorned; and critical liberals — even critical moderate conservatives — have their integrity challenged and their patriotism held in derision. It is not easy to speak out, much less to engage in civil disobedience. And yet in many generations there are occasions when we ought to do just that.

In retrospect, I should have done more. I should have mounted more compelling open protests. I should have engaged in more of what theologian and social ethicist Reinhold Niebuhr once called prophetic specificity: naming the names of public evil.

Central American sojourn[2]

Tom Wilkens

Under arrest in El Salvador

Everything in El Salvador is polarized and politicized. Everything. The church. All forms of power. Education, from elementary through university. The divisions run very deep. And they play politics for keeps. They play with their lives and with their deaths. Roman Catholic Archbishop Óscar Romero lost his life for siding with the poor of El Salvador. His successor is, understandably, far more cautious.

Lutheran Bishop Medardo Gómez regularly puts his life on the line for the victims of El Salvador's civil war. In August he was at the Honduran border trying to facilitate the return and resettlement of hundreds of Salvadoran refugees who had been living in UN camps in Honduras. Just being there was an act of courage for a man who regularly receives death threats for helping these people.

We saw some of the people that he, along with the Lutheran World Federation, has assisted. We visited El Lago repopulation community, an agricultural cooperative outside of San Salvador. The lakeside setting is breathtakingly beautiful. But the political realities are not. Eugenio, one of the community leaders, has been twice arrested, questioned, tortured, and then released by the army. If it happens again, he said quite matter-of-factly, he will not survive.

We got a taste, ever so small, of Eugenio's reality. The very next morning a half-dozen uniformed and heavily armed (with M-16s) Treasury Police, along with several plain-clothed officers, appeared at our hotel. They rounded up our group, arrested us, and took us to their headquarters.

You have to understand: if you are Salvadoran, this is your worst nightmare come true. The Treasury Police have the worst reputation for interrogation, torture, and more. We were not Salvadoran, of course. Five of us held US passports, four Canadian, and one Swedish. We were harassed and intimidated; we were lied to and were not permitted to contact the embassy. But our lives were not on the line.

Still, it was a sampling of the terror that permeates that society. It was an unforgettable reminder of what the polarities mean to ordinary Salvadoran citizens, and how every word and gesture in that culture is given political interpretation. Oppression there is not a nuanced abstraction; it is the coarse stuff of daily existence. What amazes one is that the victims — of war, of the 1986 earthquake, of grinding poverty — the victims push back. They are not resigned, but resolute; not despairing, but hopeful.

The one who epitomized that for me on this trip was Rosa (not her real name). She is a teenaged single mother whose urban squatters' settlement is under frequent siege by government and police. Her eyes occasionally danced with humor, yet her voice intoned quiet defiance. The powers of darkness and death in El Salvador have more to fear from Rosa than from the armed rebels. And they know it. That is why the rebels have died by the thousands, but the Rosas by the tens of thousands.

Under a ceasefire in Nicaragua

The Nicaraguan ceasefire went into effect in March. It continues to hold, but by no means perfectly. While we were in the countryside of Matagalpa, we heard the first report of a *Contra* ambush in which several civilians were killed. News stories later confirmed what we had heard. Such occurrences are not unusual, although it is unusual for them to get reported in the US press.

Life is hard for most people in Nicaragua. It is hard for the *campesinos* (farmers and farmworkers), who face classic high costs/low prices/tight credit problems compounded by the dislocations present in a nation on a war footing. But at least employment and subsistence are available in the rural areas. And many of the farmers have organized cooperatives that help them deal with the credit crunch and equipment needs.

Urban dwellers, on the other hand, are in much worse shape: unemployment, underemployment, and food shortages are widespread. The Nicaraguan economy appears to be in a shambles. Monetary policy decisions have resulted in several currency devaluations: one happened the week before we arrived and another the week after we left. There are shortages of all kinds, and yet a black market in consumer goods thrives in Managua.

Will it all collapse? A Stanford economist who spoke to us thought not, if for no other reason than that the Eastern bloc countries will not permit the Nicaraguan economy to collapse. He explained something of his own fascination with the Nicaraguan experiment with a "mixed economy," an economy in which capitalism has a place but the capitalist sector is excluded from the top level of economic policy decisions. The high-roller capitalists resent this, of course. Some of them told us so, in no uncertain terms.

The question, as I see it, is this: Is an economy designed to benefit the poor viable? The US answer is a resounding "No!" We even have US theologians publishing books (odes, really) in which moral silver linings are discovered in the immoral clouds of greed.[3] The poor benefit by default, not by design. We're talking basic "trickle down," folks.

On another front, there are signs that some of the polarizations so prevalent in Nicaragua may be moderating. For example, the conservative Roman Catholic hierarchy is beginning to make some statements indicating a willingness to reach accommodation with the progressive popular church movement within Catholicism there.

On a more personal level, I find that I pray more in the Third World. I think that there are two reasons. First, I am more acutely aware of just how much there is to be thankful for. Second, I am also more acutely aware of how vulnerable we all are. There are few illusions about security and immortality that can be sustained in the Third World. It is not, of course, that we are more secure or less mortal in the First World. We are simply more able to sustain illusions.[4]

Under the veneer of prosperity in Costa Rica

Education was a major focus of our travel seminar. We visited nineteen sites in eighteen days, interviewing primary and secondary school teachers, university faculty and administrators, and federal ministers of education. We saw campuses that would rival those in the US in terms of physical plant and classrooms so under-equipped that there were not even any chalkboards. We visited a university spray painted from one end to the other with leftist graffiti (in El Salvador) and an academy where the students were regularly exposed to a rightist bias (in, as it happens, Nicaragua).

One of the most interesting encounters took place at the University of Costa Rica in San José. Meeting with about a dozen of their faculty, we soon began to see a fault line emerge in their ranks. Several of the more outspoken faculty were against the traditional model of education, which in their view is used as a political tool to control the population. They advocated "popular education," that is, education designed to give people the means to control more of their own destiny. Other faculty members were clearly troubled by this, and muttered comments about subversion and communism. The traditionalists hold the power; the progressives feel repressed.

The University is something of an archetype of Costa Rica. On the surface, things seem calm and prosperous. Below the surface, there are tensions and problems. If you were to visit Costa Rica after any of the other Central American nations, your first reaction would be a sigh of relief: here, at last, is something comfortingly familiar. Hotels and stores abound; the performing arts flourish; even the architecture has a first world/European flavor.

The veneer is thick enough to sustain the impression of peace and prosperity for most visitors, I should think. But once one begins to talk with people from various sectors of Costa Rican society, the veneer wears thin. Changes in the nation's fiscal policy, for instance, have rendered small farmers vulnerable and angry. They demonstrate their predicament and frustration by blocking major roads in the nation. Church leaders and seminary professors know about the growing poverty and attempt to shape their programs to deal with that ugly reality.

Perhaps a brief excerpt from my notebook can best convey how the Costa Rican church responds to the situation:

> In the evening we went to a Protestant church service. It was a congregation made up of people from the Pentecostal and Evangelical traditions who have caught the progressive spirit. There were people there from Chile, Bolivia, Panama, El Salvador, Canada, and the US. We all reported on work among the poor in our respective countries (no illusions here; they were well aware that we would have poor in our midst). The congregation's members then reported on their work — it was impressive and humbling. At one point in the service, we joined hands in small circles of prayer for the poor in each of the countries represented. Poor Costa Ricans prayed with me for poor North Americans. It was one of the most moving worship experiences I have ever had.

There is an integrity to life in Central America that I seldom see here. There is an understanding that all of life coheres, that every dimension impinges upon every other dimension. There is far less compartmentalization, far less effort to keep education and economics and politics and religion discrete. This is risky business; compartmentalization seems safer and cleaner. Yet integration is, I think, a far healthier approach to life.

Under obligation in the US

The group with which I had traveled met again this past August — with other travel seminar participants who had gone to China, West Africa, or Eastern and Western Europe — for a debriefing. Each group composed an open letter to the North American church, copies of which were sent to, among others, the presiding bishop of the Evangelical Lutheran Church in America and the president of the Lutheran Church-Missouri Synod. The letters attempted to summarize the deepest, most lasting impressions of our sojourns. My group's letter can serve also as my own summary statement:

> What did we discover during our 18-day itinerary in El Salvador, Nicaragua, and Costa Rica this past June? We discovered US policy implemented as a war on the poor. We found the indigenous church working creatively to deal with the effects of that war and the international church working cooperatively with the indigenous church.
>
> What did we discover in Central America? We discovered strong women engaged in difficult struggles. We saw women confronting historical stereotypes and contemporary crises, and women preparing for a broad spectrum of leadership roles.
>
> What did we discover on our pilgrimage? We discovered our own cultural cocoons. And we were helped — not always gently — to break out of those comfortable yet constricting habitats.
>
> What did we discover in this sector of the third world? We discovered the relevance of liberation theology. We came to sense Christ's presence among the poor; and we came away considering seriously the prospect of Christ's absence among ourselves.
>
> What did we discover on this brief Latin American journey? We discovered a fierce, fearless grasp of the gospel. And we learned to be learners, to be tutored by those of low estate, to have our perspectives challenged and our bland, often blind confidence subverted.
>
> There is much to be done in Central America. But first, for North American Christians at any rate, there is much to be discovered — including, perhaps, a rediscovery of the gospel itself.

Such a letter is both pretentious and presumptuous. It is pretentious because it represents so little experience in Central America (my own cumulative total is a scant two months). It is presumptuous because it assumes that the North American church might actually listen to Third-World voices and visions.

Is that assumption valid? The true test lies not with presiding bishops and presidents, but with pew-sitting (and pew-avoiding) Christians. Are we ready to hear reports from "the underside of history"? Are we willing to exchange the moral indifference of excessive individualism or the moral impotence of unrealizable expectations for a meaningful and manageable sense of moral obligation vis-à-vis the third world in general and Central America in particular? If these questions have no urgency among us, then perhaps prophetic eccentricity — when God is the center, all else is off-center — has finally been overwhelmed by pathological egocentricity.

I do see signs of hope, even in the academic ivory tower: students trying to come to grips with matters of global injustice, faculty engaged in internationalizing their curricula, and administrators pursuing mutually supportive relationships with Third-World educational institutions. I invite dialogue — on the pages of our campus newspaper, the *Lone Star Lutheran*, or in some other forum — about further possibilities and opportunities.

Response:
What did I discover in Honduras?

Kim Wilkens

My dear friends, remember what you were when God chose you. The people of this world didn't think that many of you were wise. Only a few of you were in places of power, and not many of you came from important families. But God chose the foolish things of this world to put the wise to shame. God chose the weak things of this world to put the powerful to shame. What the world thinks is worthless, useless, and nothing at all is what God has used to destroy what the world considers important.　　　　　　　　　　　　— 1 Corinthians 1:26-28; CEV

I remember hearing the story from my dad of his arrest in El Salvador and gunfire heard in the Nicaraguan night. It scared me and made question his sanity for wanting to continue to visit Central America. My parents have since had many third-world experiences in their extensive travels and they keep going back. This seemed like a strange addiction to me, but about a year ago, I felt the desire to go to Central America. I asked my dad if he would accompany and mentor me on a short-term mission trip.

I think trying to describe the trip I took to Honduras will be a lot like trying to describe the impact having a son has had on my life. Until you've had your first child, you will not grasp the enormity of the transformation that will take place in your life. I suspect it is also true that until you've lived with the residents of a third-world country, even for a brief time, you can't possibly understand their life or the impact they can have on yours.

I discovered peace

My family provided unconditional support for my desire to travel to Central America. They also left no room for excuses on my part not to do a trip. My dad and I spent several months looking for a short-term mission trip to hook up with and eventually discovered that a mission team to Honduras was forming at my church. Even though this trip was something I knew I needed to do, I was never entirely comfortable with the idea. I wrote this in my journal before I left:

> Instead of getting more excited about the trip, I'd become more nervous. As the technology person, I've been feeling some pressure to have something prepared for the trip, but with no clear idea of exactly what that might be. I finally found comfort in Psalm 119. For some reason "I live here as a stranger" seemed to sum up how I feel about living on earth with me here in middle-class America and many Hondurans living over there in poverty. Living here is a waypoint, it's a learning center, it's an opportunity to connect to others and God, it's not about being comfortable or having everything you desire.

Even the night before we left, I found myself thinking that I must be crazy — why in the world did I need to go to this third-world country? Why was I leaving my husband and son and my comfortable life? Before we left on the trip, we were asked to invite several people to be prayer partners with us on this adventure, to pray for guidance and direction for the Honduras Mission team. Even though they were physically spread across the US, just knowing they were thinking about and praying for the team and me was very powerful and when I landed in Honduras all my anxiety and fears vanished. I felt peaceful the entire time I was in Honduras and I am now convinced that prayer is a powerful thing.

I discovered joy

I'm not exactly sure what I had expected out of the trip; probably things like hard work, rough living conditions, language barriers, and new foods. What I did not expect was an overwhelming sense of joy. From the day we landed to the day we left, I felt full of joy from the experiences I had and the relationships that developed. In fact, months after the experience I'm still feeling the afterglow of the effects of Honduras. I hope they never go away.

I know part of the joy came from working at the school with the children. As I worked in the computer lab, fixing computers and setting up the network, a steady stream of kids stopped by to hang out with me in the afternoons. In particular, two boys, David and Alejandro, worked with me for a couple of afternoons. Even with our language differences, they provided me with much needed help and support wiring the lab and installing applications. They were such a blessing to me and I hope that they feel ownership of the lab since they helped build it.

I also found joy in the worship experiences. There was such an authentic hunger and desire for God and a willingness to let God shape their lives. In my journal, I wrote "I have seen the words to the song *Hungry* lived out in flesh and 'blood this week.'[5]"

It's difficult to explain this joy because I did also experience the paradoxes of peace vs. violence, hope vs. fear, joy vs. despair, and wants vs. needs. I've experienced these paradoxes in the US too, but in Honduras the divide between the haves and the have-nots is so vast that these paradoxes become much more striking. Perhaps it was the joy in discovering that, when I left my comfort zone and the distractions of the stuff I've accumulated, I found myself in the presence of God. It was a presence that I could feel with all my senses. It was an experience of God I had never had before. In Honduras I could see that God has chosen "the weak things of this world to put the powerful to shame" (1 Corinthians 1:27; CEV).

I discovered truth

Truth came from an unlikely source. Raul was a gang member in Los Angeles. He was born in Honduras, but grew up in the States with his mother. He got into some sort of trouble in the US that resulted in his deportation. His family in Honduras will not accept him back. He is a disappointment to them because he can no longer provide income from the States. Honduras has a 40% unemployment rate. Raul had no clue how to live in the third world and he hit rock bottom.

Somewhere in this bottoming out, he hooked up with the Gerizim community[6] and they have faithfully nurtured him. He's been back in Honduras almost two years now and he's moved beyond the culture shock and pain. Raul was one of our translators. The week we spent with him, he was both literally and figuratively on fire with the Holy Spirit. He ran a fever much of the time he was with us, but it didn't slow down his ministering to us. He finds so much comfort in the grace God extends and he wants to dedicate his life to preaching the good news. As a gang member, he did not expect to live long. He said that all the gang members he knew were either dead or in jail. He knows he's been given a second chance.

Raul was constantly studying the Bible (sometimes three translations at once) and somehow gleaned insights that pertained directly to our lives. His enthusiasm for the word was contagious. During our time together, Raul shared carefully chosen verses with various members of the team. Here's the truth I discovered with Raul's help:

> I have learned to be satisfied with whatever I have. I know what it is to be poor or to have plenty, and I have lived under all kinds of conditions. I know what it means to be full or to be hungry, to have too much or too little. Christ gives me the strength to face anything.
> — Philippians 4:11-13; CEV

I believe in a better way

Ben Harper has a song called "Better Way." I heard it the day I returned from Honduras and it does such a good job of summing up the experience for me. I especially like how he expresses the need, despite everything the world throws at us, to believe in a better way.[7]

Chapter Endnotes

1. Abrams pleaded guilty to two misdemeanor counts of giving false testimony to Congress about the Iran-Contra affair. In return, the special prosecutor agreed not to pursue more serious felony charges. At the very end of his presidency, George H. W. Bush pardoned Abrams and other defendants involved in the Iran-Contra scandal.
2. An article published initially as a four-part series in the campus newspaper, the *Lone Star Lutheran*, following a third visit to Central America in June of 1988 under the auspices of the Lutheran Educational Conference of North America.
3. Michael Novak, an American Roman Catholic philosopher, journalist, and diplomat, was at this time one of the most outspoken supporters and defenders of capitalism. See his *The Spirit of Democratic Capitalism* (Madison Books/University Press of America, 1982).
4. The illusion of security and immortality was finally shattered for us on 9/11.
5. "Hungry (Falling on My Knees)" by Kathryn Scott (kathrynscott.blog.spot.com/).
6. The Gerizion Church community in Tegucigalpa Honduras runs a school, a medical clinic and a feeding program. This community has seeded over 100 churches throughout Honduras and Central America.
7. Ben Harper, performer, "Better Way: Both Sides of the Gun" (Virgin Records, 2006).

CHAPTER 5

HOMILY FOR A COMMUNITY OF FAITH AND LEARNING

Background essay

Tom Wilkens

The homily that follows was rooted in the Salvadoran portion of the previously described Central American sojourn in 1988. During our days there, the group had the opportunity to visit three universities: the National University of El Salvador, Central American University, and Dr. José Matias Delgado University. I gave brief descriptions and impressions of each university in the homily.

I want to focus here on my experience at Central American University. Our host was the Vice-Rector[1] of the University, a Jesuit priest named Ignacio Martín-Baró. Father Martín-Baró was a soft-spoken scholar with special interests in mental health and human rights. He was a courageous advocate for the poor and oppressed — speaking frequently in El Salvador and throughout the world and writing extensively. But most often he brought to bear pressure for positive change behind the scenes and sought to provide the skills and tools for making change largely through the University curriculum and classes.

Even his low-key approach was too much for the powerful oligarchy in El Salvador. The year after our visit a quasi-military death squad murdered Father Martín-Baró, his housekeeper and her daughter, and five other Jesuit priests on the faculty.[2] There were widespread international expressions of outrage. But there was very little change in US policy, a policy that was supportive of the repressive regime there. In truth, the Salvadoran government likely could not have survived without our substantial financial assistance.

It appears that Father Martín-Baró may have had something of a premonition of his fate. He knew very well the difference in context between university life in El Salvador and in the US. He once commented:

> "In your country," Ignacio Martín-Baró remarked to a North American colleague, "it's publish or perish. In ours, it's publish *and* perish."[3]

I have known, ever so briefly, a martyr. Though I wish that were not the case, that Father Martín-Baró might still be alive, nonetheless I am grateful that his life touched mine. Two different worlds: he and I lived in two different worlds. He knew mine much better than I knew his. He knew about the ivory towers and ivied halls that North American academics inhabit. Yet he was not bitter about my advantage juxtaposed to his disadvantage. Instead, he made a quiet case for my finding ways to be more supportive of the people he served, the people for whom he ultimately gave his life.

I have tried. I have tried to report the realities that I was seeing in Central America in articles written for publications; to advocate for peace and justice in my preaching; to raise the critical ethical and theological issues in my ethics and contemporary theology classes; and to share with my students something of the experience that I had had by taking them on field trips to the Texas-Mexico borderlands and eventually on a service-learning mission to Costa Rica and Nicaragua. To what avail? I could measure my students' mastery of information and their critical ability to process it. But I could never measure the changes in their hearts, the transformations of their inner beings. I have no access to that; no teacher does. As a result, and as with so much that really counts in life, it is a matter of faith and hope, not a matter of certainty based on hard data.

Of course, my own life was not on the line — not even my academic life. I had a department chair who supported my ventures into the developing world and its theologies. I had a college administration that helped to secure grants for my language study and travel. And I had teaching colleagues who, while they may not have been fully clear about my evolution as a theologian and professor or may not have agreed with my "take" on national and international developments, nonetheless ranged in their responses from quiet tolerance to outspoken endorsement. To whom much is given, namely me, much is — and should be — expected.

Nor was my family life on the line. My wife, Betty, deftly masked her anxieties about my safety. This allowed me to travel to places well off the tourist track. Eventually she was to join me on these journeys to the developing world and, especially after our retirements, to participate in service missions around the globe. Our two children had, I think, during the decade of the '80s only a vague awareness of and a nominal interest in their father's travel destinations and theological development. This would change in subsequent years. Our son has become an enthusiastic supporter of his parents' volunteer efforts in developing-world settings. And our daughter asked me to join her on her first international service mission in February of 2007 (see her response in the previous chapter). To whom much is given, namely me, much is — and should be — expected. Still, in the strange and surprising life of faith and logic of the gospel, these gifts and expectations have not been burdens. They have been, rather, sources of growth and joy.

The situation in Central America today has changed in some ways and yet has stayed the same in others. The poverty remains extensive and oppressive; it would be worse without the relief and development efforts of church groups and other international NGOs (non-governmental organizations). The violence continues to be widespread and intense, though more of it today stems from urban street gangs and less from civil strife and quasi-military groups. And contemporary US policy seems to result in benign neglect more than the malevolent involvement in the affairs of the Central American nations that was so prominent in the '80s and before — stretching all the way back to the mid-nineteenth century. However, our current indifference is not an adequate alternative to our previous interference. We must notice and then respond to their reality of suffering and want in creative, non-paternalistic, non-manipulative ways.

Homily for a community of faith and learning[4]

Tom Wilkens

The text

> Do you want to be shown, you senseless person, that faith apart from works is barren? Was not our ancestor Abraham justified by works when he offered his son Isaac on the altar? You see that faith was active along with his works, and faith was brought to completion by the works. Thus the scripture was fulfilled that says, "Abraham believed God, and it was reckoned to him as righteousness," and he was called the friend of God. You see that a person is justified by works and not by faith alone. Likewise, was not Rahab the prostitute also justified by works when she welcomed the messengers and sent them out by another road? For just as the body without the spirit is dead, so faith without works is also dead. — James 2:20-26

Introduction

We have heard a good deal about community during this first month of chapel talks. Those talks have been uniformly thoughtful, well articulated, and helpful. I am not one to look a gift horse in the mouth and so I will continue with what has been a winning theme. I will use a clause from this week's epistle lesson as my point of departure: "faith apart from works is dead" (James 2:26). The thesis that I should like you to ponder is this: a community of faith apart from works is dead.

A tale of three Salvadoran communities

A public community:
the National University of El Salvador

To begin, I want you to accompany me on a very brief tour of three communities in El Salvador. They are three universities: the state university, a Roman Catholic university, and a private university. Our first stop is at the oldest of the three institutions, the National University of El Salvador.

At one time the National University was one of the strongest and most prestigious institutions of higher learning in Central America. Now it is a physical mess and a fiscal basket case. What happened? What happened were student uprisings in the 1960s, faculty and staff protests in the 1970s, and the occupation and partial destruction of the campus by the army in the 1980s.

Today the graffiti-covered buildings deteriorate for lack of a maintenance budget, the faculty and staff wonder each payday whether and how much they will be paid, and the students struggle — for the most part unsuccessfully — to stay in school. Less than 5% of the students who matriculate graduate.

Why has all of this come about? Because a generation ago the university community — faculty, staff, and students — redefined their mission. They undertook a mission to correct the cruel inequities and injustices of Salvadoran society. As a political corollary of that mission, they began to protest publicly the structures of privilege and power in El Salvador. They refused to accept the *status quo*. Their strategy called for the intellectual community actively and overtly to support the oppressed and exploited majority in their country. And for this the university reaped the whirlwind of government wrath.

A Roman Catholic community:
Central American University

Our next stop is the campus of Central American University, a Roman Catholic institution run by Jesuits. This university was founded in the 1960s. It was intended to be an alternative to the emerging chaos at the state university, to be a tranquil island of academic calm in the churning sea of social unrest. It worked. Central American University is beautiful: the buildings are well equipped; the lush landscape is well manicured. There's no graffiti here.

Is this Roman Catholic school really so different from the state university? In tactics, yes. In goals, no. Central American University has defined its primary mission as the critique of structures of privilege combined with the creation of functional alternatives. The political corollary of this mission is an institutional commitment to keep pressure — not always public — on the government for change. Their strategy is to encourage faculty to critique the Salvadoran situation as an essential part of their academic work and within their academic disciplines. A few of you may remember Jon Sobrino, the liberation theologian who spoke here four years ago. Sobrino is from this university. He speaks and writes, critically and constructively, out of his discipline. He also has had threats and attempts on his life.

The students at Central American University are discouraged from joining parades of protest. But they are encouraged to orient their studies toward the plight and problems of the poor. They are being prepared to cooperate with the poor in rebuilding the nation. That's a tall order. Revolution is a piece of cake compared with the task of rebuilding a polarized, war-torn nation.

A private community:
Dr. José Matias Delgado University

Our final stop on this quick tour is Dr. José Matias Delgado University. Founded in 1977, this private university was intended — in the words of its Vice-Rector — to be a university where the students would come to study, not to engage in political activities. Apparently they do study. Sixty percent of those who matriculate, graduate. And the graduates are in demand: they find employment in government and business.

The primary mission of this university is to provide technically skilled people to run the government and the private sector economy. There is also a political corollary: *de facto* support for the political, economic and social *status quo*. Their strategy is not only to stay off the streets but also to stay away from controversial issues. That cannot be easy in this cauldron called El Salvador. On the other hand, perhaps it is the easiest of the alternatives. It is surely the least threatening, both to the university and to the power people.

Implications for US academic communities

What have these three universities — with their differing missions, political agendas, and strategies — to do with higher education in the United States? More specifically, what has this to do with our community of faith and learning?

It seems to me that all three alternatives have been exercised by US institutions of higher learning — allowing, of course, for very real contextual differences. The option taken by the students and staff of the National University of El Salvador — namely, engaging in ideological reflection, embracing a political agenda, and hitting the streets — this option has been exercised by some students in the US, especially during the '60s. I'll not argue the merits or demerits of this alternative (I do think that there are both). I simply offer the observation that Texas Lutheran College is likely a century or two away from seriously considering it.

That is not the case with the option that the private Dr. José Matias Delgado University represents. In fact, it has been Texas Lutheran's primary option until now: that is, rigorous job-oriented training coupled with the denial of a political agenda. In truth, we even have a long and honorable theological tradition in which to ground our practice. It has to do with the idea of vocation and the notion that occupations performed well are the primary means of fulfilling obligations to our neighbors. We could do worse, much worse. But I also think that we can do better.

I think that we are beginning to do better. I see signs that we are seriously considering the option that the Roman Catholic Central American University embodies: rigorous life-oriented learning coupled with the recognition of political agendas. We are beginning to see — perhaps most clearly through our movement into international education — that our institutional mission and academic program need some redefinition and elaboration to take into account institutional responsibilities that transcend the parochial imagery of ivory tower and ivied halls. Hit the streets? No. Hit the issues that trouble and terrorize large sectors of the human community? Yes. Create graffiti? No. Create networks of mutual support with third- and fourth-world peoples, schools, and churches? Yes. Alienate our traditional constituency? No. Educate our constituency *and ourselves* with respect to new realities, responsibilities, and opportunities? Yes.

A community of faith apart from works is dead. But we are not lacking in works. And we are not dead. Those aren't the issues. The issue is the quality of the works, the center of their gravity, the vision they are meant to realize. We are, I suggest, at a time of unique opportunity, great promise, and scary options. Let us be of good courage and good cheer.

Response:
Where is your Antioch?

Kim Wilkens

Some of the followers from Cyprus and Cyrene went to Antioch and started telling Gentiles the good news about the Lord Jesus. The Lord's power was with them, and many people turned to the Lord and put their faith in him. News of what was happening reached the church in Jerusalem. Then they sent Barnabas to Antioch. When Barnabas got there and saw what God had been kind enough to do for them, he was very glad. So he begged them to remain faithful to the Lord with all their hearts. Barnabas was a good man of great faith, and he was filled with the Holy Spirit. Many more people turned to the Lord.

Barnabas went to Tarsus to look for Saul. He found Saul and brought him to Antioch, where they met with the church for a whole year and taught many of its people. There in Antioch the Lord's followers were first called Christians.

During this time some prophets from Jerusalem came to Antioch. One of them was Agabus. Then with the help of the Spirit, he told that there would be a terrible famine everywhere in the world. And it happened when Claudius was Emperor. The followers in Antioch decided to send whatever help they could to the followers in Judea. So they had Barnabas and Saul take their gifts to the church leaders in Jerusalem.

— Acts 11:20-30; CEV

Where is your Antioch, your community of faith and learning? Is it dead or dying? Is it alive and growing? Before you can figure out *where* your Antioch is, you need to know *what* an Antioch is. From the description in the book of Acts it sounds like:

- Antioch is a community of faith (Barnabas, a man of great faith, went to Antioch and he recognized God at work in the community and he begged them to remain faithful).
- Antioch is a community committed to hear God's calling (the Lord's power was with them and many people turned to the Lord).
- Antioch is a community with an outward focus (they told outsiders, the Gentiles, the good news and sent whatever help they could to Judea).

Glenn McDonald, the author of *The Disciple-Making Church*, says that each of us needs an Antioch — one or more settings in which we can be ourselves in the company of a few other faithful people. He goes on to say that "we will be greatly blessed if we have found at least one place where it is safe to 'try on' and 'try out' the various visions to which God may be calling us — where we can hear the truth about ourselves without fear; where trusted friends can help calibrate our inner tuners to hear the voice of God; and where those same colleagues are willing and able to bless us on our way".[5]

Why is having an Antioch important? I have discovered that I have several Antiochs and that they are critical to my spiritual growth. The most obvious is my family, especially my husband, my son, my parents, my brother, and my mother-in-law. They provide unconditional support and love.

I've also experienced Antioch community with the Honduras mission team. I understand that achieving true community is rare. According to M. Scott Peck, author of *The Road Less Traveled* and *Beyond*, most groups of people only achieve pseudo-community, where the assumption is that everyone is the same, with the same goals in mind, and that everybody will play nice. True community requires experiencing the chaos of our differences and the breaking down of barriers to communication such as "expectations, preconceptions, and prejudices and emptying ourselves of the need to heal, convert, fix or solve."[6]

We had a diverse team, the most obvious difference being the age range: from seventeen-year-old Kalie to my 69-year-old dad. We also discovered that we had various backgrounds, skills, and gifts and in the short span of a week we became a community "in which spiritual accountability, truth-telling, and listening to God were priority activities."[7]

Finally, I am blessed to find Antioch in the people at Peace Lutheran Church in Charlottesville, Virginia. At Peace, my home congregation, I have found a community that is committed to an outward focus, to serving others, and to going in Christ. Because of their support, their prayers and their commitment to hear God's call, I have been given so many opportunities to grow in Christ.

Where is your Antioch? Is it part of a community that listens to your doubts and fears? Are they trying to hear God's call? Are they going out into the world? Do they challenge you to leave your comfort zone?

Chapter Endnotes

1. Vice-Rectors are the true leaders of Latin American universities; the office of Rector is honorary.
2. Jon Sobrino, mentioned in the homily that follows and throughout this book, was also on that faculty and likely would have been murdered if he had not been attending a conference outside the country. Two of Sobrino's recent works on Christology were put on "notification" by the Vatican in an action made public on March 14, 2007, continuing the conservative hierarchy's harsh attitude toward liberation theologians since the earliest years of John Paul II's papacy. Soon thereafter Sobrino's colleagues in the Ecumenical Association of Third World Theologians expressed their solidarity with him in a collection of essays entitled *Getting the Poor Down from the Cross: Christology of Liberation* (2007), available as a free download at servicioskoinonia. org/LibrosDigitales/LDK/EATWOTGettingThePoorDown.pdf. The book also serves as a good survey of current Latin American liberation theology by some forty theologians.
3. Ignacio Martín-Baró, Adriann Aron (ed.), Shawn Corne (ed.), *Writings for a Liberation Psychology* (Harvard University Press, 1994), 2.
4. A homily presented at Texas Lutheran College, on September 23, 1988.
5. Glenn McDonald, *The Disciple-Making Church* (FaithWalk Publishing, 2004), 93.
6. M. Scott Peck, *The Road Less Travelled and Beyond* (Touchstone, 1998), 272.
7. Glenn McDonald, *op. cit.*, 95.

CHAPTER 6

WHO, WHAT, AND WHERE IN THE WORLD IS GOD?

Background essay

Tom Wilkens

In the early '90s, several of our theology majors came to the department faculty with a request. They pointed out that the faculty had control not only over the curriculum but also over discipline-related co-curricular activities such as guest speakers and symposia. They said that they would like to have an annual theological event over which they had jurisdiction: they would choose the subject area to be explored, the format of the program, and the guest presenters. They thought the concept would be a hard sell. It was not: we faculty thought it was a great idea. We committed some departmental funds to the endeavor and helped the students to identify other funding sources.

Over the years they have sponsored some outstanding events, ranging from a one-evening panel discussion by local faculty to multi-evening series of presentations by distinguished visiting lecturers. The topics the students chose were interesting and relevant. The paper that follows was delivered at their first program. The theme, which they actually asked me to help formulate once they had chosen the subject area (they were looking for a title jazzier than "The doctrine of God" or "My understanding of God"), was "Who, what, and where in the world is God?" Four faculty members gave brief presentations, followed by a question and answer period chaired by a student. My paper contains as good a summary as I have ever composed of the fundamental theology I have synthesized over the past quarter-century. It also reveals some fissures in that theological foundation.

For one thing, I live and articulate my faith out of two realities. There is little question that, theologically, I am schizophrenic. There is, however, some question as to whether or not my schizophrenic theological condition is a disabling disorder. The paper may give some clues. It exposes in the broadest of terms the first- and third-world, or developed- and developing-world, formation of my life, faith, and theological deliberations.

The paper makes reference to process philosophy and theology, which are characteristically developed-world movements. They are often hierarchical and abstract. The hierarchy is intellectual, not institutional; subtly patronizing, not overtly demanding. Their basic frame of reference for thinking things through is the abstract sub-discipline of philosophy called cosmology. Their fundamental category within that sub-discipline — by which they seek an understanding not only of the universe but also of God — is dynamic change, not static permanence.

Without naming them, the paper also shows the influence of liberation theologies, which are typically though not exclusively developing-world phenomena: they tend to be more concrete and egalitarian. Liberation movements and the theologies they generate focus on issues rather than ideas or ideals; they function in a bottom-up rather than trickle-down mode. They understand the world and God primarily from social, political, and economic perspectives; that is, from the standpoint of the social sciences — not of philosophy or cosmology. And they seek more than understanding: they seek to transform the world.

Over the past quarter of a century, I have been shaped generally by both worlds and specifically by both process and liberation theologies. It has not been easy, since these two theological streams can have such different sets of concerns, assumptions, and methods. Yet I find the directions they move and the conclusions they draw to be complementary, not contradictory.

There were already efforts to integrate these two tributaries back in the '70s, such as Schubert Ogden's *Faith and Freedom: Toward a Theology of Liberation.*[1] Ogden is a process theologian. I thought his approach to liberation theology was quite elitist and condescending. He regarded liberation theology as "merely" practical (an attitude not unknown among systematic theologians with respect to practical theology) and nearly devoid of the necessary theoretical underpinnings. His goal was to provide the missing theory. The challenge for me, conversely, has been to hold both theologies in high regard and to high critical standards, standards not just from the philosophic tradition but also from the social sciences. Has it been difficult? Yes. Has it also been stimulating and rewarding? Extraordinarily so.

Not all process theology follows the Ogden paradigm. For example, John Cobb has connected his metaphysical concerns with a most practical orientation, focusing on areas such as ecology and economics and on issues such as sustainability and justice. I once had the privilege of inviting Dr. Cobb, now emeritus professor at the Claremont School of Theology and Claremont Graduate School, to teach a session of my Contemporary Theology seminar. I have had similarly positive classroom experiences with liberation theologians such as José Miguez Bonino from Argentina and also Elsa Támez, who spoke with my students during a travel seminar in Costa Rica. Mostly, however, I have been mentored in process theology by books and tutored in liberation theology by rural peasants and urban poor in Latin America.

Who, what, and where in the world is God?[2]

Tom Wilkens

I was the one who helped the students dream up the title for this little inquisition and — wouldn't you know? — I got it wrong. That is to say, I placed the interrogative pronouns — who, what, and where — in the wrong order. I'll correct that right now, and take the questions up in what I consider to be a more appropriate order.

The first question, then, is this: Where in the world is God? I consider that to be the primary issue because it occurs to me that where one thinks that one encounters God has the most profoundly shaping influence on one's resultant impression of God. The cocoons of the monastery and university and suburb yield very different visions than the cacophonies of the marketplace and *colonia*. My own most recent theological mentors have come from the *colonia*, not from academia.

Where in the world is God? Where the struggle for social justice takes place: there God is both *at* and *on* the side of the poor and the powerless. Where in the world is God? Where expressions of human love take place: there God is among people relating together in both small and large communities of concern. Words shared and sacraments celebrated in contexts of struggle and communities of loving concern mediate God's presence in life-affirming ways. Most other liturgical activities are reduced to empty, godless routines by an apathetic neglect of neighbor or become indictments — though largely unrecognized as such — of stiff-necked pride in ourselves, our *cultus* or our culture.

One further note about God's presence: it cannot be taken for granted. God's absence is an awful possibility and an occasional actuality. Not only can God be silent; God can also be gone. Thus it is a mistake to attribute omnipresence to God. That leads to the next question: what in the world is God?

God's whatness is not static. God's whatness changes. It changes by virtue of God's own decisions to create and to relate. *Creators* impart portions of themselves to their creations. For example, God invests a significant share of God's power in creation and in creatures, including us, and thus God is no longer omnipotent in the sense of holding and exercising all power.[3] God also decided to continue to relate to creatures. *Relaters* become vulnerable, open to inevitable though not predictable change. People primarily, though other species and even the inanimate environment secondarily, have an impact on God's becoming.

On this matter, the matter of what God is, I confess that for an elaboration of my ideas I have drawn upon the resources of the university; upon relatively recent traditions called process philosophy and process theology; upon Alfred North Whitehead and Charles Hartshorne, Schubert Ogden and John Cobb. The essence of those traditions, as I understand them, is this: God's *thatness* — *that* God is — persists. But God's *whatness* — *what* God is — proceeds to emerge as God continues to create, to impart, to relate, to change. God's whatness is contingent and becoming, like our own. But, unlike our own, God's thatness is neither contingent nor finite.

Finally, then, who has God become? From Martin Luther, a theological giant of the sixteenth century, to Karl Barth, a theological giant of the twentieth century, a claim has been made that whatever we know of God is a function — totally and exclusively — of God's humanity.[4] The reality of God may not be exhausted by God's humanity, but our access to God's reality is wholly restricted to God's humanity.

Who in the world is this God? Your answer, to come full circle, depends on where you think God is, where God is available and accessible. In my view, God is one who plays favorites. God favors the poor, the powerless, the oppressed, the suffering. In my view — and this is as much hope as it is conviction — God is one who, while favoring the oppressed, does not thereby exclude the rest of us. But God is most clearly present to the rest of us through those who suffer, through their humanity, and even through their lack of humanity.

In my view, God is one who is committed to love and justice. Because of this commitment to non-manipulative love, God will not coerce. And because of this disavowal of coercion, coupled with the aforementioned voluntary dissemination of power, God cannot, by God's self, establish justice. To paraphrase a presidential inaugural address, God's work — the work of love and justice — must truly be our own if that work is to move forward in this world.

Where is God? God is a sometimes-present reality, here as an affirming presence insofar as we are a community of love and justice. What is God? God is an always-persisting reality whose perfection includes change. Who is God? God is a currently partisan reality whose love of the poor is passionate and love of the rest of us is remarkably patient. For me, a Christian, the where, what, and who of God are epitomized and embodied most fully in Jesus the Christ. And for me, a Trinitarian, that incarnation of the where, what, and who of God is rendered contemporary, concrete, and comprehensible by the Spirit.

Response:
Thought experiment

Kim Wilkens

"We don't know what 96% of the universe is."[5]

I used to think inside the box. I thought I could use Kim's scientific method to explain the world. My scientific method relied almost exclusively on my observations, which were limited to say the least. So using Kim's limited scientific method, I did not observe God, therefore God did not exist. Then I discovered that I had kind of been forced into this box to peacefully co-exist in the modern world, where everything is explained or rationalized away.

When I learned about postmodernism and acknowledged the struggle of dealing with paradox and truth, I discovered that I had been limiting my thoughts and myself. I'm now thinking outside the box and it is a frightening and exhilarating and humbling experience. I don't have a degree in theology or physics, so I'm going to be treading on thin ice here, but I had a thought.

Dualism

We've been dividing the world up for a long time between the natural and the supernatural, mind and matter, humanity and God. We do this because it appears to us that these entities play by different rules. I just learned that this is called dualism. I love that I can learn new things at my age.

With the advent of quantum mechanics, it appears that another duality exists between the large objects we can easily observe and tiny objects known as quantum particles. The rules that we understand or take for granted that govern large objects, such as force, mass, and acceleration, don't seem to apply to quantum particles in the same way. In fact, out of our context of understanding and being able to predict large object behavior like trajectory, speed, and location, quantum mechanics seems kind of unbelievable.

> The behaviour of microscopic objects described in quantum mechanics is very different from our everyday experience, which may provoke an incredulous reaction.[6]

Trying to read about and understand quantum mechanics is very challenging and I still don't get it. Here are just a couple of things I learned that made my head spin.[7] There's actually something called The Uncertainty Principle, which is one of the cornerstones of quantum mechanics. That's not a very comforting name. It describes that for quantum particles, you cannot measure speed and location at the same time because you can only observe one property at a time. Chance plays an integral role in the life of quantum particles. They move because there is the chance that they will. They cannot be coerced. If and when they move there is no predicting the chance where they will end up. Nothing is certain. Everything is possible. And here's the kicker: Everything in our world is made up from quantum particles. How can they behave so differently? How does any order or predictability come out of this chaos?

Human Quarkiness

On the one hand this is mind-blowing stuff. How can you make sense of something that can't be predicted and leaves so much to chance? On the other hand, it sounds a lot like humans. Don't we tend to be unpredictable, often moving by chance, choosing whether to interact or not. Isn't this our God-given gift of free will? Why is it so surprising that our most fundamental building blocks have this gift as well?

God's Enormity

So we find ourselves living in a world where the small particles are behaving chaotically and the large objects are behaving more predictably. This got me thinking that maybe the largest object of all would be the most predictable, the most reliable, and the most stable. We often think of the vastness of space as a scary thing. We seem so small and insignificant. It is awe-inspiring, but now I think it should also be comforting. Growing up in Texas, I always heard that bigger is better. Maybe it really is.

Let me know Your enormity because You are always there, You are steadfast. Let me know my tininess because my life is chaotic and unpredictable. Let the quantum particles of my being search and adhere to You. Amen.

Chapter Endnotes

1. Schubert Ogden, *Faith and Freedom: Toward a Theology of Liberation* (Abingdon Press, 1979).
2. A paper delivered at a colloquy (fall term, 1992) organized by the student Department Assistants of the Department of Theology and Philosophy, Texas Lutheran College.
3. See the homily in ch. 16 for further elaboration of my views on the omnipotence of God, an elaboration indebted to process philosophy and theology. On the matter of change in God, see my background essays in chs. 8, 10, and 30.
4. This idea, at least incipient in Luther's incarnational theology, becomes more fully explicit in Barth's *The Humanity of God* (Westminster John Knox Press, 1988), especially the second chapter.
5. Science Friday, Big Questions in Cosmology, Friday, April 3, 2009, www.sciencefriday.com; Michael Turner, Professor, Departments of Astronomy and Astrophysics and Physics, Kavli Institute for Cosmological Physics, University of Chicago.
6. Wikipedia, "Introduction to quantum mechanics," en.wikipedia.org/wiki/Basics_of_quantum_mechanics.
7. Find more information about quantum mechanics from Abarim Publications, "Quantum Mechanics, Chaos theory & Reliability of the Bible," www.abarim-publications.com.

Can anything good come out of Norway? Yes. Edvard and Henrik; Else and Leif; and Hans. Each graced in a different way. Each a channel of grace, creative or redemptive, in a unique manner.[7]

Response: In good company?

Kim Wilkens

My husband and I recently watched *In Good Company*. The film is about a young executive on the fast track. In a corporate merger, he takes over the management job of someone much older and more experienced and that older person is demoted and has to work for the young guy. The young guy is all about his career, his house, his car, and his status to the detriment of his marriage, his social life, and his health. The young guy is not as ruthless in pursuit of the bottom-line as his superiors, but he feels the pressure and does what he feels has to be done (firing employees and having his team work longer hours). Through a relationship with the older man's daughter, the young man begins to understand the goals he has set for his life may not bring true fulfillment.

I didn't get it while I was watching, but I now realize my career at IBM mirrored many aspects of the young man's career. I was on the fast track. When I became a manager, I was younger than any of my employees. I was all about making it in a man's world, high performance appraisals, being respected, and a strong work ethic. I thought I was fair, but in retrospect I think I was pretty ruthless. I didn't understand people who didn't put career first. If I didn't respect the ideas of someone else, I would railroad over them if they were in my way or I would simply ignore them. The rewards were promotions, praise, and travel, but the drawbacks were a failed marriage, a lack of social skills, and an unhealthy lifestyle.

I'm lucky; I'm living my second chance. But I sometimes miss the rewards of my previous life. I wonder why it is so difficult to be satisfied doing good work without desiring praise and to make sacrifices instead of wanting more. When I started reading Donald Miller's *Searching for God Knows What*, his interpretation of the fall from Genesis not only blew me away, but also gave me insight into this age-old dilemma.

Reading Genesis has always been a problem for me. I can believe in the science of evolution. I have problems with a universe created in six days, a Garden of Eden, Eve created from Adam, a tree of life, a serpent that speaks, the fall of humankind. And, of course, it irks me that Eve bears so much of the burden for this fall. So, I have been categorizing this story as a myth devised to explain creation in ancient times and ignoring it. Donald Miller has me thinking about it again.

> Man is wired so he gets his glory (his security, his understanding of value, his feeling of purpose, his feeling of rightness with his Maker, his security for eternity) from God and this relationship is so strong, and God's love so pure, that Adam and Eve felt no insecurity at all... But when that relationship was broken, they knew it instantly. All of their glory, the glory that came from God, was gone... All of the insecurity rises the instant you realize you are alone.
>
> If man was wired so that something outside himself told him who he was, and if God's presence was giving him a feeling of fulfillment, then when that relationship was broken, a man would be pining for other people to tell him that he was good, right, okay with the world, and eternally secure.[8]

I do believe there is something missing in our make-up that we are looking for to make us whole. It's the basis of religion. Scientists have puzzled over it. B.F. Skinner thought it could be generated with behavior modification. Maslow put it at the top of his human needs hierarchy and labeled it self-transcendence. Sigmund Freud described it as our unconscious mind. All these explanations provide insight into this missing element, but none have thoroughly explained or fixed it.

I can appreciate the idea that we're wired to know our creator, to understand our creator's will for us, and to find fulfillment in this relationship. I get that somehow our connection to our creator got damaged or broken. I don't understand how this happened, but I see that it causes us to not feel whole. It's obvious to me that we spend our lives looking for wholeness, fulfillment, and security to fill this void. It explains a lot of stupidity in the world as we go *looking for love in all the wrong places.*

Is there an antidote? Jesus told his disciples that there is, but it is a radical procedure: "whoever wishes to become great among you must be your servant, and whoever wishes to be first among you must be slave of all." Talk about countercultural! Glenn McDonald, author of *The Disciple*

Another preliminary point needs to be addressed in this essay. Prior to delivering the homily, I had asked Jayme and Dale Wratchford — a student couple, both with experience in theater; Dale was one of our brightest and best theology majors — if they would pantomime the Hosea text while it was being read. I thought this might increase the impact of the text. I had no idea. After chapel, Jayme and Dale told me that they had almost called me to refuse to do it. While they rehearsed the pantomime it became, they said, excruciatingly — almost impossibly — difficult to do. They felt very deeply that it represented a marriage or a relationship gone pathologically awry. They were loathe to participate, to get so involved — which is what good actors do with their material.

They did not call me. They went through with the performance. And it was very painful. Why is it that at times when I pipe the tune, others end up paying the piper? In this instance it likely was because I was insensitive to what the text might mean to and how it might impact a young couple still quite early on in their relationship and even earlier on in their marriage. I did not notice. Noticing is an important prerequisite for learning the more profound lessons of life and preventing or alleviating the more profound pains of life.[2]

Finally, I raise issues in this homily that I do not resolve. I do not always have the humility or the honesty to do this: I share the modern human hope that loose ends can be tied together and the human *hubris* that I can pull it off. I need constant, even forceful reminders that this is not so. My daughter's postmodern perspective is a helpful, powerful antidote to my smug confidence in this pursuit.

God and the imagery of sexual love[3]

Tom Wilkens

Introduction

If you are over forty, either physically or psychologically, I may be about to ruin this hymn for you. If you are under forty, either physically or psychologically, I may be about to renew your interest in it.

If you have the hymnal open in front of you to "Jesus, priceless treasure," let me ask you to conduct an experiment. I want you to read the first verse silently. But when you do it, substitute the name of your spouse or your most romantic friend or fantasy person for the name "Jesus" and the title "Lord." Take a few moments and read it to yourself with the new name inserted.

> Jesus, priceless treasure,
>   Source of purest pleasure,
>   Truest friend to me:
> Ah, how long I've panted,
>   And my heart has fainted,
>   Thirsting, Lord, for thee!
> Thine I am, O spotless Lamb;
>   I will suffer nought to hide thee,
>   Nought I ask beside thee.[4]

What I hope you have discovered, in your silent reading, is an almost embarrassingly passionate love poem. In fact, this hymn started out as a love poem penned by a seventeenth-century German poet named Heinrich Alberti. About a decade later, the German hymn-writer Johann Franck borrowed Alberti's passionate poem and turned it into a passionate hymn. *Too* passionate, as it turned out. The German clergy regarded the hymn as too sensual for congregational use, and it took a long time for it to become widely accepted.

This small episode in liturgical history raises several interesting questions. But I would like to focus on just one: should a community of faith utilize the imagery of sexual love in giving expression to its understanding of God? It is not a new question. Many medieval mystics decided that, while the powerful imagery of sexual love is always open to unhealthy distortion, its strength could be used to good effect in elucidating the most intimate dimensions of our relation with God. For example, one of the primary images of the divine — human union employed by Christian mystics in their effort to describe the intense intimacy of that union is the image of the divine marriage.

There is a related issue, even more disturbing, raised not by this hymn but by the biblical text that I am about to read and that Jayme and Dale Wratchford will give visual interpretation. It is the issue of God and the imagery of spousal abuse. The imagery is from marriage gone destructively wrong. Please listen and watch.

The text

Plead with your mother, plead — for she is *not* my wife, and I am *not* her husband — that she put away her whoring from her face, and her adultery from between her breasts, or I will strip her naked and expose her as in the day she was born, and make her like a wilderness, and turn her into a parched land, and kill her with thirst.

Upon her children also I will have no pity, because they are children of whoredom. For their mother has played the whore; she who conceived them has acted shamefully. For *she* said, "I will go after my lovers; they give me my bread and my water, my wool and my flax, my oil and my drink." Therefore I will hedge up her way with thorns; and I will build a wall against her, so that she cannot find her paths.

She shall pursue her lovers, but not overtake them; and she shall seek them, but shall not find them. *Then* she shall say, "I will go and return to my first husband, for it was better with me then than now."

She did not know that it was I who gave her the grain, the wine, and the oil, and who lavished upon her silver and gold that they used for Baal. Therefore I will take back my grain in its time, and my wine in its season; and I will take away my wool and my flax, which were to cover her nakedness.

Now I will uncover her shame in the sight of her lovers, and no one shall rescue her out of my hand. I will put an end to all her mirth, her festivals, her new moons, her sabbaths, and all her appointed festivals. I will lay waste her vines and her fig trees, of which *she* said, "These are my pay, which my lovers have given me." I will make them a forest, and the wild animals shall devour them. I will punish her for the festival days of the Baals, when she offered incense to them and decked herself with her ring and jewelry, and went after her lovers, and forgot me, says the LORD.

Therefore, I will now allure her, and bring her into the wilderness, and speak tenderly to her. From there I will give her vineyards, and make the Valley of Achor a door of hope. There she shall respond as in the days of her youth, as at the time when she came out of the land of Egypt.

On that day, says the LORD, you will call me, "My husband," and no longer will you call me, "My Baal." For I will remove the names of the Baals from her mouth, and they shall be mentioned by name no more. I will make for you a covenant on that day with the wild animals, the birds of the air, and the creeping things of the ground; and I will abolish the bow, the sword, and war from the land; and I will make you lie down in safety. And I will take you for my wife forever; I will take you for my wife in righteousness and in justice, in steadfast love, and in mercy. I will take you for my wife in faithfulness; and you shall know the LORD.   — Hosea 2:2-20; italics mine

God and the imagery of spousal abuse

Several weeks ago I attended a convocation of teaching theologians where the book of Hosea was the grist for our dialogical mill. The portion of Hosea that was just read became the basis for a lecture and a sermon by two women. Both women, quite independently, came to the same conclusion: God is portrayed in this text as an abusive spouse, following a familiar pattern of alternating rage and regret. Both women have seen that pattern again and again through abused women they counsel.

That's an appalling conclusion. It evokes many troubling questions. For instance, is that pattern of abuse actually in the text? And if it is, would the author/editors of Hosea have been consciously aware of the behavior model they had chosen to portray God's anger and love? I don't have definitive answers to those questions. But I do know that two very competent theologians — both trained to read things *out of* texts rather than *into* them — two talented women, both experienced in dealing with spousal abuse, see the pattern there. I think we must take their insights seriously. Jayme, Dale, and I have tried to do so this morning.

It is when I have taken seriously people who suffer — because of race or gender or sexual orientation or some other prejudice-triggering reality that simply never permits the pain to go away completely — it is when I have taken such people seriously that I have learned the most theologically. You are present throughout the global village. You permeate that collage of cultures called America. And you are also here, in this community of faith and learning: people who suffer abuse because of race or gender or sexual orientation or some other prejudice-triggering reality. Here. Among us. A part of the "us," though often marginalized or pressured to be unreal in order to prevent marginalization. In the past three years, for example, I have learned the most, theologically, from a gay student. I owe that young man not only a debt of theological growth but also a debt of human anguish that I can only imagine and can never repay.

Rather than attempt to answer all the troubling questions that the Hosea text arouses, let me respond in what I hope is a constructive way to an underlying theological problem. The problem is this: how to portray God's transcendent power without obscuring God's immanent love. It is not easy, but I think that a late fourteenth- and early fifteenth-century Augustinian monk has done it quite well. Our closing hymn, written by

Bianco da Siena, uses the imagery of light to depict both the love and the power of God. This imagery of light — warm and soothing, on the one hand; laser-like and surgical, on the other — this imagery also was used by earlier mystics with insight, sensitivity, and control. I commend it to our imaginations.

> Come down, O Love divine;
>> Seek thou this soul of mine
>> And visit it with thine own ardor glowing;
> O Comforter, draw near;
>> Within my heart appear
>> And kindle it, thy holy flame bestowing.
> Oh, let it freely burn,
>> Till worldly passions turn
>> To dust and ashes in its heat consuming;
> And let thy glorious light
>> Shine ever on my sight,
>> And clothe me round, the while my path illuming.[5]

Response:
Restoration

Kim Wilkens

Encountering images of sex and violence in the Bible should not be surprising. Actually, I didn't fully appreciate the extent of this until stumbling upon a website called The Brick Testament.[6] Seeing some of these scenes recreated with Legos® is kind of shocking. What is surprising to me is the apathetic response toward these descriptions today. More disturbing is the use of select passages out of their context in the Bible and from the world they were created to boost a personal agenda of righteousness.

It seems that the Bible shows us many examples of the problems that occur when sex is rooted in violence and not love. There are stories and retellings of sexual thoughts and deeds outside of loving relationships that are about power and gratification. The one that really gets to me is the story of Sodom and Gomorrah, so often cited as a justification to judge homosexuality as a sin when to me it is so clearly about power, mob mentality, and gang rape. Lot's offering of his virgin daughters in place of the "strangers" is heartbreaking to me. What was he thinking? How can that be in the Bible? I also find Hosea's text casting God as the spurned husband capable of and justified in physical violence toward his wife troubling. It seems like a very bad metaphor.

I usually love metaphors. One of my "jobs" is to come up with sermon images that get projected during worship. It's so much easier to find or create images when a metaphor can be found to represent the material. When I was working on Easter images the theme was restoration. I gave the images an "old movie in need of restoration" kind of look to help convey the idea of restoration. I was looking for a Last Supper image and I stumbled upon this article about Leonardo's masterpiece, describing how it has been through many restorations.

> Leonardo, always the inventor, tried using new materials for Last Supper. Instead of using tempera on wet plaster (the preferred method of fresco painting, and one which had worked successfully for centuries), he thought he'd give using dry plaster a whirl. His experiment resulted in a more varied palette, which was Leonardo's intent. What he hadn't taken into account (because, who knew?) was that this method wasn't at all durable. The painted plaster began to flake off the wall almost immediately, and people have been attempting to restore it ever since.[7]

So here's a metaphor that popped into my head. The Bible is a masterpiece that was created using the invention of the written word versus the tradition of oral history used for centuries before. The intent was to harness the rich and diverse collection of stories, history, wisdom, poetry, prophecy and first-hand accounts of God's work in the world, but the medium had some unexpected drawbacks. The most obvious is the problem of translation. There are twenty English translations on biblegateway.com alone. Apparently there are even much-debated, different styles of translation (such as formal equivalence, dynamic equivalence, and paraphrase). Like paint flaking off a masterpiece, there are words that have become obsolete and are in need of having their meaning restored. I wonder how many translations have been misguided attempts at restoration. If the words need to be translated, what about the metaphors?

Hosea uses a powerful metaphor of a marriage gone horribly wrong to describe God's relationship with Israel. Maybe one thing we've missed with this metaphor is the age-old adage that it takes two to tango. When a marriage goes wrong, one party or the other may have exacerbated the conflict, but the very nature of conflict is that it takes two.

The Hosea text also seems like a mixed metaphor where two mutually exclusive responses to a marriage in conflict are presented. The wife (Israel) has behaved very badly, breaking the covenant of marriage by being unfaithful in body, soul, and mind. In version one, the husband (the Lord) is understandably upset and is therefore able to justify his actions of retribution and revenge. In version two, the husband's response to his wife is to speak gentle words of hope, reconciliation and peace. Where is the justice in that? Does the husband really expect words alone to change the wife's behavior?

In our modern day world, I think we can imagine ourselves as the reckless wife, making one bad choice after another, but when we tie the two versions of the broken marriage story into one, we come away terrified of the abusive husband and distrustful of the whispered promises from the abusive spouse. I wonder if this story is missing the "but." God could choose to respond to a world that is so often in conflict with God's will with vengeance, a very human and justifiable response, *but* instead no matter how unkind, unfair, unfaithful, unaware, unworthy, or unwanted we treat our relationship with God, God continues to seek restoration with us.

> "I will give you justice, fairness, love, kindness, and faithfulness. Then you will truly know who I am." — Hosea 2:19-20, CEV

Chapter Endnotes

1. Almost any of Tillich's numerous writings will either elaborate or illustrate his method of correlation. See Tracy's *Blessed Rage for Order: The New Pluralism in Theology* (University of Chicago Press, 1975), a difficult but rewarding work, for an amplification of his refinement of the method. Both Tillich's method in general and Tracy's book title in particular, making the intensity of his quest for intellectual order explicit, clearly indicate that they are modern, not postmodern, theologians.
2. This lesson was initially brought home to me by Henri Nouwen in his *Reaching Out: The Three Movements of the Spiritual Life* (Doubleday, 1975), a book that I used for several years as a text in a course titled Religion and Culture Today.
3. A homily presented at Texas Lutheran College on October 7, 1994.
4. "Jesus, Priceless Treasure" words by Johann Franck 1618-1677. In the public domain.
5. "Come Down, O Love Divine" words by Bianco da Siena, d. 1434. In the public domain.
6. Brendan Powell Smith, *The Brick Testament*, www.thebricktestament.com.
7. Shelley Esaak, "About.com: Art History," *Leonardo da Vinci — The Last Supper*, Art History. arthistory. about.com/cs/leonardo/a/last_supper.htm.

CHAPTER 10

BEING ONE FAMILY WITH GOD

Background essay

Tom Wilkens

The religious right has surveyed and then registered a claim for the "family values" turf. The religious center and left seem unable to put together effective counter-claims. This is one of the reasons I have been uncomfortable using the term "family" as a metaphor for the church. In my mind, it has become too narrowly defined and understood in too static a way — that is, too detached from broad and dynamic biblical notions — to serve well as either an equivalent for or an explication of the term "church."

And so, as I said in the beginning of the next homily, I was not at ease with the theme chosen for my congregation's annual retreat: "Being one family with God." But I had come on board as the preacher of the day well after the theme had been chosen and the retreat agenda set. Thus I had to deal with it. It is a good discipline to be confronted with these situations from time to time.

In the homily, I spoke about the changing family and I spoke in a largely positive manner. The religious right would have been upset. To be more specific and contentious, the religious right does not really embrace family values: they embrace family principles. There is a difference.

In western culture, there are two major streams of ethical thinking. One we call deontological ethics (from the Greek word *deóntos*, meaning duty), wherein moral obligations are spelled out in terms of laws or principles — principles that are understood to be divinely inspired and absolute by those Christians who function morally within this frame of reference. Deontological ethics, in its purest form, operates with a palette of black and white — with no multiplicity of options in moral choices either sought or tolerated. An act is either moral or immoral, right or wrong. There is no middle ground; there are no shades of gray.

The other stream we call teleological ethics (from the Greek word *télos*, meaning end or goal), wherein moral obligations are elaborated in terms of consequences and values. Teleological ethics can operate with a highest or absolute good: for Christians that would be God. But it also recognizes that the rest of goods and values are not absolute. Teleological ethics holds that moral decisions are made in a grayscale milieu. To put it indelicately but accurately: for Christians who operate morally within this scheme, God alone is absolute; everything else is up for grabs. This sounds downright scary, if not even crazy. It could drive a person to trust in God instead of rules or a rulebook.

I belong to the teleological camp. This does not mean that I hold no strong moral convictions or values. I would hope that this is clear by now. But it does mean that I have to be willing to reassess my convictions and values at every turn or challenge. Now you know my homiletical dilemma: I had a theme with a hijacked metaphor as its focus, infused with some inappropriately absolutistic moral principles, and an audience comfortable with the situation. But there is more.

I have inherited a Christian tradition that in some significant ways had become more Greek than Hebraic in its orientation. And I would be speaking to a congregation that, by and large, embraced this tradition. That is to say, on an issue central to this whole subject, they would be inclined to regard immutability or unchangeableness — an ideal of ancient Greek culture — as the epitome of perfection. Not only would they want no change in God (see my paper in chapter 6); they also would want no change in basic human institutions, such as family.

It would appear that I was about to enter a moral and cultural minefield. However, that depiction is far too dramatic. In truth, the minefield image is not even close to the reality of the situation I faced. By this time, 1995, Faith Lutheran members had lived with me for over a quarter of a century. They had become accustomed, through annual adult study classes I taught and occasional homilies I delivered, to giving me a fair hearing. And they had become quite tolerant of my atypical views and perspectives. It would be no different on this occasion.

Something I still have not forgotten happened after the Sunday morning retreat service was over. I was standing on an outdoor patio, waiting for the camp dinner bell to sound, when a boy of ten or eleven came up to me and thanked me profusely for the sermon I had just given. His thanks were heartfelt; it was obvious to me that he had not been put up to it by his parents. But before I was able to engage him in any sort of conversation, he ran off to join his buddies at play. Why had he approached me, some distance away from the worship space and some minutes after the worship time? What was there in the homily that could touch a small boy?

I have to say this, although you have probably already guessed it: I have never given a children's sermon and I never will. I would not have the slightest clue as to how to do a homily for children or even how to begin to prepare one. I do not think of kids when I put a homily together, other than to restrain my pen if I am tempted to use some vulgar language to make a point (if I actually wanted to do this and needed a precedent, Luther at times used barnyard vocabulary in his preaching). I think of adults. I believe the homily that follows illustrates this. And yet, apparently it spoke in a helpful way to a young boy. As I have been rereading the homily in preparing this essay, I continue to puzzle over that.

A closing comment for this essay: through baptism, a gracious God finalizes our adoption papers. Through sharing in the Eucharist, that same gracious God sustains our membership in God's family. But participation in the Eucharist is also an act of both courage and humility: it identifies us with generations of God's loving servant people, God's faithful suffering people, and God's hopeful martyred people.

Being one family with God:
the rhetoric is easy, but the responsibility is not[1]

Tom Wilkens

Introduction

The theme selected for our weekend retreat, "Being one family with God," would not have been my choice. I prefer the metaphor of community to that of family when I think about the church. But I have discovered over the years that it is usually good to be encouraged to rethink one's position. I have been doing this for the past couple of weeks and it has been helpful for me to clarify my thoughts about family and church. So in this morning's sermon I will address the theme of "Being one family with God." But I will add a sub-title: "the rhetoric is easy, but the responsibility is not." Or — to put it more simply — the talk is easy, but the walk is not.

As I read and reviewed some things, especially certain portions of the biblical literature, I was reminded of an important truth about family: the family is always changing. Surely the family may be changing more rapidly in the twentieth century than in previous times. But family has never been stable, if by stable we mean permanent in shape or function or definition. And so I would like to share a few thoughts about the changing family from three perspectives: the Old Testament, the New Testament, and contemporary America.

The changing family: some Old Testament perspectives

Many books and articles have been written about these three perspectives; so let me be very selective in saying just a few things about each one. First, with respect to Israelite notions of family that emerge through the Old Testament, I am always struck by the *inclusive* definitions of family that were operational there. Family in Israel was not typically nuclear or even molecular. Family often included father, mother or mothers, sons, daughters, concubines, slaves, servants, resident aliens, and the needy. And family values and obligations included *all* of those people. That's a far cry from the narrow way we tend to define family and family values today.

Another fact that emerges in the Old Testament is that family patterns changed when life circumstances changed. As Israel underwent the transitions from pastoral to agricultural to urban life settings, family also underwent transitions. Even high officials could be criticized if they did not change rapidly enough. The warm embrace of monogamy in the Eden story of creation, likely published at about the time of King Solomon, perhaps also served as a subtle critique of his polygamous lifestyle. The Israelites faced real problems, as we still do, in attempting to balance the need to change with the times over against the desire to retain some core features from the past. They simply could do it at a more leisurely pace than we have been challenged to do in our day.

The changing family: some New Testament perspectives

As we turn to the New Testament, and look at the origins of the Christian church, we find that it began as a "house church." It was also a church of households: whole households were brought into the community of Christian faith through the baptism of adult members of those households. And again, those households or families bore more resemblance to the inclusive Old Testament models than the smaller, more exclusive models of family in recent history.

What I wish to focus on in the New Testament, however, is the way in which Jesus is portrayed as dealing with family. For one thing, when Jesus had to face transition, he apparently felt comfortable with change and perhaps even innovation with respect to family. Reading what is usually cited as Jesus' sixth word from the cross from the Fourth Gospel:

> When Jesus saw his mother and the disciple whom he loved standing beside her, he said to his mother, "Woman, here is your son." Then he said to the disciple, "Here is your mother." And from that hour the disciple took her into his own home.   — John 19:26-27

At that most poignant and painful moment in his life, Jesus reconfigured his own family.

For another thing, Jesus went far beyond the Old Testament in giving an even more inclusive definition of family. The Gospel of Mark presented it this way:

> Then his mother and his brothers came; and standing outside, they sent to him and called him. A crowd was sitting around him; and they said to him, "Your mother and your brothers and sisters are outside, asking for you." And he replied, "Who are my mother and my brothers?" And looking at those who sat around him, he said, "Here are my mother and my brothers! *Whoever does the will of God* is my brother and sister and mother."   — Mark 3:31-35; italics mine

"Whoever does the will of God is my brother and sister and mother." So what in the world is the will of God? The author of Luke apparently asked the same question. When he retold that story about Jesus he made an interesting and helpful clarification:

> Then his mother and his brothers came to him, but they could not reach him because of the crowd. And he was told, "Your mother and

your brothers are standing outside, wanting to see you." But he said to them, "My mother and my brothers are *those who hear the word of God and do it.*"   — Luke 8:19-21; italics mine

"My mother and my brothers are those who hear the word of God and do it." If Jesus truly meant that, then the sustaining membership fee for Jesus' family seems to be very high: hearing the word of God and then doing it.

The word of God says, "Love your neighbor as yourself." *Do it.* Could that possibly mean that a tithe on all my income for the church and other charitable groups should be a minimal expectation rather than an impossible dream? After all, the tithe still leaves a whopping 90% for my biological or legal family. It seems to me that members of Jesus' family probably ought not find the tithe either unreasonable or impossible if we take the rhetoric of the church as family seriously. The rhetoric — the talk — is easy; the responsibility — the walk — is not.

The word of God says, "Love your enemies and pray for those who persecute you." *Do it.* Could that possibly include the vicious bomber of the Oklahoma City federal building? The rhetoric is easy; the responsibility is not.

The word of God says, "Give food to the hungry and drink to the thirsty, welcome the stranger, clothe the naked, and visit the imprisoned." *Do it.* On just that last point alone — visiting those in prison — every member of Faith Lutheran who can read and write has the opportunity to visit prisoners of conscience once a month by writing a short letter for Amnesty International. Yet less than 5% of us do it. The rhetoric is easy; the responsibility is not.

That's the bad news. None of us has the price of admission into Jesus' family. And not enough of us pay the sustaining membership fee of hearing the word of God and doing it.

The good news is that the price of admission has been paid for us by God through Christ Jesus. The further good news is that we have some marvelous examples of sisters and brothers in Christ in this congregation, sisters and brothers who hear the word of God and do it — among their family in Faith Lutheran or *Las Milpas*,[2] among their family in the city of Seguin or the global community. And if you were to ask these exemplary sisters and brothers how they manage to hear the word of God and do it, most of them probably would respond with some embarrassment that what they do is no big deal and certainly no reason to boast. If they were to wax biblical they might say something like "it is not I, but Christ who lives in and through me." Or if they were to wax theological they might well credit the grace and power of God, which always seems sufficient.

But let's not make God's grace cheap. The confessional prayer that opens the liturgy each week must be understood as an open admission that we have not paid the sustaining membership fee in Jesus' family — hearing God's word and doing it. If we are aware of this then perhaps the declaration of forgiveness which follows that confession of sin and shortcoming can have an impact, can empower us to trust the grace of God to change us, can help us move from somewhat dysfunctional to more fully functional membership in Jesus' family.

There seems to be more bad news. Membership in Jesus' family may not build up the nuclear biological or legal family. In fact, it may tear the nuclear family apart. Discipleship is divisive. We read in Luke:

"I came to bring fire to the earth, and how I wish it were already kindled! I have a baptism with which to be baptized, and what stress I am under until it is completed! Do you think that I have come to bring peace to the earth? No, I tell you, but rather division! From now on five in one household will be divided, three against two and two against three; they will be divided: father against son and son against father, mother against daughter and daughter against mother, mother-in-law against her daughter-in-law and daughter-in-law against mother-in-law." — Luke 12:49-53

I'm not really sure that I can handle that text or that I want to handle it. One thing seems clear, however: at a minimum, what we have here is a reality check for the family of Jesus. Insofar as the church represents the family of Jesus, it is to be inclusive — as the previous gospel texts indicated. Yet insofar as the family of Jesus represents commitments that run counter to culture's values, the family of Jesus is divisive.

That's the bad news. The good news from those who have actually tried Jesus' countercultural way — that it's better to give than to receive, that rendering service is better than receiving service, that you must lose your life if you want to find a life with any prospect of fulfillment: you know the kind of countercultural stuff I'm talking about — those who try Jesus' countercultural way report that it actually works. The good news is that the deepest joy of life comes to those who travel the way of the cross. How odd of God to plan it that way. How good of God to show us the way in Jesus the Christ.

The changing family: some contemporary perspectives

Some years ago, the United States mined the harbor of Nicaragua's major seaport. We were taken to court, the World Court in the Netherlands, and found guilty of violating international law. We then told the World Court to take a running leap. We said that we were not going to be held accountable to international law, that we were not going to relinquish one iota of our national sovereignty.

The question for us this morning is quite similar, actually: are we going to relinquish any of our nuclear family sovereignty, to say nothing of our individual sovereignty, to the sovereignty and claim of Jesus? The bad news is that if we are true to our cultural values, even if we are true to so-called American family values, we likely will not place the claim of the broadly inclusive family of Jesus ahead of the narrowly exclusive claim of the nuclear or biological family. If we are true to our cultural values, at least as I see and understand them being widely practiced today, then I should think that the honest and honorable thing for us to do would be to stop using the rhetoric of family in the church. The rhetoric is too easy; the responsibility is definitely not.

The good news is that there are some clear signs that this congregation is moving in the direction of taking the rhetoric of family very seriously. We have articulated some major goals as an inclusive, outward-reaching family of Jesus in the mission, vision, and strategy statements approved last fall. We have undertaken to give Christian nurture and financial support to those who prepare for ministry in a larger church that is trying very hard to be inclusive and outward reaching. My son, among others, is the grateful recipient of that nurture and support. We are embarking on expanding the role of Faith Lutheran in our lives and community through the calling of a second pastor. If we will continue to have the courage of our commitment to the whole family of Jesus, God has promised something that the pursuit of happiness cannot attain: the joy of life that not even death can overcome.

But perhaps the most immediately significant work we have to do as a congregation is to increase our vigilance to make sure that *everyone* is included as *a fully participating and valued member* in the family of

110

Faith Lutheran: single people, single parent families, divorced adults and the children of divorce, blended families, widows and widowers, young folks and old folks. And I stress *increased vigilance*, for some of these people find barriers to their sense of belonging, of contributing, of having their needs met in the family we call Faith. Let me repeat: some people find barriers to their sense of belonging, of contributing, of having their needs met in the family we call Faith. Occasionally the barriers may be active: veiled attitudes that nonetheless act like electronic fences to keep some people away from the center of our life together. Perhaps mostly the barriers are passive: unacknowledged signs of benign neglect.

Being one family with God: the rhetoric is easy, but the responsibility is not. May God grant us the wisdom and courage and persistence to live up to our rhetoric.

Response:
Beloved community

Kim Wilkens

The importance of family is definitely a value that seems to have been passed down from generation to generation in the families of my husband and of my family. We are blessed to be part of families that give us their unconditional love. I'm not saying it's easy and that there aren't times of major disagreement or disappointment, but over days, months, and years we work through them and find we can still love each other. The older I get, the more I find that I am also looking for that kind of love from my church community. They are the ones with me here and now, on an almost daily basis, not miles away like much of my family.

I believe we all want to be part of a healthy, reconciled, authentic community. This is something Martin Luther King Jr. named the beloved community, one with the type of spirit and type of love "that can transform opposers into friends."[3] Depending on your experience of church, you may be thinking that either being beloved community in a congregation is a no-brainer or a pipe dream. It probably should be a no-brainer, but I'm finding it more like *I have a dream*.

Maybe we shouldn't expect congregations, made up of everyday, ordinary people to be able to form healthy communities. It's a tall order especially when you consider that we are coming together from a variety of backgrounds and experiences. What I think we share is our belief that God loves us unconditionally. Where I think we get off track, is when we start placing conditions on how, when, where, and who gets to respond to that love. We love our labels because they help us define who is "in" and who is "out."

There is a lot of disillusionment out there. Maybe this is where the emerging church movement got its start. I'm guessing some people began expressing different ways they were experiencing God's love and how they wanted to respond, but the more they opened up and shared their story, the more the traditional church shut them out for their non-conformity.

I'm part of a Lutheran church that is coming from a traditional/modern perspective. It is struggling right now to pass on the faith to an emerging generation. Within this community, I find myself the spokesperson, pot stirrer, or radical depending on whom I am speaking with on behalf of the disillusioned. I get increasingly frustrated with those who don't or won't see that there are some issues with the way we do church today that keep people away, people who may desperately need to hear about Jesus. Some days it seems like it would be easier to chuck it all and start over, to go hang out with a bunch of other people that think the same way I do. When I start down that road, I feel I may be slipping into the same trap as some of those I disagree with; that it's all about me and my needs. So instead of giving into my flight or fight instincts, I am being challenged to respond to this congregation as beloved community.

Maybe one step is to get rid of this notion of "organized religion." This term implies to me some sense of having it all together, of perfectly interlocking pieces. I think some people find the idea of organized religion comforting because they feel it offers a safe and stable environment, a sanctuary in the world of chaos around us. What a rude awakening one has when church fails to live up to this ideal. That's because, as Kelly Fryer says in her book, *No Experience Necessary*, "the church is people who are listening to and following Jesus together... We don't go to church. We are the church."[4] Well, if the church is people in community, then the church is going to represent a lot of different experiences, passions, disappointments, gifts, attitudes, disagreements, challenges, and beliefs just like the real world.

How do we do church with all these unique perspectives messing about? Here's a clue I stumbled upon when reading *Take This Bread* by Sara Miles.

> You can't be a Christian by yourself. You can't be more special or holy. I was going to be changed, too, and lose my private church for a new one I couldn't control. I was going to have to work with the people I liked at St. Gregory's, and the ones who irritated the hell out of me, and Veronica, and a bunch of strangers I hadn't even met yet.[5]

I am beginning to understand that I can't be part of community without expecting change, in myself and in others. That's scary because I'm going to have to give something up. Do I really believe it is better to give than to receive?

Becoming and being a beloved community is challenging. It seems the closer we get, the harder the issues that can get in the way become. I think Thomas Merton's quote really nails it:

> Our Christian calling does not make us superior to other men, nor does it entitle us to judge everyone and decide everything for everybody. We do not have the answers to every social problem, and all conflicts have not been decided beforehand in favor of our side. Our job is to struggle along with everybody else and collaborate with them in the difficult, frustrating task of seeking a solution to common problems, which are entirely new and strange to us all.[6]

That sounds a lot like family working through their disagreements and disappointments and at the end of the day, week, month or year, still finding and giving love to each other.

Chapter Endnotes

1. A homily presented at the Faith Lutheran (Seguin, Texas) congregational retreat on April 30, 1995.
2. *Las Milpas* is a mission congregation in the Rio Grande valley partnered with and supported by Faith Lutheran.
3. Dr. Martin Luther King Jr., *The Role of the Church in Facing the Nation's Chief Moral Dilemma* (1957).
4. Kelly Fryer, *No Experience Necessary: Everybody's Welcome* (Augsburg Fortress, 1999), 39.
5. Sara Miles, *Take This Bread: A Radical Conversion* (Ballantine Books, 2007), 256.
6. Charles Marsh, *The Beloved Community: How Faith Shapes Social Justice, from the Civil Rights Movement to Today* (Basic Books, 2005), 210.

CHAPTER 11

IN PRAISE OF GUILT

Background essay

Tom Wilkens

It is an odd title, even for me: "In praise of guilt." We Lutherans are famous, or infamous, for the loads of guilt we carry. Garrison Keillor makes a good part of his living taking well-aimed and insightful shots at Lutheran guilt on his radio show, "A Prairie Home Companion." I have already commented, in the background essay in chapter 3, that guilt does not seem to me to be an effective motivator for an improved lifestyle. Plus, there is more to criticize.

Luther and his evangelical successors have been inclined to understand and articulate their core understanding of the Christian faith in terms of a single biblical paradigm that came to dominate medieval Christendom: guilt and forgiveness — the confession of sin and its absolution. This is a powerful paradigm, but not the only one. There is, for example, the paradigm of death and life: the proclamation of the good news of life in the face of death — not just personal biological death but fatally flawed, death-inducing institutions and structures of society. This is the paradigm that held sway in the ancient world and now shapes the developing-world proclamation of the word of God by liberation theology. And then there is the paradigm of despair and hope: the proclamation that meaning is possible even when meaninglessness appears to prevail; that there is a fulfilling alternative to our empty consumer culture. This seems to be the paradigm that resonates most deeply with postmodern people.[1] Having said all of that, I persist in praising guilt. The homily that follows will say why.

Since I do not find guilt or even forgiveness to be fully adequate incentives for life changes, what does work for me? I have previously referred to hope. On the premise that this might be somewhat vague, permit me to elaborate a bit more. In 1995, when this homily was given, I was beginning to think more and more about retirement. When I think about things like this — that is, new directions for my life — I often think out loud. I begin to talk about it with family and friends and colleagues. In essence, I paint myself into a corner: I say so much about my tentative plans that it would appear impolite, if not downright embarrassing, not to act on them. And always, it seemed, the resources could be found to pull off the plans.

So I began talking about taking an early retirement and doing some overseas volunteer service projects. The two were related: to do overseas volunteer service, especially in the developing world, would require that I have a high level of stamina. I became determined not to wait until I was too old to do it.

The opportunities were there: not only many opportunities to do overseas service, but in addition the fiscal opportunity to make it happen. The University had a liberal early retirement program and I had some generously provided family resources. So after trying out the idea first by teaching a summer graduate course at an Indonesian university in 1997 and then by accompanying students on a service-learning mission to Costa Rica and Nicaragua in the spring of 1998, I submitted my resignation effective after the spring term of 1999. I was 62. Betty had retired two months earlier. We have done many international service projects since that time — usually together, but occasionally not.

This approach to life and life changes will not work over the long haul if that is all there is: public posturing and financial resources. I also have to be given the gift of hope, the prospect of making a difference — not a big difference, but at least an incremental one. It is hope, not guilt, that keeps drawing me forward. It is guilt, not hope, that keeps reminding me of how far I have to go.

In praise of guilt[2]

Tom Wilkens

The text

From now on, therefore, we regard no one from a human point of view; even though we once knew Christ from a human point of view, we know him no longer in that way. So if anyone is in Christ, there is a new creation: everything old has passed away; see, everything has become new! All this is from God, who reconciled us to himself through Christ, and has given us the ministry of reconciliation; that is, in Christ God was reconciling the world to himself, not counting their trespasses against them, and entrusting the message of reconciliation to us. So we are ambassadors for Christ, since God is making his appeal through us; we entreat you on behalf of Christ, be reconciled to God. For our sake he made him to be sin who knew no sin, so that in him we might become the righteousness of God.   — 2 Corinthians 5:16-21

Exegesis and hermeneutics

Several years ago I presented a homily with a title that apparently caught a few people by surprise. I called it "In praise of apathy." Some of you likely will find this morning's topic, "In praise of guilt," equally strange. Consider the source.

In one way or another, most of you in this assembly have come to know a German-born and educated mid-twentieth-century theologian named Paul Tillich. Many of you were introduced to him through a slender volume titled *Dynamics of Faith*[3] — a book that, though brief, nonetheless comes across as aggravatingly repetitive and needlessly jargon-filled. Yet for all that, it contains revealing dissections of faith and of doubt.

It is Tillich's analysis of the nature and role of doubt that I find par-ticularly valuable. He wrote of doubt approvingly. He wrote about the kind of doubt that calls into question the truth of propositions to which we give our assent: a veritable ocean of propositions the earlier American philosopher Charles Sanders Peirce had termed beliefs. They range from beliefs about the structure of DNA to beliefs about the sources of the Dead Sea scrolls. Tillich called this form of doubt methodological or scientific and argued that it was the major stimulus for extending the frontiers of knowledge. Without methodological doubt, science withers and dies, and the advance of technology grinds to a halt.

But it is his commentary on another type of doubt that I find even more insightful: existential doubt. Existential doubt is doubt that pertains to the faith that centers and organizes our inmost selves; to the undergirding, context-establishing axioms that give the potential for meaning and purpose in our lives. Such doubt has been viewed by many religious communities as a dangerous — even a deadly — virus, seeking to penetrate the membrane of faith and destroy it. Tillich, on the other hand, saw existential doubt as an essential component of all living faith: not external and destructive but internal and constructive, though surely also discomforting. Existential doubt keeps faith honest and real by reminding us of the enormous risk of faith. It reminds Christians, for instance, that Christianity is a faith and not a security system.

The biblical text that was read at the beginning expresses this faith and exposes the risk: in Christ God was reconciling the world to God's self. A carpenter's kid from Nazareth (an auto mechanic from Geronimo, Texas, would be a rough contemporary equivalent) is the agent of reconciliation between God and humanity. That affirmation is neither self-evidently nor demonstrably the case. It is not a conclusion to which I have come in my life. It is an axiom I keep rediscovering in my life and keep pondering as a premise for the direction and fulfillment of my life. Faith is, after all, a gift and not an achievement.

But this homily is not supposed to be about doubt and faith. It is titled "In praise of guilt." I should like to suggest, however, that there is a connection between doubt and guilt. I would hold that guilt plays a role in Christian life somewhat analogous to the role that existential doubt plays in Christian faith. Guilt helps to keep our *lives* honest and real. It provokes a healthy discomfort about our attitudes and behaviors.

Guilt has gone out of favor in the last century or so. We complain loudly about institutions or people who send us on guilt trips. Let me say that I don't think that the church is supposed to be a travel agency for guilt trips. Rarely has it been that for me. I book my own trips, thank you. However, the church *does* provide a travel guide service, for which I am grudgingly grateful. I need a guide to point out that my guilt is real because my dehumanizing thoughts and attitudes are real; my destructive words spoken and constructive words unspoken are real; my bad deeds done and good deeds undone are real. Theologies or philosophies that attempt to replace guilt with a comprehensive no-fault life policy are fraudulent. Get real. Get honest. Guilt requires a thick coat of forgiveness, not a thin cloak of therapy or rationalization. And forgiveness, like faith, is not achieved: it is given.

And so, once again, the text: in Christ God was reconciling the world to God's self. Reconciliation presupposes distance: not spatial or emotional distance, but moral distance. Here we confront the mystery — that is, the sacrament — of reconciliation. It is the mystery that God in Jesus the Christ has closed the moral distance. It is the mystery of fully deserved guilt dissolving in fully undeserved forgiveness.

The church, I think, has not done so badly in its attempt to keep us real about our moral life. For the church has in its tradition, and continues in some of its branches today, the practice of confession and absolution, of the admission of guilt and the declaration of forgiveness. In the ELCA's *Lutheran Book of Worship* it is called the Brief Order for Confession and Forgiveness. It is a service of disclosure, not of defensiveness. It is a service of forgiveness, not of faultlessness.

A clean heart. A new creation. A reconciliation. When these are declared, savor the peaceful embrace of forgiveness for a moment. It won't last. There will be occasions for confession and forgiveness tomorrow and the next day and the next. It's the way human life works, even for the pious — perhaps especially for the pious. Nelly Ritchie, a Methodist pastor in Argentina, put it this way:

> Nothing separates us from God like a piety that is sure of itself. Nothing draws us closer to God than acknowledgement of the grace of pardon, the offer of a new chance for abundant grace.[4]

Forgiveness is a marvelous gift. But don't bad-mouth guilt. Guilt seems to be one of God's primary set-ups for grace. And grace, in turn, seems to be God's primary secret for a life of meaning and purpose, though not necessarily of comfort and ease.

Response:
Christianity, poverty and contradictions

Kim Wilkens

> Contradictions have always existed in the soul of humanity. But it
> is only when we prefer analysis to silence that they become a constant
> and insoluble problem. We are not meant to resolve all contradictions
> but to live with them and rise above them and see them in the light of
> exterior and objective values which make them trivial by comparison.
>
> *Thoughts in Solitude*, by Thomas Merton[5]

I'm afraid I have a hard time with Merton's idea of silence in the
face of contradiction. For me, this is especially true when thinking about
the Christian response to poverty or more specifically the white, middle-
class, mainline Christian church response to poverty. This response often
seems full of contradictions. In so many places and so many ways, Jesus
directs his disciples to give up everything to follow him. And yet our
church institutions don't seem to model this kind of sacrificial giving.
Priority is given to the building, infrastructure, salaries, and internal programs, with resources for the work of mercy and justice put on the bottom
of the list. One of the fallback positions in this community that drives me
crazy is using Jesus' statement about the poor in Mark 14:7 as a "get out
of jail free" card.

> You will always have the poor with you. And whenever you want
> to, you can give to them. But you won't always have me here with
> you.
>
> (CEV)

Do you really know what issues are facing the poor in your community? If your answer is no, that's okay, they will always be there. Not
really sure you have the time or resources to help right now? That's okay,
you can give to them whenever you want.

The Webster Dictionary's definition of guilt is "to make someone feel
guilty, especially in hopes of getting them to do something." I want to do
that. I don't want to hear any more justifications; I want to hand out some
guilt!

But when I look at how this verse applies to me, I see Jesus' statement as more of a direct correlation to how I choose to live. Instead of

stepping on my holier-than-thou soapbox, pointing out where everyone else is failing the system, I feel convicted to look at my own behavior. If I am honest with myself, there is poverty because of me. I need to stop thinking of poverty as a problem out there; it is a by-product that I cause by my consumption and my waste. Until I change, I will always have the poor with me.

Maybe that is why Merton prefers silence to analysis in the face of contradiction. In the analysis, we can get caught up in guilt, fear, inertia, weariness, depression, pride, and priorities. In the silence we can see where we live in the contradiction and we can choose to change.

Chapter Endnotes

1. Paul Tillich first articulated these three paradigms in *The Courage To Be* (Yale University Press, 1952). I have found Tillich's analysis enormously helpful, though his close association of each paradigm with a particular era (ancient, medieval, modern) too limiting. The paradigms also have value for understanding different contexts of life today — such as the developed or developing world — and different stages of an individual's life in any generation.
2. A homily presented at Texas Lutheran College on November 17, 1995.
3. Paul Tillich, *Dynamcis of Faith* (Harper & Row, 1957). See Kim's analysis of the faith and doubt in her essay, "doubting faith," in ch. 19.
4. "Women and Christology," in Elsa Támez, ed., *Through Her Eyes: Women's Theology from Latin America* (Orbis Books, 1989), 87.
5. Thomas Merton, *Thoughts in Solitude* (Farrar, Straus and Giroux, 1999).

CHAPTER 12

WHAT'S LUTHERAN ABOUT LUTHERAN HIGHER EDUCATION?

Background essay

Tom Wilkens

Many religious bodies in the US are deeply involved in education. Some, such as the Roman Catholic Church and the Lutheran Church-Missouri Synod, have invested the bulk of their educational resources in primary and secondary schools. And others, such as the Evangelical Lutheran Church in America (ELCA) and several other mainline Protestant denominations, have put much more of their educational effort into colleges and universities. Those priorities have had consequences: many outstanding schools but fewer outstanding institutions of higher education in the former cases; and exceptional colleges and universities but far fewer quality primary and secondary parochial schools in the latter instances.

Another significant issue, especially as it applies to colleges and universities, has to do with the nature of the relationship between church bodies and their institutions of higher learning. In recent decades, for example, an increasingly conservative papacy and hierarchy have exerted tighter control over Roman Catholic colleges and universities and also over Roman Catholic theologians teaching in public universities. Baylor University had to deal with a similar situation in its relationship with the Southern Baptist Convention, an issue Baylor at least partially resolved by wresting control of its governing board from the Convention. Baylor wants to keep its Baptist identity without, however, relinquishing control to an external entity. On the other hand, some ultra-conservative church-related colleges and universities welcome close ties and strict oversight by their sponsoring bodies. Finally, there are colleges and universities founded by religious groups that over the years have weakened or even severed the ties with their originating bodies. Once diminished, those ties are difficult to make stronger — as a recent president of Trinity University in San Antonio discovered when he tried to strengthen that institution's relationship with the Presbyterian Church.

This issue also confronts Lutheran colleges and universities, though sometimes a bit differently. I still remember a former president of Texas Lutheran remarking to me that he was sure it would remain a church-related college, at least on his watch. He was less sure that the denomination involved, the ELCA, had remained a college-related church with traditionally strong commitment to and support of its institutions of higher learning. Yet by and large, ELCA institutions of higher learning have retained viable and valuable church connections — differing from time to time and place to place — without losing control of their educational programs.

So what's Lutheran about Lutheran higher education? Lutheran higher education has a serious and growing commitment to academic freedom, at least among the colleges and universities affiliated with the ELCA and especially since the mid-twentieth century.[1] I recall a new faculty member, a political scientist hired at the same time I had been in the late '60s, who previously had attended and taught at state universities. A couple of years later he confided to me that he had had concerns about academic freedom at a church-related college, but that he found more of it at Texas Lutheran than at the state universities with which he had been affiliated. Government officials can apparently be more interfering and intimidating than church leaders.

It is not perfect. Some of the disciplines with greater exposure to the general public (such as theater) and to the university constituency (such as theology) are potential candidates for administrative pressure. My own institution passed this test with flying colors with respect to my discipline of theology: our administration regularly ran interference for us with a segment of the constituency that was upset with our department from time to time. On the other hand, occasionally they could not refrain from attempting to interfere with theater production schedules in an effort to forestall public criticism. Overall, however, the administration scored high marks in maintaining a setting of academic freedom. Lutheran higher education can be, and often is, a model for this kind of milieu.

What's Lutheran about Lutheran higher education? Lutheran higher education encourages careful, critical scholarship. The next story comes from my student days at Luther Seminary in St. Paul, Minnesota, a post-graduate institution, not my teaching days at Texas Lutheran, an undergraduate school. A cadre of a half-dozen of us students gathered around Professor Edmund Smits, affectionately known as Papa Smits, a theologian from Latvia who came to Luther Seminary as a displaced person after World War II. In a perpetually ongoing seminar in patristic literature and theology, Smits taught us a love of the writings and of the insights of the early church fathers. My own later doctoral research and dissertation dealt with seven letters composed by an early second-century Syrian bishop named Ignatius of Antioch.

One day Smits came to the seminar with some news that had him excited. Anders Nygren, a world-renowned theologian and philosopher from Sweden, was going to deliver a series of evening lectures on philosophy of religion at the University of Minnesota. They would be free and open to the public; we seminar students were encouraged to attend as many as our schedules would permit. In addition, Smits — who apparently knew Nygren from his time in Europe — had invited Nygren and us to his home following one of the lectures. But Papa was concerned: he admonished us not to be our typical brash North American selves but rather to behave in a deferential manner toward Nygren, who would be more used to that demeanor from his European students.

We were not disrespectful but we certainly were not timidly deferential, either. We had read Nygren's *magnum opus*, titled *Agape and Eros*, and we had developed some serious reservations about his understanding of the appropriate relation between Christianity and culture. So we questioned and we probed. Obviously, Nygren was more than capable of the intellectual fencing that ensued. What saved our skins with regard to Papa Smits was that at the end Professor Nygren expressed his thanks for a stimulating evening. He had not expected us to be familiar with his work in so much detail and to be so energetic in discussing it with him. He had found at least some evidence of careful, critical scholarship where many

Europeans thought there was little if any of it. Nygren was impressed; Smits was disarmed; we were off the hook.

What's Lutheran about Lutheran higher education? Lutheran higher education promotes wide-ranging thought, especially in the under-graduate programs — a practice that roots back to Luther himself. Most Lutheran colleges and universities have a required core curriculum that stresses intellectual breadth and encourages thinking across disciplinary boundaries. I firmly believe in this. It is one of the reasons that I was happy to stay in an undergraduate situation rather than aspire to seminary teaching. I do not think that I could have flourished in a place where there were only other theologians with whom to interact.

In my case, the broad interaction I thrived upon was encouraged and facilitated at an institutional level. My university had a series of academic deans committed to multi-disciplinary learning, specifically to team-teaching across disciplinary lines. I team-taught courses more than fifty times during my tenure at Texas Lutheran, with colleagues from nine different departments. These were tremendously stimulating learning experiences for me and also, I have to think, for the students. But they were also quite costly learning experiences for the institution in terms of its commitment of faculty resources.

What's Lutheran about Lutheran higher education? I have some more things to say about this in the paper that follows, given in a setting where many in the audience had shared a classroom with me. It turns out that Lutherans — who tend to do very well at parsing the past, tolerably though inconsistently well at engaging the present, but not so well at framing a future — have a track record of vision and innovation in this area.[2]

What's Lutheran about Lutheran higher education?[3]

Tom Wilkens

Just in case there is someone here who is not familiar with the Lutheran legend, let me begin by observing that the Lutheran movement was born out of a university matrix. Martin Luther became professor of

Bible at Wittenberg University in 1512. When he posted the 95 theses on the Wittenberg castle church door five years later, Luther was serving also as a pastor. It seems that he was the first church relations officer, connecting university and parish, in the Lutheran movement.

In addition to that university tie, some of the most significant developments in Lutheran history were nurtured early on in university settings. One such development was Pietism, which got underway late in the seventeenth century. Philipp Jakob Spener is generally credited with initiating the Lutheran version of Pietism. While he was a pastor at Frankfurt am Main, Spener organized weeknight sessions consisting of Bible study, prayer, hymn singing, and the sharing of faith in small groups that he called *collegia pietatis* — colleges or communities of piety.

Spener was instrumental in the founding of a university at Halle in 1694. That university became the hub of Lutheran Pietism for much of the eighteenth century. Luther's successors in the professoriate at Wittenberg concluded that Pietism was a crock. The Wittenbergers formulated scores of charges of heresy against the Halle pietists. Meanwhile, Pietism at the university in Halle had come under the able leadership of August Hermann Franke. He had called his pietistic gatherings *collegia philobiblica* — colleges of love of the book, that is, the Bible.

American Lutheranism was profoundly influenced by all of this, especially through clergy who were trained at Halle and then served parishes in the American colonies, and most especially through Henry Melchior Muhlenberg. Included in Muhlenberg's long list of accomplishments was his organizing of the first synodical structure in American Lutheranism in 1748: the Ministerium of Pennsylvania. The first American Lutheran college, Gettysburg, was established within its boundaries in 1832. In 1988, that synod found its way into the Evangelical Lutheran Church in America.

Besides such structural and spiritual ties between the Lutheran movement and the university, are there curricular ties other than the obvious presence of departments of theology and of required courses in theology in American Lutheran universities? There are. Let me mention just one historical example. Luther and his younger colleague Philipp Melanchthon, professor of Greek and theology at Wittenberg, engineered an impressive reform of the universities and schools in Germany. They promoted the inclusion of many more of the creative impulses of renaissance humanism in the school and university curricula than had ever been there before. For his efforts with the schools, Melanchthon came to be called the "Preceptor [Teacher] of Germany." Luther, by the way, not only worked to reinvigorate German university education; he worked to eliminate one-fourth of the professional curriculum.[4]

So then, what's Lutheran about Lutheran higher education? It seems to me that what it means to be Lutheran in higher education in America today is to be willing to provoke and perhaps even to lead the charge for the reinvention of higher education in America today. "If it ain't broke, don't fix it," you say? While it is surely not a universally held view, I tend to agree with the legion of critics who say that American higher education is broken. I disagree with some of the more prominent critics who invite us to go back to the future for therapy.[5] An even stronger case likely can be made for the brokenness of American schools. But since American universities are not yet a part of the solution, my working assumption is that we are a part of the problem — all of us in all of our disciplines.

Luther thought that German education in his time was broken. Luther and Melanchthon convinced the German educational establishment to bet the future of German education on an infusion of humanism. And those two professors did it from the weak power base of a very young and small university.

Where do you think that we, in our weakness and smallness, should be encouraging American higher education to place its wager and risk its future? If we aspire "to become the premier undergraduate institution in the liberal arts, sciences and professional studies in the Western US,"[6] then we must not only place our own bet but we thereby also call the hands of the rest of the players in the game. We say, in effect and with as much nerve as we can muster, look at us and you are looking at the future.

Yes, it is a David and Goliath scenario. But remember two things: first, Luther was a David and not a Goliath. Second, David and Luther prevailed. Will we prevail? Will we engage and lose? Or will we simply cede this match as a strategy to stay in the contest, an understandable move as we prepare to encounter the Southern Association for our decennial accreditation?[7]

As an endnote let me observe that today the reason you non-Lutherans among us might have cause to be anxious has little to do with Lutheranism as religion, at least not in a narrow sense of religion. Rather it has to do with the potential for raising more cultural hell than you may wish to handle if we were to take the Lutheran tradition in higher education more seriously. Education is one of the few cultural domains where Lutheran origins were not predominantly conservative. On the other hand, we Lutherans may well need those of you who are not Lutheran to remind us of our own innovating educational heritage — as a British Methodist (E. Gordon Rupp)[8] and an American Quaker (Roland Bainton)[9] were needed to reintroduce English-speaking Lutherans to their own theological and historical roots nearly a half-century ago.

Response:
A Montessori approach to church

Kim Wilkens

As I try to follow discourse on the Emerging Church, I wind up reading lots of blog. It can get pretty frustrating because the Emerging Church movement is a moving target and I don't really have the time it takes to go beyond just skimming the surface of the dialog. However, every once in a while I'll stumble across a blog entry that provides a great snapshot into the state of the movement. One such article was Frank Viola's open letter, *Will the Emerging Church Fully Emerge? An Invitation for Serious Reflection and Open Dialogue*, where he examines strengths and weaknesses of the emerging movement. What particularly caught my eye was the primary weakness he describes because it applies not only to emerging church but every church, and I think is certainly relevant to the state of education across the board.

> The Emerging Church phenomenon has wonderfully articulated some of the major flaws of the modern church, yet like all of its predecessors, it has failed to identify and take dead aim at one of the chief roots of most of its ills.
> I firmly believe that the taproot of most of the problems that plague the church in modernity is the clergy system. To put a finer point on it, Protestant Christians are addicted to the modern pastoral office. The pastor is the all-purpose religious professional in the modern Protestant church, both evangelical and mainline.

Please note that my critique is not an attack on pastors as people. Most pastors in the Emerging Church are gifted Christians who have a heart for the Lord and a genuine love for His people. It is the modern pastoral office and role that I believe is profoundly flawed, and few of us have ever questioned it.

Let me unpack that a bit. My experience in this country and overseas over the last seventeen years has yielded one immovable conclusion: God's people can engage in high talk about community life, Body functioning, and Body life, but unless the modern pastoral role is utterly abandoned in a given church, God's people will never be unleashed to function in freedom under the Headship of Jesus Christ. I have had pastors vow to me that they were the exception. However, upon visiting their congregations, it was evident that the people did not know the first thing about functioning as a Body on their own. Neither were they given any practical tools on knowing the Lord intimately and living by His life. The reason is that the flaws of the modern pastoral role are actually built into the role itself.

The pastor, by his mere presence, causes an unhealthy dependence upon himself for ministry, direction, and guidance. Thus as long as he hangs around delivering sermons, the people in the church to which he belongs will never be fully set free to function on their own in a church meeting setting. Further, the pastoral office typically destroys those who populate it. Jesus Christ never intended for anyone to shoulder that kind of enormous responsibility and power.[10]

I keep thinking about this observation of pastoral leadership. Can you imagine a church without a pastor? How would that work? My church has been trying to do something far less radical, moving away from pastor-centered leadership to empowered lay leaders and teams. It is an exciting time and it's very challenging and so slow. We set off on this new vision in 2005 and we're still struggling. I believe it is so difficult for even the best-intentioned pastors to equip his/her members because of the way most of us grew up learning.

I am by no means a Montessori expert, but having experienced vicariously the results of such an education on my son and through my own experience teaching technology in a Montessori environment, I can begin to appreciate how this "radical" approach to learning could be helpful in the church. Here are some basic characteristics of a *Montessori education*[11] and how they might relate to church.

Stages of development

Montessori recognizes and values the unique needs of children at different developmental stages and integrates this understanding into the educational environment. The community of the classroom provides a safe and secure place for children to develop self-esteem and confidence, while they learn to be responsible and caring members of society.

Church leaders recognize people are at different stages in their faith journey and provide appropriate building blocks for growing faith. The church provides a safe and secure environment for exploring faith.

Child-centered

The Montessori approach challenges the conventional methodologies wherein teachers "fill" children with knowledge. The Montessori teacher acts as a guide, an inspiration, and a remover of obstacles, so children can follow their natural inclinations to explore and grow.

Church leaders act as a guide, an inspiration, and a remover of obstacles so that members can follow their natural inclinations to explore and grow their faith.

Independence

Montessori philosophy emphasizes functional and intellectual independence as crucial to human development. Montessori encourages children, from the earliest ages, to use their practical and intellectual skills to meet their own everyday needs and pursue academic learning. Montessori communities promote self-sufficiency in social relationships as well, providing tools and language for children to solve conflicts and negotiate peacefully.

Church leaders encourage members to use their skills to meet the needs of the church. The church community promotes and encourages self-sufficiency.

Process versus product

Montessori utilizes a guided discovery approach to learning. Montessori guides (teachers) present lessons to children as "keys" to open the door to learning. Learning outcomes come about naturally, often spontaneously, sparked by student-driven interest. Montessori allows the process of learning to unfold authentically until the child is ready to demonstrate mastery.

Church leaders allow people to explore their faith authentically in a non-judgmental environment.

Skills for life

Montessori emphasizes learning through all five senses, not just through listening, watching, or reading. Learning is an exciting process of discovery, leading to concentration, motivation, self-discipline, and a quest for knowledge that lasts a lifetime. Montessori schools group children in different age groups, forming communities in which the older children mentor the younger children.

The church community forms small groups where learning and mentoring take place.

Chapter Endnotes

1. There are over forty Lutheran colleges and universities in the US and Canada; 28 of those institutions, including Texas Lutheran, are associated with the ELCA.

2. A much more detailed elaboration of my views on Lutheran higher education is contained in "Vocation and Higher Education: Some Lutheran Perspectives and Prospectives," a chapter in *Vision and Revision: Old Roots and New Routes for Lutheran Higher Education* (Division for College and University Services, American Lutheran Church, 1977), pp. 39-79. That paper was written during a sabbatical year as a Research Fellow at Luther Seminary, which included a weekly seminar involving other Lutheran college faculty, from several disciplines, on sabbatical leave.

3. A paper delivered at the Sittler Faculty Forum, Texas Lutheran University, April 11, 1996.

4. Of the four professional studies available in late medieval universities — theology, medicine, civil law, and canon law — Luther sought to eliminate canon law as no longer needed or relevant.

5. See, for example, Allan David Bloom's *The closing of the American mind: how high er education has failed democracy and impoverished the souls of today's students* (Simon & Schuster, 1988).

6. *President's Vision Statement*, Texas Lutheran University, 1.

7. The Southern Association of Colleges and Schools is a regional accrediting agency for institutions of higher education. Colleges and universities need to be reaccredit ed every ten years. Losing accreditation is a devastating blow for any school.

8. See especially E. Gordon Rupp, *The Righteousness of God: Luther Studies* (Hodder and Stoughton, 1953), which sparked a generation of scholarship about Luther's theology in the English-speaking world.

9. See Roland Bainton, *Here I Stand: A Life of Martin Luther* (Abingdon, 1950), which became the standard English-language biography of Luther for a generation.

10. Frank Viola, "Present Testimony Ministry," *Will the Emerging Church Fully Emerge?*, 2005, www. ptmin.org/fullyemerge.htm.

11. The following text is borrowed heavily from the definition of **A Montessori Education** created by Wendy Fisher, Head of School at the Montessori Community School, Charlottesville, VA.

CHAPTER 13

TWO HOMILIES ON ROMANS 13:1-7

Background essay

Tom Wilkens

"On the one hand ... and on the other." Like Tevye in *Fiddler on the Roof*, I have repeated these phrases countless times. I did it in the classroom, where one of my responsibilities was to present different positions and arguments on many issues. "On the one hand ... and on the other." Early on in my teaching career I tried very hard not to tip my own hand; not to let the students know my stand on an issue lest they adopt (or reject) it too quickly; not to let my own biases show through in the discussion.

I must have become quite good at it. I remember a student at our Randolph Air Force Base program, a man well above the typical eighteen to twenty-two-year-old undergraduate age range, coming up to me after the course had concluded to thank me for the class that semester. I thought that I detected an edge of sarcasm in his voice. He then went on to say that he admired a church-related college for permitting an atheist to teach a theology course. He was serious both in his assessment of my belief system or lack thereof and in his thinly veiled criticism of Texas Lutheran. Perhaps he did not recognize my "on the one hand ... and on the other" approach for what it was: a pedagogical technique. Perhaps he read my willingness to look at every viewpoint, even to insist upon it, as a sign that I had no faith of my own.

"On the one hand ... and on the other." Maybe I had become too good at it. I never stopped the practice of arguing as well as I could for different points of view — even atheism. However, I also began to let the students know where I stood on some significant issues, especially if they asked, but not too soon: not before they had agonized over the difficult dilemmas and hard choices placed before them.

Actually, I had condescendingly underestimated my students. They were not lemmings. They would not follow a professor's views blindly. Sooner or later it dawned on most of them that we all have biases; that we all probe faith and perceive God through lenses that refract the light of what we are examining onto our own distinctive screens of life. Objectivity is a goal toward which we may strive; it is never something that we have in hand. Strict objectivity is a figment of the imagination, even in scientific investigation. It is better to recognize our biases, make them as transparent as we possibly can, and thereby exercise some control over them.

In the homily that follows I took my "on the one hand ... and on the other" style into the pulpit. Today two quite distinct hermeneutical or interpretive roads lead out of the Epistle of Romans lesson for that week. Each hermeneutical approach served, in sequence, as a starting point for a homily. I made my best effort to elaborate each interpretation honestly and convincingly. Some in the audience, though by no means all, knew that I was not personally convinced of the first, more traveled approach to the text. One friend told me afterwards that initially she thought I had taken leave of my senses. I believe she felt that I had finally cracked under the pressure of supporting too many minority reports and lost causes in the Christian community. She turned out to be relieved once the second homily got underway. Many others likely had the opposite reaction: they would have become very uncomfortable once I no longer was looking at the text in the customary way.

Is it ever appropriate to preach in this manner, to introduce a tension between perspectives without even attempting to relieve that tension? Perhaps it is appropriate in the academic venue where I did it, but not in a parish setting. Perhaps both. Perhaps neither. My own opinion is that it is a good idea, not a bad one, occasionally to leave the pulpit with some questions still open — either unanswered or with more than one plausible answer. I did that in the following homily. I would do it again with this text from Romans. I have seldom done it with other texts, at least so explicitly and thoroughly, in either academic or parish environments.

In the second homily, I note but do not detail crucial and consequential shortcomings in the German Christian response to Nazism. Betty and I have two good friends from Germany who take this very much to heart: Wilfried and Christa Kürschner. Wilfried is a professor of linguistics at the *Hochschule* in Vechta in Lower Saxony. Until her recent retirement, Christa taught religion in a *Gymnasium*, where German students prepare for university. Whenever we visit places representing the highest and best of German culture with them, such as Weimar with its rich literary and musical heritage, they insist that we also visit neighboring sites of Germany's Nazi nadir, such as the Buchenwald concentration camp with its grisly legacy of violence and death. Christa always did this with her students when she took them on field trips. They both are determined that the German people never forget that having a refined secular culture and a sophisticated Christian heritage is no guarantee that unspeakable savagery will not break out in their midst. Are we any less vulnerable?

While Wilfried and Christa are too young to have clear personal memories of World War II, they do have chilling remembrances of the Cold War — especially Wilfried. His family lived in East Germany. Wilfried escaped, but much of his family did not. He had to endure many years of long waiting periods to get permission to visit them and then undergo the pain of parting — each time not knowing whether or not he would ever see them again.

We were with them on their first visit to Berlin following the destruction of the Berlin Wall and the reunification of Germany. Wilfried stood motionless and nearly incredulous at the Brandenburg Gate, tears streaming down his face, as he recalled the sorrow that the Wall had visited upon his and so many other families over the decades. It was a most poignant moment for him, and meaningful to us because he shared it.

Two homilies on Romans 13:1-7[1]

Tom Wilkens

The text

Let every person be subject to the governing authorities; for there is no authority except from God, and those authorities that exist have been instituted by God. Therefore whoever resists authority resists what God has appointed, and those who resist will incur judgment. For rulers are not a terror to good conduct, but to bad. Do you wish to have no fear of the authority? Then do what is good, and you will receive its approval; for it is God's servant for your good. But if you do what is wrong, you should be afraid, for the authority does not bear the sword in vain! It is the servant of God to execute wrath on the wrongdoer. Therefore one must be subject, not only because of wrath but also because of conscience. For the same reason you also pay taxes, for the authorities are God's servants, busy with this very thing. Pay to all what is due them — taxes to whom taxes are due, revenue to whom revenue is due, respect to whom respect is due, honor to whom honor is due.

— Romans 13:1-7

The first homily

One of the most significant revolutions in western history took place early in the fourth century of the Common Era. Within a twenty-five year time frame, the Christian church moved from a position of no legal status in the Roman Empire — having experienced either sporadic or systematic persecution for nearly three hundred years — to a position of favored legal standing in the Empire.

As one might expect this new favored status for Christianity affected the interpretation and application of texts such as Romans 13:1-7 for the next sixteen centuries. Political and ecclesiastical realities have changed continuously, and often substantively, throughout those centuries. But the interpretation of Romans 13:1-7 has remained remarkably stable. In truth, I am convinced that the meaning of the Romans text and its proper practical applications appear to be virtually self-evident to a majority of American Christians. That makes this homily easier: easier for me to compose and easier for you to comprehend.

As an exemplar of mainstream interpretation of this text, let me briefly refer to Martin Luther. In his 1520 *Treatise on Good Works*, at the point where Luther was explaining the fourth commandment — which obliges us to honor father and mother — Luther wrote:

138

The third work of this commandment is to obey temporal authority, as Paul teaches in Romans 13 and Titus 3, and Saint Peter in 1 Peter 2... the task of temporal power is to protect its subjects and to punish theft, robbery, and adultery, as Saint Paul says in Romans 13, "Authority does not bear the sword in vain; it serves God with it, [and is] a terror to evildoers, but the protector of the good."[2]

And in his 1523 treatise entitled *Temporal Authority: To What Extent It Should Be Obeyed*, Luther stated:

First we must provide a sound basis for the civil law and sword so no one will doubt that it is in the world by God's will and ordinance.[3]

Luther then cited Romans 13 as a biblical warrant for the obligation of individuals to obey temporal authority in all but a few narrowly defined, theoretical circumstances in which passive disobedience might be appropriate.

In 1525, Luther referred to our text from Romans several times as a biblical basis for his refusal to support a peasant revolt in southern Germany. A year later, he quoted the Romans text as an endorsement of the profession of soldiering. To be sure, there were nuances in Luther's handling of Romans 13 that were unique. Nonetheless, he remained in the mainstream of Christian hermeneutics — a stream that has flowed into our own century, indeed into our own decade. Romans 13, filtered through this interpretive tradition, has led almost inevitably to a harmonization — if not homogenization — of Christian confession and national culture. American Lutherans have national songs in their hymnals, as do most denominations. The Houston Lutheran Chorale just two weeks ago presented a program on campus in which distinctively Christian music and clearly patriotic numbers were woven into a seamless cloak. The program was well received, and why not? Our temporal authorities are under God no less — perhaps even more — than in Luther's day.

The second homily

I have another homily on the same text. There is a minority view of this text, a view of somewhat more recent vintage. It is the view that Romans 13 has been manipulated into playing a very negative and destructive role for the past sixteen centuries.

J. C. O'Neill, in a commentary titled *Paul's Letter to the Romans*, put it this way:

> These seven verses have caused more unhappiness and misery in the Christian East and West than any other seven verses in the New Testament by the license they have given to tyrants, and the support for tyrants the Church has felt called to offer as a result of the presence of Romans 13 in the canon.[4]

Ernst Käsemann, in his *Commentary on Romans*, agreed:

> Almost inevitably ... the exhortation has stood in the shadow of metaphysics of the state or an interrelating of church and state in salvation history. The doors have been opened in Christianity not only to conservative but also to reactionary views even to the point of political fanaticism.[5]

But it is my own colleague, Norm Beck, whose challenge to the mainstream interpretive tradition of Romans 13 I find most intriguing and very plausible. In his study titled *Anti-Roman Cryptograms in the New Testament: Messages of Hope and Liberation*, Beck writes:

> When Paul wrote to followers of Jesus in Rome itself, the center of Roman power and of the activity of the zealous advocates of Roman Civil Religion, it was important for him to be as careful as possible to code his derogatory comments about Rome, Caesar, and the zealous advocates of Roman Civil Religion in cryptograms that would be especially subtle. It was also advisable for Paul to write something openly that was quite positive about Rome and its governing authority so that if Paul's letter should come into their hands they would be deluded into thinking that Paul and his friends were loyal supporters of the Roman authorities. This is exactly what we have in Paul's letter to the followers of Jesus in Rome.[6]

Dr. Beck disagrees, furthermore, with the accuracy and adequacy of most translations of Romans 13. For instance, he argues that the Greek term usually translated as "be subject to" or "obey" would be better translated as "respect the power of." To quote Beck again:

> Seen in this light, Romans 13:1-7 is not so much a concise statement of support of the divine right of kings as it is a wise and very subtle anti-Roman cryptogram intended by Paul to save Christian lives until

God would act through the means that God uses to remove the oppressors and to accomplish God's will.[7]

This is a very different reading of the text, so different that it has suggested to Dr. Beck and others that many New Testament texts — including Romans 13 — have two different meanings, for two different audiences. The meaning of Romans 13 that registers with most of us — namely, that Saint Paul was affirming the power of the state — was meant for a non-Christian politically powerful audience. The other message — that Paul was affirming resistance to the powers of the age in ways that would least threaten Christian lives — was meant for a politically powerless Christian audience. Both messages are there, but isn't it interesting that most of us get the one intended for non-Christians and intended to be at least somewhat misleading?

Now that you have to choose, and in light of your chosen interpretive tradition: Go in peace, serve the Lord.

Response:
Go in peace, serve the Lord

Kim Wilkens

If you go to church, you probably hear something like this at the end of each worship service; it's the benediction, the last words said that will send you on your way back out into the world. But what if the message you just heard or the worship you've just experienced shakes your worldview, reopens old wounds, or reignites lingering doubts? How easy is it then to go in peace, serve the Lord?

After the bait and switch my dad uses in his homily, the closing words seem particularly taunting, almost sarcastic. My dad loves to provoke thought and discussion. I remember that students weren't allowed to sit back quietly in his class. Oh no, he would hover and then swoop in for the "in your face" question.

I don't remember many details about my early religious experiences except things like church was not an option, everybody seemed pretty sure about the whole God thing, questioning was only healthy up to a point and we didn't talk much about religion or faith at home. In retrospect, I find that a little strange considering my family background.

My mom seems to have an unfaltering faith that I will never comprehend. I believe she finds my doubts and questioning disconcerting. In the early days, I think she hoped that I would eventually just "get over it" and come to my senses. I think my dad, on the other hand, wanted me to figure things out on my own. So much so, that I felt he would often avoid talking religion, so as not to unduly influence my faith journey. Truthfully, I found both of their responses to my questioning frustrating.

Through the years, I think what my parents and I have figured out is that we don't have all the answers for ourselves or for each other, but that we do have a need to share with each other authentically and transparently. Because Christianity and Christians are full of contradictions and tensions, that peace we are to go into the world with can come in part from being in family and/or community where we can be our God-given selves.

I'm now getting a taste of my own medicine through my son. He questions every little thing with an insight and intellect that seems far beyond his ten years. I've learned there's no convincing him and certainly no worrying that he's going to take what I say without applying his own lens. If I could have the last word in any of these exchanges with Xander, maybe there is no more appropriate ending than my wish for him to be able to go in peace, serve the Lord.

Chapter Endnotes

1. A homily presented in the fall term, 1996, at Texas Lutheran University.
2. In *Luther's Works*, volume 44 (Fortress Press, 1966), 91.
3. In *Luther's Works*, volume 45 (Muhlenberg Press, 1962), 85.
4. J. C. O'Neill, *Paul's Letter to the Romans* (Penguin Books Ltd., 1975), 209.
5. Ernst Käsemann, *Commentary on Romans* (William B. Eerdmans Publishing Company, 1980), 354. Käsemann was extremely critical of the German church for its generally inappropriate and inadequate responses to Nazism.
6. Norman A. Beck, *Anti-Roman Cryptograms in the New Testament: Messages of Hope and Liberation* (Peter Lang, 1997), 78.
7. *Ibid.*, 81.

CHAPTER 14

TWO SUMMER SAINTS

Background essay

Tom Wilkens

The husband of the woman mentioned in my previous background essay, who had commented on the homily in that chapter, spoke to me after I delivered the homily that follows. He said that he had learned more than he ever wanted to know about the two saints featured in my remarks. His point: less data and more interpretation, exhortation or proclamation would make a better sermon. I agree. Or do I?

In recent years there has been a huge resurgence of interest in the telling of stories, both in the church and in society. Storytelling and memoir writing have become viewed as life-centering and even therapeutic activities, to say nothing of their entrepreneurial value. I can attest to their life-centering and therapeutic potentials. Writing the background essays for this book has been an exceptionally focusing and restorative experience for me. It remains to be seen whether it will have any commercial value at all.

Still, I can empathize with my friend and critic. I, too, have suffered through sermons that were very long on narrative, especially on storytelling, and very short on any clear point or purpose. Seminaries of mainline denominations — especially their departments of homiletics, where the chief job is to teach preaching — have apparently of late been pushing narrative as a homiletical style. American evangelicals have known about the potency of stories for generations. My complaint is not about their use but their misuse or over-utilization.

Yet here I am in this book stringing together story after autobiographical story. I have never thought of myself as a storyteller, but there is a family history of it. My maternal grandmother, Grandma Heald, came to live with us after Grandpa Heald died. I was just short of nine years old at the time. She could really spin a yarn, particularly tales about her childhood, youth, and early adulthood. And she read the canon of children's stories with a special flair. I would listen, spellbound, as Grandma read those stories for my younger sister Sue. I learned during her years with us that, in communities where she had lived as a married adult, Grandma quickly became known for her storytelling and dramatic skills. She was the organizer and often the chief player in public entertainments such as storytelling, dramatic reading, and theater.

My mother learned these skills. She also told stories — a lot of them about family and many of those with a comedic twist. Much of what I "remember" from my early childhood I recall from her telling and retelling of stories from that time. My wife has often let me know, eyes rolled up, that most of the stories I have repeated here I have told again and again — and again and again. But I am now convinced that if I had not done this, a lot of them would have been forgotten. You may be thinking that many should have been forgotten: let us not go there.

Our son Nick does all of this more skillfully than I do. For one thing, he has a much better memory, especially for episodes and experiences from his early childhood. For another, he uses stories — stories he has heard or read, but also stories that he has lived — to very good advantage and with very clear and substantive points to make.

Nick's third advantage — as a counselor, an adjunct university professor, a public speaker, and an occasional preacher — has come at enormous cost to him. He has been afflicted for most of his life with OCD (obsessive-compulsive disorder). Out of that circumstance, he approaches people, their personal concerns, and the public issues we all face together with a depth and perspective I simply cannot match.

My own life experience pales by comparison: so little pain and so much privilege. Take the next homily, for example. Does it have a weak and largely unsuccessful opening attempt at wittiness? Yes. Does it contain too much data and chronology, and too little stirring storytelling? To be sure. Is it deficient in both brain food and heart nourishment? Guilty on both counts. Nevertheless, humor me: read it anyway. Perhaps it would be more tolerable if you were to read it and the other homilies in this book out loud — the way in which they were originally shared.

Two summer saints[1]

Tom Wilkens

Introduction

I have a summer birthday and I have a complaint. Roughly one-fourth of you have summer birthdays also and thus will have an existential understanding of my grievance. During the years of childhood and adolescence, when birthdays are coveted collectibles, those of us with summer birthdays got cheated. The rest of you would get individual recognition in school, perhaps even something of a celebration during recess or at the end of the class day. But those of us with summer birthdays were all lumped into one generic group and given untimely recognition tinged with unspoken criticism for being born outside the parameters of the school year. And sometimes the vacation schedules of our friends or even our own families made it difficult or impossible to have a proper birthday party at home. It wasn't fair. We — my summer birthday colleagues and I — still bear scars. My own self-image, frankly, has never fully recovered.

Think twice, therefore, before conceiving in autumn. It may well lead to many summers of discontent for your children. But think twice, also, about dying in summer. It may well lead to your premature erasure from the collective memory of humanity. That's what has happened, to some degree at any rate, to people such as Bartolomé de las Casas of Spain and Prince Vladimir of Russia. Their lives are recommended for commemoration on July 17 and 15 — their death days, respectively — days when we're far likelier to be reminiscing about an outdoor concert or trying to remember the currency exchange rate in our foreign vacation destination than to be recalling two summer saints. They deserve better, just as summer birthday people deserve better. So I will begin to make amends.

Bartolomé de las Casas

Bartolomé de las Casas was born in 1474 into a family that had migrated from France to Seville in Spain. His father, Francisco, had accompanied Columbus on his second voyage to the New World. Francisco brought back a Native-American boy, whom he gave to Bartolomé as his servant.

Young Las Casas took a degree at the university in Salamanca and became a lawyer. He journeyed to the New World in 1502 as an *encomendero* — which was a sixteenth-century version of an entrepreneur. He became a priest in 1510 and later joined the Dominican order. This gave him both freedom of speech and material security.

Las Casas became an outspoken critic of the cruel exploitation of the indigenous people of the New World and received support from the church leadership, the Spanish crown, and the Dominican order. He often squandered that support with personal attacks on those who did not meet his own standards of social justice.

It is ironic, to say the very least, that Las Casas also argued for the introduction of black slaves into the New World. He himself took seven African slaves into South America to assist with an experiment — which failed — of establishing a separate colony for the indigenous people in what is now Venezuela.

In 1527, Las Casas traveled to Nicaragua and found that the reforms instituted by the establishment of *encomiendas* had failed. What had happened is that the people who had been enslaved by the *conquistadóres* had now become agrarian serfs. This was not good enough for Bartolomé.

In 1540 Las Casas returned to Spain, where his advocacy for the indigenous Americans had an impact on the "New Laws" of 1542. However, those laws were soon revised to diminish their beneficial effects for the indigenous people and to maximize the benefits for the Spanish and the Creoles.

Las Casas was appointed the bishop of Chiapas in 1543 and managed, on a trip to Guatemala, to offend the supportive bishop there. He retired in 1551 and returned to Spain, dying in Madrid in 1566.

What lessons are there for us as we commemorate Bartolomé de las Casas? *First*, nobody has perfect insight; in fact, none of us have perfect hindsight. Surely Las Casas can be faulted for his vision of a just world in which the Indians were included but the Africans excluded. Yet it does raise an interesting question: for what will we be faulted in 450 years?

Second, it is instructive to note the different assessments of Bartolomé de Las Casas from different times and locations. For example, the article on Las Casas in the *Catholic Encyclopedia* of 1908 had, at best, only occasional and grudging admiration for the man and his work. For the most part, the article had a negative and condescending tone. He was viewed as an anti-establishment ingrate. On the other hand, in a more recent history of Christianity written from a contemporary Latin American perspective, Las Casas is vaunted as a true hero of the faith and a pioneering soldier for social justice.

Prince Vladimir of Russia

Five centuries before Las Casas lived out his vocation, Vladimir was one of three sons born to the ruler of Kiev. Though his grandmother had converted to Christianity, at the time a very small movement in the region, his father did not.

Vladimir was made the Prince of Novgorod in 970. In a power struggle with one of his brothers after the death of their father, Vladimir killed the brother, united Novgorod and Kiev, and became the Grand Duke — all with the aid of the Scandinavians.

After some negotiations with the Byzantine Emperor, Vladimir was engaged to the Emperor's sister Anna. As a part of the arrangement, Vladimir was to be baptized. The baptism took place but then the Emperor attempted to back out of the deal. Vladimir attacked, won, and married Anna. He sent away his four previous wives.

After his conversion, Vladimir began to destroy the pagan statues and sacred sites he had constructed and established in the early years of his rule. Christianity spread rapidly in Kievan Russia. Vladimir required that his subjects be baptized. Many church buildings were constructed.

In his latter years, Vladimir gave up his military adventures and concentrated on establishing schools and an ecclesiastical court system. But at the very end of his life, concerned about his sons as successors, he marched on Novgorod against one of those sons, named Yaroslav. Vladimir died along the way.

I offer two reflections on Vladimir's commemoration. *First*, old habits die hard: not even a kinder, gentler Vladimir finally could forgo the use of force to assure his own political preference for succession.

Second, for all that and for all the internal weaknesses in Eastern Christianity at that time, Vladimir's contributions to the Christianization of Russia were considerable and memorable. God's ways often do not conform to our own canons of civility and religiosity. Or, to put it another way, God has a history of making silk purses from sows' ears. My impression of the Christian spirituality emerging in contemporary Russia is that it truly is a silk purse. It is very different from the Christian spirituality I have encountered in Spain and Latin America, but not any less authentic.

Conclusion

Finally, I should like to make three brief observations that occur to me as I remember Bartolomé and Vladimir. The first has to do with the flawed character of the commemorated. *Simul iustus et peccator* — at once justified and a sinner. That's not just Latin: it's life. *Simul iustus et peccator* — "when I want to do what is good, evil lies close at hand" (Romans 7:21). Saint Paul knew it. Luther knew it. You and I know it.

The second observation has to do with the flawed expectations of those who commemorate. *Vocatio* — vocation, our calling — requires more than role models. Christian discipleship cannot be reduced to mere mimicry of the saints or, for that matter, to mere imitation of the Christ.

The third observation has to do with a fitting epitaph for lives remembered: *soli Deo gloria* — to God alone the glory. Bartolomé's own testimony shortly before he died is, I believe, an appropriate assessment of his flawed life:

> [It was] by the goodness and mercy of God that I was called into His ministry which I did not merit, that I might attempt to protect those multitudes of peoples who are called Indians ... from the unimaginable and unthinkable wrongs, evils, and injustices which we Spaniards inflicted upon them against all reason and justice.[2]

What will be said of your flawed life, and mine, if the timing of our deaths is good and we are remembered? *Soli Deo gloria* — to God alone the glory — was the theme of the eulogy that I gave at my father's memorial service nearly six years ago. I could depart in peace if my son, with a clear mind and conscience, could use that same theme at my memorial service. *Soli Deo gloria.* That's not a bad bottom line to a day of life or to the whole of life.

Response:
Heretic, phreak and sufferer?

Kim Wilkens

heretic?

It all started on the way home from church one Sunday. I was listening to *This American Life*. "Heretics: The story of Reverend Carlton Pearson, a renowned evangelical pastor in Tulsa, Oklahoma, who cast aside the idea of Hell, and with it everything he'd worked for over his entire life."[3] Pearson was steeped in the Pentecostal tradition where it seems a great deal of emphasis is placed on saving souls. I've always had a problem with this, but it was interesting to hear how someone who bought into this worldview had his world turned upside down. It seemed to start out innocently enough. He's watching a TV program about starving refugees from Rwanda and thinking to himself that these folks haven't been "saved." What does hell mean to them, because aren't they are already in a living hell? And how can he or 100 pastors or 1,000 pastors or all the pastors or all the Christians in the world really go about "saving" everyone in the world? He finally realized that he can't and they can't and that God's probably not looking for that kind of help. So he did lots of studying and praying and decided that God was not the inventor of hell; "we do that to each other and we do it to ourselves." This got Pearson labeled a heretic in his faith tradition and radically altered his life. He's now pastor of New Dimensions whose tag line is the friendliest, trendiest, most radically inclusive worship experience! Sounds like a place I'd like.

phreak?

That Sunday afternoon the hubby and I went to a one-man play at The Gravity Lounge called "Jesus Phreak: The Story of a Very Unlikely Disciple." This unlikely disciple turns out to be a "mixer"; he wears mixed fabrics, which is prohibited somewhere in Leviticus. He grew up going to church, so he knows that "mixers" aren't welcome there. Even so, he seems to be relentlessly pursued by God. Every time he tries to move farther away, he gets nudged back. Reading the gospels, he discovers that Jesus has come for the outcasts and therefore for him.

One thing that really spoke to me personally in this show was the portrayal of a disciple being relentlessly pursued by God, even in the face

151

of the disciple's doubt and skepticism and derision. That so feels like my journey, as I kick and scream all along the way.

There was also a discussion panel after the show and the topics that came up and the people who spoke gave me a sobering reminder about how the Church and my church have been so careless toward the well-being of LGBT people. I think our fear is really just masquerading as a cautious approach toward welcoming and inclusivity, as if addressing this issue would open Pandora's box and all hell would break loose. The closing words of this discussion were — what are you willing to suffer for the gospel?

sufferer?

On the way home from our date, we listened to a program called e-town. A singer/songwriter named Steve Earle was one of the guests (my hubby is quite distressed that I don't seem to know this guy). Anyway, something he said on the show stuck with me and, luckily, it was reproduced on the website.

> I've been pretty heartbroken about the way things have gone politically in this country the last few years and I seriously considered moving someplace else ... then I figured out that I didn't have to leave the country. All I had to do was come to New York. I needed really badly at this point in my life to see a mixed-race, same-sex couple holding hands in my own neighborhood. It makes me feel safer.[4]

I get that I'd be considered a heretic in some Christian settings. I'm cool with that. I reluctantly agree that I've become a Jesus phreak. Left to my own devices, I do not think it is the path I would choose to follow, but it's the path I find myself on. I'm not so sure about this suffering thing, but I guess whether I choose to act or not, there will be suffering. If I don't act, I will suffer heartbreak at the way things are going for many churches and the people that get or feel excluded. If I act, I will probably suffer obstacles, injustices, frustration and humiliation.

So, what am I willing to suffer? I'm still trying to figure that one out. I hope I figure it out before someone has to write my epitaph.

Chapter Endnotes

1. A homily presented at Texas Lutheran University on February 7, 1997.
2. From his *Testamento del obispo de Chiapas*, given in Madrid in 1566.
3. This American Life, 304: Heretics, December 5, 2008, www.thisamericanlife.org; Reverend Carlton Pearson, pastor of New Dimensions Worship Center.
4. Etown, *Steve Earl*, December 3, 2008, www.etown.org.

CHAPTER 15

CONFORMATION CLASSES
I HAVE TAKEN AND TAUGHT

Background essay

Tom Wilkens

My parents belonged to a generation of North Americans that dearly wished for better lives for their children and were prepared to sacrifice for this goal. In my parents' case, it was not a vague dream but a focused objective. They committed early on in their marriage to help each child through a bachelor's degree program. It was not that we kids felt pressured to do it. It was simply a part of the family atmosphere that we breathed, a rarely spoken axiom or assumption of our life together. For example, it never occurred to me to ask whether or not I should go to college. The question was where I would go, and that was left to me to decide — as was the choice of major.

They pulled it off. My father owned and operated a laundry and dry cleaning business in a resort town. He made virtually all of his profit during the short summer tourist season. He often added a second shift of workers at that time. We children, from about age fourteen onward, worked for our father during those summers. My recollection is that we did not receive traditional wages or, if we did, that they amounted to little more than pocket money. But then, each year during our college careers, we got whatever it took to make up the difference in room, board, tuition, and textbook costs that were not covered by whatever scholarships and grants we might receive or part-time employment we could secure. It could count up, especially since three of the four of us started at private colleges and three of us finished there. In my oldest brother's instance, alternative employment had to be found. He had chronic back problems that would not allow him to do the heavy lifting involved at the laundry. In any event, our parents saw us all through college financially. And we all emerged from our undergraduate programs debt-free.

In my case, this arrangement went beyond college. I continued to work for my father during the summers prior to my first two years of seminary. The same deal applied. I told my dad the summer before my first year of seminary that it did not seem fair, that he and my mother were doing more for me than for my siblings. I thought that I should find some other wage-paying summer employment and take more fiscal responsibility for my education. My father said nonsense: that he really needed me to help with the summer rush and that it was as good a deal for him as it was for me. Talk about nonsense. I did not learn until my ordination as a pastor what the real reason was. I will share that part of the story with you in a few moments.

Following the first year of seminary, in the summer of 1959 while I was working at the laundry, I hired an evening tutor to teach me Latin, a language that as a math and science major in college I had not learned. My tutor was a winsome retired classroom teacher who soon had me reading brief excerpts from classical Latin authors. But she had what I regarded at the time as a serious character flaw. She actually thought that the pithy aphorisms and epigrams we were translating together comprised, along with others she had collected over the years, a sufficiently broad and deep foundation for her life. I was in one of my "if it is not long, complex, and at least somewhat obscure philosophically or theologically then it cannot be worthy of my intellectual attention" phases. How could she possibly take this simplistic stuff so seriously?

You can imagine how appalled I was later that summer when, after I had again preached at my home congregation while the pastor was on vacation, a young high school English teacher — who had also heard me preach previous summers — came up to me and said how much she appreciated my epigrammatic style of sermonizing. Epigrammatic style? Me? Mister depth and detail and complexity? I was crushed, but it was true.

It has turned out to be advantageous. Whether lecturing in a fifty-minute class or preaching a twelve-minute homily or writing a brief background essay for this book, I do resort to epigrams and other expressions that facilitate brevity. I need to use words, phrases, and sentences that carry large built-in constellations of meaning, rather than elucidating everything in great detail. The trick is to simplify and abbreviate without trivializing or becoming banal. I know that I do not always pull it off.

I was ordained as a Lutheran pastor in the spring of 1963. This simple fact had some very substantial faith behind it, most particularly the faith of my parents. I have already shared that when I was born our family attended a Baptist congregation. There was no chance, therefore, that I would be baptized as an infant. But this does not mean that nothing of sacred significance happened at the time, that God had no access to me.

I still remember my parents asking me to step away from the crowd at the reception following my ordination. They said that they had something they wanted to share with me, privately. What they told me was this: in my infancy they had taken advantage of an opportunity offered by the Baptists to dedicate children to God. I was the only one of the four siblings for whom they chose this ritual. And in that service of dedication they committed me to the full-time service of God, much like Hannah had done with her son Samuel at the shrine in Shiloh, although — unlike Hannah — they did not leave me behind in someone else's care (1 Samuel 1:21-28).

They had not breathed a word of this to me before the ordination service. And they certainly had not pushed me into attending seminary or taking a call to be a parish pastor. They never even hinted at such a course for my life. But after the fact, they were obviously delighted that it had all taken place. They believed that the seeds of faith and of a call to faithful service had been sown in the service of dedication. I believed it, too; in fact, I still do. And quite plainly, it was the reason why they had chosen to extend the financial arrangement mentioned above through my seminary years. They thought that they had contributed, by virtue of the ritual of dedication, to my decision to pursue education beyond the bachelor's degree. They felt a responsibility to help bear some of the monetary obligations that decision had incurred.

I served a southern Wisconsin parish with two small congregations, in the towns of Avoca and Lone Rock, for a little over three years. They were good years for me — learning years. For instance, I learned that a parish pastor must excel at multi-tasking, especially in a situation where there is no team ministry involved. And I learned that I was not very good at meeting the multiple demands of parish ministry.[1] There were many responsibilities that I sensed I did not fulfill well. One of the things that I thought I carried out better than the rest was teaching, including teaching confirmation classes in my parish and occasionally leading theological discussions for the conference of pastors to which I belonged. So I finally decided to quit the multi-tasking parish ministry in order to prepare to enter the more focused teaching ministry in a college or seminary setting. It was then that I went off to graduate school in Scotland, with Betty accompanying me and our two-year-old daughter, Kim, in tow. My developed-world generated and oriented theological education would continue in this place.

A decade later my developing-world generated and oriented theological education began, first through the traditional academic medium of books and then through the non-traditional means of hands-on experience. Let me tell you about one more of my developing-world mentors. I never got to meet him in person. He had been a Salvadoran archbishop. He was murdered in 1980, four years before my first visit to El Salvador. I have stood at his plain tomb in the sparsely decorated cathedral in San Salvador. I have read his writings. But most importantly, I have encountered him through Salvadoran Christians whom he so profoundly influenced both in his life and in his death. His name was Oscar Romero.

Monseignor Romero coined an expression that has had much currency in Latin American theology and some even in North American Christianity. He called his theology a "theology of accompaniment." That expression describes how he lived out his episcopal calling: he accompanied his people on their journeys through life, especially the ordinary people of El Salvador whose lives were troubled — marked by cruel and dehumanizing injustice, poverty, and violence. This style of his ministry as a bishop, a ministry of accompaniment, finally convinced the power people that they would have to get rid of him. And so they hired an assassin. In the milliseconds that it takes a bullet to move from a hard metal barrel into a soft human body, Oscar Romero became a martyr.

These occurrences from my past have kept percolating in my mind and heart. They may help to explain the interpretations I share and the conclusions to which I come in the following homily. For one thing, I am more fully persuaded than ever that we do not choose God: God chooses us. And I have had my horizons vastly expanded as to the means — especially the people — through which the Spirit of God's call to faith, hope, and love comes and is continually renewed and reshaped.

For another, and central to the argument that ensues on the next pages, from 1983 — the year of my first full immersion, or baptism, into the developing world — onward I became increasingly convinced of the transformational potential of ministries of accompaniment and of the theologies that grow out of those ministries. I grew to be less exclusively reliant on traditional teaching techniques and more committed to sharing my developing-world experiences or, better yet, providing my students firsthand encounters with developing-world realities through field trips and service-learning projects.

Conformation classes I have taken and taught[2]

Tom Wilkens

The text

Do not be conformed to this world, but be transformed by the renewing of your minds, so that you may discern what is the will of God — what is good and acceptable and perfect.   — Romans 12:2

Exegesis and hermeneutics

That is not a typo or a misprint on your worship sheet this morning. I am going to speak about conformation classes, not confirmation classes

What is a conformation class? A conformation class consists of a set or series of learning experiences that impose methods for achieving and assessing results in the learning process. Conformation pertains to the dimension of learning that prompts us to call the fields of study on this campus "disciplines." The word discipline connotes order, control, and diligent training. Ideally, the discipline of learning arises from within the learner; practically, discipline is very often externally imposed.

I have both taken and taught conformation classes. Today I am less aggrieved about that as a student and less repentant about that as a teacher

159

than I was a generation ago. Conformation classes set limits. They do not liberate the mind or release its creative potential. And yet, as I was reminded some thirteen years ago in a paper delivered here by Rabbi Arnold Jacob Wolf, discipline and limits are co-requisites of creativity and freedom. Sinai or law is the yin to the yang of Exodus or liberation.

Pablo Picasso's incredibly creative artistic achievements emerged out of an early mastery of the traditional techniques of art. The innovative musical genius of a Beethoven or a Bernstein grew out of early discipline in the traditional techniques of musical composition. Martin Luther's reformation activities and Martin Luther King Jr.'s civil rights achievements are inconceivable apart from the low-profile years of disciplined learning that served as prologues to their high-profile public lives and contributions.

But what of this morning's text: "Do not be conformed"? Are there unwise and unwarranted conformities that we ought to avoid? Are there unhelpful and even unhealthy conformation classes? Yes, on all counts. In truth, I think that conformation classes must be viewed largely in negative terms if that is all they are: exercises in conformity, preparations of protégés. The yin of conformation always should be balanced by the yang of transformation.

"Do not be conformed to this world." Clearly that imperative warns against uncritical and unchallenged conformity. Yet it is not a call to an undisciplined life or mind. The call is to be transformed, to be renewed, somehow to transcend the very cultures that, while they nurture us, also often anesthetize us and render us overly docile. Education means, literally, "to lead out" — not to remain forever in the field or the discipline but to step away to get a different perspective, a broader view, a larger vision, a better estimation. Education entails transformation, and transformation requires some distance from the familiar and the customary, from areas where our competence is high and our confidence may border on arrogance.[3]

I would like all of the classes I teach to be both conformation and transformation classes. I agree with one of our international students who wrote a campus newspaper column last month praising the values of disciplined classroom learning, of detailed examination and appropriation of past cultures, and of methodical inquiry into present realities. But I also agree with one of my colleagues who spoke in chapel several weeks ago about the values of critical distance — of counterculture, if you please — which is central to the genius of Lutheran higher education. Conformation and transformation. Yin and yang. A delicate balance. I achieve it far less often than I fail.

When and where have I had success in keeping the balance, both as student and as teacher? I learned another lesson nearly a generation ago. I used to think of field trips, internships, travel seminars, and immersion experiences as peripheral or even gimmicky, and likely beneath the dignity of higher education. But no longer. The most transforming experiences that I have had in my life have come through immersion, through travel that went well beyond tourism. For example, each time I go to the developing world and stay long enough to connect and notice and share and serve and be served, I am transformed. I am — to use the term former presiding bishop Chilstrom employed to describe his experience with the people of the church in El Salvador — I am converted.

I think I achieve that balance between conformation and transformation in my teaching on those all-too-rare occasions when I go with students to places where they can experience someone else's culture and observe someone else's take on goodness, acceptability, and perfection. And where, with respect to the discipline I teach, they can see someone else's incarnation of the gospel of Jesus the Christ. I accompany a few students to places like that. I encourage others to go without me. And I try, haltingly and never with sufficient effect, to bring some of it into my classes on campus.

There is no magic here: the disorientation caused by hands-on culture shock or the challenges to our mindsets posed by vicarious cultural experiences through readings, lectures or media presentations don't always lead to renewal and transformation. But they always hold the possibility. In a few moments, as you hear the concert choir sing an anthem in Chinese, will you silently curse my thoughtless neglect to print the available translation on the worship sheet? Or will it be an occasion for you to wonder what it might be like for our Asian ESL (English as a Second Language) students those first few days of their swim in our strange culture and difficult language? Will it be a reminder to you that you may not *fully* comprehend *anything* in your own language, or that another language may be able to communicate profundities that your own language cannot bear? Will it have some small power to transform us, or will it reconfirm us in our uncritical ways — uncritical, that is, of our own ways, though often critical of the ways of others?

If I were asked whether or not I favor a mandatory component of service learning in the curriculum of Texas Lutheran University, today I would answer, "Yes, I do." Service learning holds real promise for transformation, as we heard in last Monday's chapel. Perhaps the idea is worthy of some Planning Committee time or faculty workshops or Student Government Association consideration. It could be a way of translating that extraordinari¹⁻ moving tribute to Mother Teresa here in this place two weeks ago into a most meaningful educational policy with life-changing potential. If implemented, however, service learning also should be required of all faculty and staff. It would never do for the students to become more balanced in their learning and in their lives than the rest of us. Balancing conformation and transformation is never easy and, like mystical insight, never more than fleetingly realized. But it is a worthy quest, perhaps the defining quest, for a community of learning and faith.

Conclusion

Do not be conformed to this world — to this age with its frayed intellectual collars and increasingly homogeneous cultural styles; with its dehumanizing prejudices and destructive behaviors — but be transformed by the renewing of your minds, so that you may discern what is the will of God: what is good and acceptable and perfect.

Response:
The curse of knowledge

Kim Wilkens

The problem is we have no memory of what it is not to know. And so our churches, led by people plagued with the curse of knowledge, provide experiences and design services that feel right to people who know stuff, but totally miss the boat when it comes to people who don't.
Pop Goes the Church by Tim Stevens[4]

I would bet you didn't realize that taking a class or learning a lesson would come with a curse. I didn't. Can it really be the more you know, the more you're cursed? That's not what those public service announcements imply. Gaining knowledge is certainly empowering and a blessing, but it can also make us forget what it was like not to know. I think we sometimes develop amnesia about the journey of discovery. We are often left with some answers, but not many of the questions or the failed hypotheses that got us there.

I'm feeling the curse. With a call to emerging ministry hanging over my head, what am I doing? Still planning contemporary and traditional worship. Why? 'Cause that's what I know how to do. What I sense and what I can't quite put my finger on is how to get beyond the knowledge to the calling. I'm feeling the tension of trying to follow a distant call versus being the best I can be here and now with the knowledge I think I have mastered.

> But God chose what is foolish in the world to shame the wise; God chose what is weak in the world to shame the strong; God chose what is low and despised in the world, things that are not, to reduce to nothing things that are, so that no one might boast in the presence of God.
> — 1 Corinthians 1:27-30

I think it's time to get a little foolish, so I've been compiling my foolish wish list:
- a cure for my amnesia, so I experience empathy not indifference
- worship experiences that don't assume everyone is on board with the whole God thing
- Sunday school teachers that don't assume every child is on board with the whole God thing
- welcoming and inviting to those with differing beliefs and actually respecting them and their faith walk
- more concerned with being Christ followers than being Christian
- challenging people to live like they're blessed to be a blessing
- not challenging people to sing hymns and recite creeds they don't necessarily get
- excellence in worship based on the Spirit's presence not on the mechanics of worship

What are your foolish wishes?

Chapter Endnotes

1. I wrote an article some years later in which I contended that letters of call to ministers contained overly ambitious job descriptions — nearly twenty duties stipulated at that time in my church body. I argued that the list should be drastically reduced, to give pastors the opportunity to focus and develop areas of solid competence. See "Ministry, Vocation and Ordination: Some Perspectives from Luther" in *The Lutheran Quarterly* XXIX.1 (February, 1977), 66-81.
2. A homily presented at Texas Lutheran University, November 21, 1997.
3. For some additional thoughts on transformation, see the paper titled "A rough guide to transformation of consciousness" in ch. 25.
4. Tim Stevens, *Pop Goes the Church: Should the Church Engage Pop Culture?* (Power Publishing, 2008).

CHAPTER 16

THE LAST HOMILY

Background essay

Tom Wilkens

My love for music began at a very young age. From as early as I can remember, my father — with an interest that belied his eighth-grade education — regularly tuned in to the Saturday afternoon radio broadcasts of Metropolitan Opera productions. During my years in the lower grades of elementary school we had a music teacher who came into our classroom a few times a week to teach us folk songs and to play, on a piano or a phonograph, some of the standard pieces of western classical music. I thoroughly enjoyed it. And though I never learned to play a musical instrument, I have sung choral music most of my life.

The joy that music elicits in me — joy experienced regularly in hearing and sometimes in performing melodies, harmonies, and even occasional discordant intervals — grew while singing in our high school choir. The director had us constantly reaching for and sometimes attaining at least a modicum of mastery of a portion of the world's great choral literature. In my high school, by the way, more prestige was attached to participating in the concert choir than playing on athletic teams. I did both, but there was never a doubt in my mind which one would win if I were forced to choose between them: it would be music. Normally I try not to wax nostalgic about the good old days. Yet in this instance I am tempted to do so beyond my capacity to resist. How many public schools today value the arts more highly than athletics? Not many, I think.

My affinity for choral music grew during my college years, when I sang in the chapel choir and in the annual Advent season performances of

Handel's "Messiah." It continued throughout my adult life as a member of various church choirs. The highlight of my musical avocation came during the 1980s when I sang with the Texas Bach Choir, a San Antonio-based group dedicated to performing the Baroque and Classical choral repertoires.

Lutheran colleges and universities typically have a deep commitment to music education and musical performance. Texas Lutheran was no different. There were expectations, with resources to facilitate their realization, that the Concert Band and the Concert Choir would be outstanding organizations. They rarely disappointed. And my wife and I rarely missed their concerts.

I almost always requested that the Concert Choir sing in chapel when I spoke. In addition to taking great pleasure in the music, this was also my hedge against a poor turnout for the chapel service: more people attended whenever the choir sang. And so I asked the director, Sigurd Christiansen, if the choir would sing for the service in which I would give my "last homily." I had already chosen a hymn for the service. The choir began preparing two anthems. When I saw the music Christiansen had chosen, I decided to use the anthem and hymn texts as the basis for my homily. I had little difficulty relating them to the "last homily" motif.

This was my last homily while in the employ of Texas Lutheran University, but not my last homily ever. In retirement I have continued to do guest preaching on campus, in congregations inside and outside of Texas, and overseas. These preaching opportunities continue to serve as occasions to proclaim a word with consoling priestly or challenging prophetic dimensions and to articulate a theology with more focus and yet also more openness.

I have never been a soloist. Occasionally I have sung in duets or quartets, but mostly I have been a member of larger choral ensembles. I sometimes think of my preaching in a similar way: it looks like solo work, but I really function as a member of the chorus. At times, to carry the metaphor a bit further, I sense that the director is calling upon me to intone some prophetic dissonance. At other times I am asked to sing several measures of priestly harmony. But none of it works, especially the dissonance, if I do not remember that I am a chorister and if I do not listen very carefully to the rest of the choir.

Retirement is surely a significant time of transition. And this transition does not always go smoothly. Over the years I have known some teachers who were quite anxious about the prospect of retiring. They worried about the losses: the loss of close relationships with colleagues and students, the loss of an important structure for their lives, and the loss of the level of income they had achieved and to which they had become accustomed. College professors often talk a good game about the need for and even the exhilarating promise of change. But we do not always take our own advice. We often fear change in our own profession and in our own lives, especially when the umbilical cord of employment — perhaps even of our self-esteem — is about to be cut.

Possibly, at age 62, I was still naïve. Perhaps I did not appreciate the gravity of the situation, the seriousness of the transition, or the possibility that so many things could go so wrong in retirement — especially the adverse things associated with aging. And yet, I did not fear it. I welcomed retirement as an opportunity, the kind that young children so willingly and expertly embrace: a chance to continue to reinvent oneself in terms of life goals and lifestyle.

I do not pretend to be pulling off this reinvention business as well as a child. My habits are more deeply ingrained, my preferences are more narrowly defined, and my energies are more quickly exhausted than they used to be. Nonetheless, I do try. And while it may not be the most profound or existentially meaningful thing in the world, I did recently purchase a digital piano. I think it is high time, now that I am in my seventies, that I finally learn how to play a musical instrument.[1]

The last homily[2]

Tom Wilkens

The first text: "The Lord is a mighty God" by Felix Mendelssohn

The Lord is a mighty God and a mighty ruler, over all creation.
(Altered; sung by the Texas Lutheran University Concert Choir;
Sigurd Christiansen, director)

The first part of the last homily

The Lord is a mighty God but not, I suspect, an almighty God.[3] I would like to remove the expression "Almighty God" from our theological vocabulary. I know: it won't happen. This is an eleventh-hour effort by a notoriously naïve promoter of lost causes. Even the mere suggestion of ceasing to refer to God as almighty is enough to send some people into theological disarray, as I was reminded in one of my classes last week.

So why do I make the suggestion? What would be lost? What would be gained? I don't think that much would be lost. It turns out that the expression "Almighty God" shows up much more often in our liturgical life than in our supposedly normative biblical tradition. In the New Testament, for instance, the Greek word which is usually translated into English as "almighty" — *pantokrátor* — occurs only ten times, nine of those times in the book of Revelation. The author/editor of Revelation clearly regarded Rome as a great power. We can argue whether Rome's power was exercised for good or evil or perhaps some of both. But surely we can agree that it was real power exercised in real ways in the real world.

In such a context, I should think, the theological point being made was not that God holds all power — that God is almighty — but that God's power is sovereign. Even mighty Rome is answerable to a greater power: the sovereign power of God. Or, as Paul put it in his letter to the Philippians, in the final analysis every knee shall bow in acknowledgment that Jesus the Christ is also the Lord.[4]

So what do we lose if we address God as Sovereign Lord, not as Almighty God? We lose a number of ideas about God consistent with the notion of almightiness. We lose a God who is invulnerable. We lose a God who is impervious to change or, in the older terminology, immutable. We lose the Unmoved Mover of the philosopher Aristotle, scarcely a cause for deep grief.

168

What do we gain? We gain a vulnerable God. We gain a suffering God. We gain God as a waiting father, cut to the quick by our arrogant departures and overcome by joy at our humble returns. We gain God as a mother hen, anxious for her wandering chicks. We gain God as a caring shepherd who prefers to engage the sheep through voice recognition rather than by the threat of a stout stick or a barking dog. We gain a God who knows something about weakness, not just strength; about losing, not just winning; about death, not just life.

If that is what we gain by regarding God as sovereign in power, but not all-powerful, then I'm ready for the change. And I suspect that this is the God who has been trying to reach out to us all along: a God whose power, whatever else it might accomplish, does not shield the heart of God from occasional pain or the hand of God from occasional weakness.

The second text: "Mothering God, you gave me birth" by Carolyn Jennings

Mothering God, you gave me birth
in the bright morning of this world.
Creator, source of every breath,
you are my rain, my wind, my sun.

Mothering Christ, you took my form,
offering me your food of light,
grain of new life, and grape of love,
your very body for my peace.

Mothering Spirit, nurt'ring one,
in arms of patience hold me close,
so that in faith I root and grow
until I flow'r, until I know.[5]

(Sung as the hymn for the day)

The second part of the last homily

The Lord is a fathering God yet also, I suspect, a mothering God.[6] One of the great theological issues concurrent with my tenure at Texas Lutheran has been the gender issue. It seems almost omnipresent. It manifests itself in matters ranging from the roles of women in church and society to the gender bias of our language.

I belong to what appears to be a growing segment in both church and society which holds that the issues are important, the problems significant. But within this segment there is little agreement as to strategies or tactics to deal with gender bias. For example, some would like to de-gender our God-talk. On this matter I find myself agreeing with the German systematic theologian Wolfhart Pannenberg, who holds that de-gendering is not really a good idea. There is, he argues, too much essential and irreplaceable content in the notion of God as father in our tradition to lay that notion aside. The problem, it seems to me, is not with male-gender metaphors for God. The problem is with male-biased communities of faith neglecting to nurture and be nurtured also by female-gender metaphors for God.

Therefore, maybe bringing more gender balance into our God-talk is the answer. One approach to this that has gained some support is to focus on the Third Person of the Trinity — the Holy Spirit — as a promising point from which to expand our appreciation for the feminine side of God. This focus is augmented at times by an emphasis on God as Wisdom — Sophia in Greek — the embodiment of God as feminine, perhaps even of God as Goddess.

However, I prefer the approach taken by the hymn we sang a few moments ago. Its words are based on a text by a woman named Julian of Norwich, a medieval mystic whose contemplative life focused on the mystery of divine love. The hymn is traditional in that it is Trinitarian. It is non-traditional in that it declares a feminine side to each Person of the Trinity: mothering God, mothering Christ, mothering Spirit. I suspect that for Julian of Norwich God was bi-genderal.

Again, what do we gain by breaking out of a male-exclusive mindset with respect to God? We gain half of the world's population as potential theological mentors and spiritual guides, whose mentoring and guidance come out of the very depths of their identity and experience as women and of God as woman. As a man, I gain perspective on God mediated through feminine identity and experience, but only if women agree to be my tutors and I agree to be tutored. Some women have agreed; sometimes I agree. Not always. The community of God's people needs more women as guides, more men under their guidance, more access to the mothering vocation of God.

The third text: "The Evening Primrose" from "Five Flower Songs" by Benjamin Britten

When once the sun sinks in the west,
And dewdrops pearl the evening's breast;
Almost as pale as moonbeams are,
Or its companion star,
The evening primrose opes anew
Its delicate blossoms to the dew.
And, hermit-like, shunning the light,
Wastes its fair bloom upon the night;
Who, blindfolded to its fond caresses,
Knows not the beauty he possesses.
Thus it blooms on while night is by;
When day looks out with open eye,
Bashed at the gaze it cannot shun,
It faints and withers and is gone.
(Sung by the Texas Lutheran University Concert Choir)[7]

The third part of the last homily

The Lord is a generous God and even, I suspect, a profligate God. I remember a professor who was also my chief mentor at seminary commenting on an offering hymn many of us have sung. The first verse goes like this:

We give thee but thine own,
Whate'er the gift may be;
All that we have is thine alone,
A trust, O Lord, from thee.[8]

Not true, the professor would insist. Think about the theology of what you sing or say or hear, he would urge. This little liturgical ditty presumes the doctrine of a stingy God, a God who never really lets go of anything. Is God actually like that? Or is God truly generous, recklessly extravagant, unashamedly wasteful? Charge God with profligacy, but never with stinginess.

John Clare (1793-1864) wrote the poem titled "Evening Primrose" that Benjamin Britten (1913-1976) set to music. Think about the theology of what you sing, choir members. Think about the theology of what you hear, chapel attendees. The Lord is not just generous. The Lord is a downright wasteful God. The Lord creates a universe so large and so rapidly expanding that it beggars the imagination. It's more than we need.

171

It's more than we can fully investigate or comprehend, maybe even more than God intended. Perhaps God got a bit carried away.

Consider the evening primrose, which wastes its fair bloom upon the unseeing night. It possesses a beauty that will never be perceived, a beauty that the light of day will destroy. How utterly extravagant. How gloriously wasteful. I suspect that God has a streak of creative wantonness.

God's profligacy is not the wastefulness of unwise use or unsustainable consumption. God's profligacy is the wastefulness of unbridled generosity — providing more beauty and space and grace than can ever be enjoyed or explored or exhausted; providing more love and hope than even the killing grounds of Cambodia or Kosovo or Columbine can absorb and destroy. God is generous to a fault — much like the fault of the mother to my children; much like the fault of the mother and of the uncle to my grandchild.

The Lord is a mighty God, a mentoring mother God, a stunningly generous God. The Lord is a suffering God, a nurturing father God, a wildly creative God. And for those of us named Christian — originally a term of derision, subsequently and again today a catalyst for persecution — for us the Lord is Jesus.

Let us pray:

> Come, Lord Jesus. Accompany your people as we continue to make transitions in the days and years ahead — some larger and publicly acknowledged, others smaller and scarcely noticed, yet all of them important in the tapestry of our common life. Amen. Come, Lord Jesus.

Response:
Send your love

Kim Wilkens

I wish I could quote song lyrics or bundle a CD with this book. In my original responses to my dad's chapters, I was often inspired by a song title or lyrics, and I used them in my writing. Then I found out that quoting song lyrics in a book is a big no, no. I had to update 14 of my responses to remove lyrics. I tried to keep most of the references to the song titles, so you might see a glimmer of how these songs have touched me.

Music has been a consistent, positive force in my life. Unfortunately, not in the creating or making of it (oh how I wish I could carry a tune or write brilliant lyrics), but in the receiving of it. There are songs that have gotten me through rough times and others that help me celebrate the joys. There are songs that get me through melancholy and songs that can pull me out of a funk. When I really connect with a song, I find myself creating a music video in my head. Maybe that's because I grew up on MTV. I love creating music videos for worship. The right image with the right lyrics can be powerful.

I know our God receivers are damaged because we have such a hard time hearing Her, but sometimes I think She sings to me through a song. Today, it's "Send Your Love" by Sting.[9] The repeating chorus is about sending your love into the future. I think this gets right to the heart of the matter as it summarizes well what God has been and is up to on planet earth, continually sending Her love here and now and into the future. I think that's what God wants us to do. What would sending our love into the future mean? For me, it's pretty easy to identify what it doesn't mean. It's not expecting anything in return or knowing what effect it will have or fulfilling some hidden agenda or about taking control.

I think my dad has identified some of what it might mean. If God has and is continually sending His love into the future, then He is not looking for power. If God has and is continually sending Her love into the future, then She is willing to nurture and make untold sacrifices for Her creation. If God has and is continually sending His/Her love into the future, then the Lord is stunningly generous.

Lord, thank you for sending your love here and now and into our futures. It is an amazing gift. Please help us to follow your lead as we send our love into the future. Amen.

Chapter Endnotes

1. For some further thoughts on retirement, see the background essays in chs. 17 and 18.
2. A homily presented at Texas Lutheran University on Friday, April 23, 1999.
3. See the paper titled "Who, what, and where in the world is God?" in ch. 6 for some additional thoughts on the notion of omnipotence.
4. With respect to the Hebrew scriptures, the expression *El Shaddai* is traditionally translated as Almighty God, a practice that goes back to the King James translators of the early seventeenth century. *El Shaddai* more likely means Mountain God or Sufficient God.
5. Text copyright Jean Janzen, admin. Augsburg Fortress. Used by permission.
6. This part was later expanded into a stand-alone homily. See "The mothering vocation of God" in ch. 26.
7. "The Evening Primrose" was composed by Benjamin Britten in 1950.
8. "We Give Thee But Thine Own" words by William W. How, 1823-1897. In the public domain.
9. Sting, *Send Your Love: Sacred Love* (A&M, 2003).

CHAPTER 17

AFTER THE TOUR GUIDE WAVES GOOD-BYE

Background essay

Tom Wilkens

After 31 years of teaching, I retired from Texas Lutheran University at the end of the spring semester in 1999. Around the middle of that final term the campus pastor asked me to give a "last lecture," the kind of thing one would deliver as a valedictory at the conclusion of an academic career. It was an interesting exercise that taught me, among other things, the difficulty of summarizing and prioritizing the lessons learned over a long professional life in just a short talk.

Toward the end of the semester, my wife and children organized a truly festive retirement party, attended by many colleagues, friends, family members, and former students. A lot of nice words were spoken. I no doubt flatter myself by thinking that many of the things said were actually meant. And of course, there was also some good-natured "roasting" involved.

Betty and I both took early retirements with a view to doing short-term volunteer global service missions. I had tested the waters in 1997 by teaching a summer graduate course in theology at Satya Wacana University in Salatiga, on the island of Java in Indonesia. And in May of 1998 Betty and I accompanied a number of Texas Lutheran students on a service-learning mission to Costa Rica and Nicaragua, involving a construction project and working with orphaned children. These experiences persuaded us that we could do these sorts of things and that they were worth doing.

In the years of my retirement I have thus far participated in eight additional global service missions: to China, South Africa, Costa Rica, Russia, Italy, Guyana, Lithuania, and Honduras. They have ranged in length from eight days to four months. I have taught theology and ethics at two seminaries; taught English as a Foreign Language (a much more accurate way to describe it than English as a Second Language) at a university, a college, and an elementary school; and assisted in construction, medical, and technology projects in three Latin American settings. Betty has accompanied me, engaging in a variety of service activities, on six of these service missions. In addition, she has done two on her own.

The work and the participation in the lives and communities of international sisters and brothers in Christ constitute only one-half of this calling to which we periodically respond. The other half consists of reporting on the overseas realities that we encounter to our sisters and brothers back home. We do this together through programs and presentations that we make in churches, schools, and universities. And I do it alone in the papers I have written and the homilies I have preached in my retirement years. All of the homilies and papers in the remainder of this book will show, to a greater or lesser extent, the impact of this current vocation of ours.

It is a vocation: we no longer have jobs but we still have vocations or callings. The call to international service looms large in our lives. But we also engage in service on the home front, ranging from mentoring elementary school children and young single moms to leading a group dedicated to fund-raising for the local symphony and participating in their program to provide classical music encounters for area school children. The challenges to us are great; the rewards for us are far greater. I sometimes need to interrupt people who are preparing to get teary-eyed about our dedication to service and remind them that Jesus really meant what he reportedly said: it is better to give than to receive (Acts 20:35). To use an oft-repeated line from Luther's *Small Catechism*, this is most certainly true. The term sacrifice somehow seems inappropriate to describe what we do or, more to the point, what God does through our lives these days. It turns out that we always receive, in so many ways, much more than we give.[1]

The piece that follows flowed out of two months of travel and service in China during the summer of 1999. It was our first service mission in retirement and we did it together. The paper gives a fairly comprehensive summary of what we saw, what we did, and what we learned during our travel and work there. But I think that one element in the report requires a little more elaboration and some corrective tweaking.

I wrote in the paper about the underground or unregistered church. This refers most particularly to those Christians in China whose roots are in what we in the West would call Protestantism, especially the more aggressively evangelical Protestant bodies. Most of them would feel compromised by the kind of power the Chinese government exercises over the officially registered church. And so they refuse to register, to permit governmental oversight of their religious lives. These underground Christians have experienced persecution, sometimes severe. There is also an ongoing struggle between the Chinese leadership and the Vatican over control of the Roman Catholic Church in China. In retrospect, I think that the article was too upbeat and effusive about the registered church and too uncritical and reticent about the tremendous problems that many underground or unregistered Christians still face in China today. We did not, it became quite clear in subsequent conversations with a fellow professor who was also a political refugee from mainland China, get the whole picture.

After the tour guide waves good-bye[2]

Tom Wilkens

Our tour of central and eastern China was over. The transition to the EFL (English as a Foreign Language) program was punctuated by a move from a four-star to a two-star hotel. It would continue on the weekend with an orientation held at a hillside retreat center.

We had begun the sixteen-day tour in Shanghai, with its western-style waterfront building facades regaining some of their former splendor. We ended in Hong Kong, with its unforgettable skyline. In between was a myriad of sights and sounds, of tastes and smells: the Great Wall of China; the Forbidden City in Beijing; the contrasts of prosperity and poverty; the Terracotta Warriors of Xi'an; the polluted yet stately Yangtze

River; the pure Li River seen through the mists of a summer rain; the odor of incense at the very active Buddhist temples; the delicious foods and new-found dexterity with chopsticks. All of this, and more, would serve as context for our work when we returned to Mainland China to begin our teaching.

Betty and I joined four other short-term Evangelical Lutheran Church in America volunteers in Hong Kong for our initial orientation. There we were introduced to the modest ELCA China Program and to the impressive campus of the Hong Kong Lutheran Seminary. Betty and I also had a second opportunity to worship with the people of Truth Lutheran Church in downtown Kowloon, this time with the celebration of the Eucharist.

Early the following week in Nanjing we joined 74 other US volunteers, forty of them from the Lutheran Church-Missouri Synod, for a four-day orientation to the Summer English Program sponsored by the Amity Foundation. The Amity Foundation, an arm of the Chinese Christian (read "Protestant") Council, also sponsors other educational, medical, and development programs.

After the orientations we traveled to Linyi, located in Shandong Province in eastern China and began our assignment at Linyi University. Our teaching team consisted of five Americans, including Chicagoan Sarah Olson, whose six-foot height and blonde hair drew a crowd wherever she went; South Dakotan Clayton Olson; Bill Davis, a Methodist from Colorado; plus a Scot, Pamela Gordon, a recent graduate of an *alma mater* of mine — the University of Aberdeen in Scotland. The group was thus both ecumenical and international. Our classes ran from 8:00 to 11:30 a.m. and from 2:30 to 4:30 p.m., Monday through Friday. Our students, middle school and high school English teachers from throughout the region, labored very hard to improve their English speaking and listening skills. They were a joy to work with.

Through all of this, we learned new things about China and left some long-held prejudices behind. Let me give a few examples:

Fiction: Bibles are illegal in China and need to be smuggled into the country. *Fact*: Millions of Bibles are printed and distributed legally in China every year. We toured a plant that prints Bibles. We saw some of those Bibles in the church pews in Linyi.

Fiction: The church cannot grow in China because religion is illegal and evangelism is therefore impossible. *Fact*: It is estimated that there are over fifteen million Protestant Christians in China today, in churches that are registered or in the process of registering with the Chinese Christian Council. The underground or unregistered church may be much larger. Two new congregations are formed every three days. They worship openly and legally. While it is true that foreign missionaries are banned and all public forms of evangelism are outlawed, the church in China grows rapidly — more rapidly than in the US — through the witness of lifestyle ("see how they love one another") and by personal evangelism (much like the ancient church).

Fiction: China has no seminaries and therefore cannot train church leaders. Or if it does have seminaries, they teach something other than true Christianity. *Fact*: We visited one of the major theological seminaries in China: Nanjing Union Theological Seminary. The president of the Seminary spoke to us. There is little doubt in our minds that the faculty there teaches "the faith once delivered to the saints." There are not enough seminaries and there is a leadership shortage. We Western Christians need to become inventive enough to find new ways to help our sisters and brothers in Christ in China without being intrusive or imperious. The Western powers once forced China to submit to drug traffic which it did not want but which the West found profitable. We will not be allowed today to impose our particular (peculiar?) Western interpretations and practices of Christianity upon China — nor should we.

Enough sermonizing. We were called "experts" in China, but we learned just as much as we taught. On one occasion, for instance, we were invited into a modest Chinese home to learn how to make *jiaozu*, a delicious stuffed dumpling. We then joined the family for the meal, which included six other dishes. It was a most pleasant evening.

We began with an extensive tour of major cities, historical sites, and natural features of China, crisscrossing its eastern half by plane, boat, train, and bus. We ended with a shorter circle tour of Shandong Province, traveling by van, bus, and plane. In between we met, taught, and learned from many people at the University in Linyi. On the one hand, we were privileged and pampered. On the other, we worked hard under developing-world conditions in the summer heat.

Two months of contrast. Two months of enrichment. Two months of challenge to deeply rooted biases, long-held stereotypes, and out-dated information. It certainly was worthwhile for us. We hope that it will prove to be worthwhile for others also.

One way it could be worthwhile for others is for us to convince some of you to do similar things. Many US churches help their members make connections with overseas volunteer projects designed by the indigenous churches. Check their web sites. For example, if you belong to a church body that in turn belongs to the National Council of Churches of Christ, it can serve as your conduit into the Amity Program in China. But there are many other opportunities and many other agencies.

We do quite a bit of international traveling and highly recommend it, for both the pleasure and the perspective it gives. For countries that may present some problems with respect to travel infrastructure accessibility or reliability, we suggest booking an organized tour. But in addition, we recommend that you remain abroad after the tour guide waves good-bye and engage in some sort of volunteer activity. It could change your life, for the better. It could change other people's lives, for the better. It requires a willing heart, an open mind, a flexible spirit, and, typically, a bachelor's degree — the very things with which a Texas Lutheran University grad is equipped. Everything else, such as financial assistance or matching talent to need, can usually be located or negotiated. As the Nike Corporation has said so often, "Just do it." At least they got something right.

Response:
Walking the labyrinth

Kim Wilkens

Sometimes when I'm working on these responses to my dad's writing, I struggle with what thread or train of thought to pick up on. Often there seem to be too many choices, but in the case of this chapter, I just didn't feel a connection to something that I could relate to my life. So, it may be a stretch, but what I finally identified with is the idea that we don't always get the whole picture. One way I was reminded of this truth is through an experience of walking the labyrinth on July 1, 2008. Here's what I wrote about that experience.

It's amazing how something kind of cheesy can also be kind of profound. Peace is borrowing an indoor labyrinth this week and I had my first chance to walk it today. I've heard about walking the labyrinth for several years now, especially amongst the Emerging crowd, so I've been wanting the chance to try it.

As you walk into the labyrinth, you are supposed to release and let go of the details of your life. For a few minutes, I couldn't let go of the cheese factor, walking barefoot on a canvas palette painted with a purple maze. Next I found myself going through my mental to do lists. No, I reminded myself, I'm not supposed to *do*, I'm supposed to *undo*. Then I started noticing where I was walking. At times I would get close to the middle and then be led away again. That's interesting. I tried not to cheat and look ahead to what was coming next and before I knew it I was in the center.

Now I don't know what labyrinth protocol is on silence or not, but I decided to walk the labyrinth with background music. While I'm in the center, Alison Krauss started singing "A Living Prayer,"[3] a song about laying down control of your life and handing it over to God, and that is totally how I'm feeling today, but I know it won't last.

I think the labyrinth is a good metaphor for my faith journey. Sometimes I feel like I'm just moving in circles, as my faith ebbs and wanes, but is never fully formed. Then there is the rare occasion where my faith crystallizes into truth, purpose and understanding. However, as the seconds, minutes, hours and days pass, my faith tends to get muddled up as I circle back out of the labyrinth. I guess I just need to remember to return to the journey, especially when it seems kind of cheesy and hopeless.

Chapter Endnotes

1. For additional thoughts about retirement, see the background essays in chs. 16 and 18.
2. An article written after two months in China during the summer of 1999 and appearing initially on Texas Lutheran University's website.
3. Alison Krauss and Union Station, *A Living Prayer: Lonely Runs Both Ways* (Rounder/ Umgd, 2004).

CHAPTER 18

OLD PROFESSORS NEVER DIE, THEY JUST FADE AWAY

Background essay

Tom Wilkens

The next six of my presentations share some common ground. They all grew out of our second international service project in retirement: four months of volunteer work at Umphumulo Lutheran Theological Seminary, located at that time in rural South Africa. Betty helped to staff the Seminary library and also taught English as a Foreign Language to students still struggling with their English-language skills. I taught courses in Christian ethics and church history. The semester there reconfirmed our decision to take early retirements so that we could do such projects while we still had the health and stamina required.

Retirement is a problematic issue for many people. It has not been difficult for me, though the ease of my transition required a fairly radical rethinking of the views about work and retirement that dominate our culture. This rethinking may have begun, at least subliminally, with a workplace discussion at our family laundry and dry cleaning business about a half-century ago.

I recall speaking with my dad after it had become clear that none of the children would take over the firm he had worked so hard to nurture. I asked him if he had any concerns about this. Would there be any lingering regrets when he retired that the family business would not remain in the family? Not at all, he said in his response to my query. The business was for him merely a means to the end of caring for the family and seeing to the education — the higher education — of the children. By this time, my brother Frank held an MBA from Harvard and brother Jim a PhD from Cornell. Dad was at the halfway point of meeting an important goal he and our mother had set. It would be fully achieved when my sister Sue and I both finished degrees.

My father knew intuitively what it took me several years to learn and then to assimilate into my world-view: there is a difference, a crucially significant difference, between being and doing. We must take care not to suppose that our being, and with it our sense of worth and dignity, is somehow contingent upon our doing. Doing — our study, our work, our child-rearing, even our leisure — should be understood as an expression of our being, of who we are and what our lives are about, and not as the basis or source of our being. Doing cannot establish, enlarge or sustain our fundamental identity. Our being at its deepest level is an endowment, not an accomplishment.

Occasionally I used to lay out the following two scenarios with my students, both having to do with my eventual retirement from Texas Lutheran University. The first scenario went something like this: I announced my plan to retire and was overwhelmed by the heartfelt responses expressed by parades of people stopping by my office. First came the students, tearfully begging me to remain in my teaching post lest their educations suffer irreparable damage. Then my faculty colleagues stopped by, mournfully maintaining that the ranks of the faculty could never recover from my departure. And finally members of the administration, nearly overcome by the gravity of the situation, assured me that the institution might well fail if I left my position. I felt incredibly honored by this outpouring of sentiment and quite guilty about my decision to retire. Perhaps I should reconsider.

The second scenario was quite different: I announced my retirement and was underwhelmed by the reaction. The department quickly wrote a job description. Soon after that the University initiated the search for a new teacher. There were over 100 applicants, each superbly skilled and all more qualified than I. At the conclusion of the search process, the University offered a contract to an outstanding young scholar and it was accepted. The University subsequently bade a public farewell to me, with kind remarks and genuine institutional sincerity, but it did not miss a beat in its academic program. It turned out that I was a replaceable cog in an educational machine and the machine, always undergoing assessment and procuring new parts, just kept getting better.

Which scenario, I would then ask my students, is likelier to be the case when I retire? After the brief and inevitable calculation as to whether or not they could risk being honest with me on this matter, the response was always the same and always correct: the second scenario would probably be closer to the reality when my retirement came. And it was. What was the point of the exercise? To alert students to the dangers of attempting to use their occupations as means of validating their value as human beings because, among other reasons, it could lead to debilitating personal and relational consequences with the loss of their jobs and to growing fears at the prospect of their retirements.

Old professors fade away: it is our lot in life. It is not a sad or a bad lot at all. Retirement is good. However, this would not be so if my worth and significance as a person were on the line with all the decisions I continue to make about what to do or not do, and with the "success" or lack thereof I have with those choices. Not to bear that burden is truly liberating and exhilarating. It is a concrete expression of what Lutherans call living out of the gospel rather than according to the law. It is a gift.

I am often asked these days how I am doing. "Better than I deserve," I reply from time to time. It seems to take many people aback. When they recover, some of them smile knowingly and agree that this is true for them, too. Others disagree. They try to reassure me, and themselves, that we deserve the good lives we are leading. I am not at all convinced; I am simply appreciative.[1]

Old professors never die, they just fade away[2]

Tom Wilkens

The title for this article paraphrases or, more accurately, parodies a line from General Douglas MacArthur's stirring farewell address delivered nearly a half century ago to the cadets at West Point. At one time the commandant of West Point and later the supreme commander of allied land forces in the Pacific theatre during World War II, MacArthur said

185

with much emotion shortly before he left the podium signaling the sunset of his career, "Old soldiers never die, they just fade away."

Neither his wistful statement, borrowed from a much earlier popular song, nor my twisted title are, of course, true. We all do die: in my case, just not quite yet. Meanwhile, I fly away. Last summer my wife, Betty, and I flew to China. We did some volunteer teaching at Linyi University, located several hundred kilometers southeast of Beijing. You can read about it in an article titled "After the tour guide waves goodbye," posted on the Theology/Philosophy Department page of the Texas Lutheran University website.[3]

This past January we flew to South Africa. Currently we serve as volunteers at Umphumulo Lutheran Theological Seminary, located in KwaZulu-Natal Province about an hour-and-a-half's drive outside of Durban. The rural setting is incredibly beautiful and especially lush right now with the summer rains. We are living quite comfortably in the Seminary guesthouse, just a short walk from the campus.

But all is not well in this Eden. The litany of South Africa's ills could be very long indeed: a burgeoning crime rate; a growing HIV-positive/AIDS rate (already 36% in this province, 18% nationwide); serious environmental degradation; a 52% unemployment rate. I could go on and on. Yet the overall impression we have of the people and their spirit is upbeat and hopeful. Their present reality, seemingly a statistical nightmare, is nonetheless better than the past horrors of apartheid.

The Evangelical Lutheran Church of Southern Africa (ELCSA) and its Seminary here at Umphumulo also have problems. Many of those problems, though not all, stem from insufficient financial resources. In addition, the church feels threatened by charismatic movements and by literally hundreds of independent religious groups active in southern Africa. And the Seminary sometimes feels like a neglected stepchild of the church, lower on the church's priority list than it should be if it is to perform well its function for the church. But despite all of the needs and difficulties, our experience has been mostly positive. The people, from the Rector (the Reverend Dr. Musa Biyela) to the students (a record enrollment of over one hundred this year), have been exceptionally welcoming and hospitable.

Our days here have fallen into something of a pattern. Betty works in the library each weekday morning and teaches some English for first-year students. I teach classes in ethics and church history for third- and fourth year students and take my turns leading chapel services. There are two chapel services each weekday and most Sundays. Before classes we gather for matins or morning suffrages. After supper there is a variety of liturgies, ranging from evening suffrages to services of healing. And the singing, mostly *a cappella*, is glorious.

Eucharistic services here are fascinating syntheses of high-church formality and low-church spontaneity. On the one hand, they include elaborately vested celebrants, incense-bearing acolytes, and traditional chanting. On the other hand, there are congregation-initiated hymns, prayers, and vocal responses to well-delivered sermon lines. The new participant quickly becomes both captivated and inspired.

Even though Umphumulo is remote, it still attracts a steady stream of international visitors. They range from backpacking German students to a retired American couple to a media-attracting head of state. Prime Minister Bondevik of Norway came to the Umphumulo parish church on a recent Sunday to note the role played by nineteenth century Norwegian missionaries in establishing the Lutheran presence among the Zulus. The Evangelical Lutheran Church in Southern Africa is now the largest church in this province. This is due in no small part to the Norwegian missionaries at Umphumulo. They built a school and a hospital and established congregations. The school was for decades a teacher training college, until the state removed it during the apartheid years. The Seminary relocated here in the 1960s to take advantage of the facilities. The government runs the hospital now in the post-apartheid era.

For all of the legitimate criticisms that can be leveled against nineteenth-century European and American missionary efforts, there nevertheless remain important positive contributions. The descendants of those who were initially evangelized acknowledge these even today. They remain grateful for the proclamation of the gospel and for the provision of education, two powerful forces that sometimes converge to liberate people in unexpected ways. Such is the story, at least in some tellings, of the remarkable transition from apartheid to freedom for the majority of South Africans this past decade. Political liberation must soon be accompanied by more economic and social participation, lest the gains be lost in a cauldron of violence and despair.

On a more personal note, we had a wonderful surprise upon our arrival in Umphumulo. We discovered that one of my former students and one of the best — Eric Modisane, a South African who graduated from Texas Lutheran in 1981 with a theology major — is on the faculty here teaching Greek and New Testament. It truly is a small world after all. When I am no longer able to fly away, perhaps I can fade away with fond remembrances of people and places and times past on a globe that has shrunk significantly during my itinerary upon it.

For now, there are more memories to be made. Accompanied by some twenty members of our home congregation, we will fly to Costa Rica in July on a brief service mission. With a twisted sense of humor that I really do appreciate, people call what we are doing nowadays "retirement." I will try to let you know when we get the hang of it a bit better.

Response:
Talk without ceasing

Kim Wilkens

"Luke, you're going to find that many of the truths we cling to depend greatly on our own point of view."

Ben in *Return of the Jedi*[4]

Talk, talk, talk, talk. Sometimes I think that's all the Emerging crowd does. Talk about theology, talk about words, talk about talking, talk about inviting others to talk.

I, too, can get caught in this mode and sometimes I'm afraid that I spend way too much time "talking;" be it on my blog, in worship planning, writing devotions, teaching technology, or updating websites. Lately, I've been especially ambivalent about my contribution to this book. I mean who really cares what I have to say? What's the point? Where's all this "talking" going to lead?

It's probably this ambivalence that made me wary when I was asked to participate in a small group. I was uneasy about starting a small group to study and "talk" about *The Heart of Christianity* by Marcus Borg. The thing is, this book has already had a profound impact on my life. Every chapter I've read has blown my mind and I literally have to take a break to let the words sink into my bones. Like this gem:

I don't think that Jesus literally died for our sins. I don't think he thought of his life and purpose that way; I don't think he thought of that as his divinely given vocation. But I do have faith in the cross as a trustworthy disclosure of the evil of domination systems, as the exposure of the defeat of the powers, as the revelation of the way or path of transformation ... as the proclamation of radical grace.[5]

Borg seems to be taking head-on many issues I have with the creeds and the modern baggage they carry as well as dismantling the facade of American Christianity, exposing a center I long to embrace. So I stopped reading the book once I knew I was doing the book study, because I wanted to wait and share my thoughts with others.

I guess that is ultimately why we talk — to share — to know and be known by others — to develop relationships. At the end of the conversation — when we're finally ready to ask "What do we do now?" — I just hope that all this talk eventually leads to action. I pray that our voices may fade away as our actions speak louder than words.

Chapter Endnotes

1. For some additional reflections on retirement, see the background essays in chs. 16 and 17.
2. Dr. Norm Beck, chair of the Theology/Philosophy Department, asked me to submit an article for the annual department review. The article is an edited collation of newsletters sent to Faith Lutheran Church in Seguin, Texas, while we were in South Africa. It appeared in the 1999-2000 edition of the *Theology/Philosophy Review* of Texas Lutheran University.
3. This article is now printed in the previous chapter of this book.
4. Star Wars: Episode VI — Return of the Jedi. Memorable Quotes. *IMDb*. www.imdb. com/title/ tt0086190/quotes.
5. Marcus Borg, *The Heart of Christianity* (HarperSanFrancisco, 2003), 96.

Chapter 19

Our Gospel May Be Too Small

Background essay

Tom Wilkens

Thinking big and thinking innovatively should be persistent hallmarks of the church. Yet often they are not. This is not to say that thinking small is always inappropriate: the gospel does indeed need to address nuclear family issues, individual lives, and personal problems. Still, this must not be done in isolation from or at the expense of the big picture: of communal, global, and even cosmic realities. Nor, in our openness to innovation, should we abandon all of our traditions. However, we regularly need to look for new ways to comprehend and convey them. And finally, we must be willing to moderate the "pack rat" mentality so often associated with religious conceptions and customs: we need to let go of some of them.

The homily in this chapter attempts to deal with a few of these matters. For example, it tries to alert us to sweeping dimensions of the gospel that often do not catch the attention of many in the Christian community. One way to enlarge our appreciation for the vast scope of the gospel is to be open to new ways of seeing, living, and understanding it. Assistance for these endeavors can come not only from within the community but also from without, including other faiths.

When I was a seminary student, one of the distinguished guest lecturers who spoke on campus was Will Herberg, a Jewish theologian and social thinker. Earlier he had published an influential study of the

American religious landscape, a book titled *Protestant-Catholic-Jew: an essay in American religious sociology* (1955). In his lecture, Herberg addressed the central Christian notion of incarnation: the enfleshment of God in the person of Jesus. He knew that in some Christian circles this ancient notion was being discussed with respect to its relevance and adequacy for people in a post-Enlightenment scientific age. Herberg offered an alternative, suggested to him by his own religious heritage. Christians would do better to use the term "enhistorization," he argued. In other words, he proposed a switch from a spatial (incarnation) to a temporal (enhistorization) frame of reference. It would fit more closely with the then-current Christian emphasis on *Heilsgeschichte*, salvation history, as a perspective from which to read the Bible and to understand the God it portrays. And it might also communicate more effectively with the secular public. Christians should speak less of the incarnation of God and more of God's enhistorization.

I thought it was an idea worth examining, though as it happens not much came of it. You will not find the word "enhistorization" in the subsequent Christian vocabulary. But what I found more remarkable at the time was that a Jewish scholar genuinely cared about the well-being of the Christian community, to the point of wanting to help us in our mission. I already knew that religious communities chronically borrow from one another, including those communities that produced the Jewish and Christian scriptures. They adopt and they adapt. But I also knew that they rarely acknowledged this borrowing and even more rarely tried to help a neighboring, perhaps even a rival, religious community.

The modern phenomenon of positive, mutually supportive interfaith dialogue had not heretofore been a part of my experience. I was more taken at that point in my life by the new prospects for ecumenical (*intra*-faith) relations. Herberg's whole approach was far different than anything I had been exposed to before, and it fascinated me. Among the things I found intriguing were his extraordinarily sympathetic understanding of Christianity and his deep insight into its meaning. He had a feel for Christianity that went far beyond scholarly analysis. In truth, Herberg regarded Judaism and Christianity as two religious expressions of one common faith.

It was not until much later, in reading some reminiscences penned by the late conservative commentator William F. Buckley Jr., that I learned Herberg, around the time he lectured at our Lutheran seminary, had been exploring the possibility of becoming either an Episcopal or a Lutheran Christian. Interestingly, it was an American Neo-orthodox theologian and sometime critic of theological liberalism, Reinhold Niebuhr, who talked Herberg out of leaving Judaism and converting to Christianity. Herberg, Niebuhr held, could make an infinitely greater contribution by remaining a spokesperson for Judaism in conversation with Christianity.

The major thesis of this book is that Christians should not always accept the views and values of culture. A major corollary of this thesis is that we need to be selectively, not uniformly, countercultural. Either the unremitting condemnation or the uncritical affirmation of culture would be much easier. But we have the more difficult task of deciding which cultural values, trends, and practices to oppose and which to encourage and at times incorporate into our faith and practice. For instance, the inclusion of music in our lives of faith is for most of us a no-brainer: the only things we are prepared to quibble about are appropriate lyrics and musical styles. Yet not all Christians have incorporated music as a part of their ritual life. Still, for me, music — including but by no means limited to the music of the church — has expanded and enriched my understanding of the gospel and my appreciation of life beyond measure. I need this kind of help. I think that most of us do. Individually we can find such help in different niches, ethnicities, and cultures across the globe. We should respect and encourage those explorations.

In this first century of the third millennium, perhaps we Christians need to look not only to culture but also to other religions for assistance in enlarging our perspective and elaborating our faith with more inclusive and pertinent vision. Will Herberg offered an idea to help Christians of the mid-twentieth century to do just that. The stakes are even higher now: interfaith dialogue and cooperation, and the mutual respect and trust that they can engender, are urgently needed and in desperately short supply in today's world. Little hearts and minds, coupled with large fears and prejudices, will keep our gospel smaller, less tolerant, and more narrowly applicable than it can and ought to be.

To show how far that I have come in my own lifetime, which also illustrates the great distance that I had to travel in this matter — given my myopic beginnings — let me end this essay with a quote from the keynote address that I gave to the Texas Conference of Churches annual meeting in 1999 on the occasion of its thirtieth anniversary. The address was titled

"Back to the future" or "Titanic — how shall we cross the millennial dateline?" I made this the first of three challenges to the delegates:

> I challenge you to participate in a shift in emphasis from ecumenical to interfaith relations. Surely the single most important ecumenical initiative in the twentieth century was Vatican II. But I remind you that Vatican II also took perhaps even more surprising initiatives with respect to inte ith relations. As I stated a moment ago, the ecumenical task never ends. Yet its context is shifting. The twentieth century was without doubt the greatest century of ecumenical activity and advance ever. And this organization made major contributions toward that end. Will people leaving the twenty-first century be able to call it the "interfaith century," and will the Texas Conference of Churches have played another major role?

Our gospel may be too small[1]

Tom Wilkens

The Text

Love never ends. But as for prophecies, they will come to an end; as for tongues, they will cease; as for knowledge, it will come to an end. For we know only in part, and we prophesy only in part; but when the complete comes, the partial will come to an end. When I was a child, I spoke like a child, I thought like a child, I reasoned like a child; when I become an adult, I put an end to childish ways. For now we see in a mirror, dimly, but then we will see face to face. Now I know only in part; then I will know fully, even as I have been fully known. And now faith, hope, and love abide, these three; and the greatest of these is love.

—1 Corinthians 13:8-13

Introduction

About a half-century ago, British biblical scholar and theologian J. B. Phillips wrote a book titled *Your God Is Too Small*. In his book, Phillips argued that many Christians in Europe and North America had very immature and underdeveloped understandings of God. They had a God who was comfortable and controllable, a God who confirmed their cultures, values, and lifestyles rather than confronting them. Phillips also complained that many Christians had a Jesus who was meek and mild: a pale Galilean in a world of much color and intensity. I think that Phillips' criticisms were on target.

For Christians today, however, the issue may be that our *gospel* is too small. Jesus is Lord, we confess, but perhaps not the Lord of all: of every sector of our lives, every relationship, every nook and cranny and moment. Jesus is the Savior, we confess, but perhaps not the Savior of the whole creation: of every star and speck of sand, of every species and not just our own. Surely Jesus is the Savior of people, we think, not of the planet or solar system or universe.

If we think this way, then our gospel may be too small. One way of looking at the theological education that you will receive at this place is to see it as an opportunity to broaden your grasp and expand your understanding of the gospel: the good news of Jesus the Christ, the Lord, the Savior.

How can the canvas on which you paint the gospel with your life and witness grow? Let me suggest that Saint Paul might be able to help you — and me — in this matter through his observation in the text from 1 Corinthians that I just read a few moments ago:

> And now faith, hope, and love abide, these three; and the greatest of these is love.

Context

In 1 Corinthians, chapters 12 and 13, Saint Paul identifies a number of the gifts of the Spirit, ranging from gifts of healing and teaching to gifts of faith and love. It looks as though the three gifts mentioned in chapter 13 — namely faith, hope, and love — represent his short list of the most important spiritual gifts. And clearly for St. Paul, the greatest gift of the Spirit is love.

Interpretation

Martin Luther had a lot of difficulty with this verse. Brother Martin simply could not accept that Paul had placed love above faith in the ranking of spiritual gifts.[2] We all know about Luther's strong emphasis on faith. It was a good emphasis and needed at the time, in the sixteenth century. And we still benefit in the twenty-first century from Luther's insights into the nature and role of faith in the Christian life. For instance, just yesterday I heard a marvelous, thoroughly Lutheran presentation

195

by the Rector, the Reverend Dr. Biyela, on the central place of faith in doing theology that will strengthen the church and benefit the world. Our Christian faith is rooted in God active over the millennia in the lives and history of God's people and in God available to us today through Word and sacrament. This faith steadies us on a sometimes-stormy course of life. Such is the greatness of faith.

But Saint Paul wrote that love is even greater: love that embodies selfless giving, love that embraces the unlovely, love that sacrifices without keeping accounts. I witnessed a marvelous act of such love three days ago.

The Reverend Abrahamse came to the afternoon orientation session fully intending and fully prepared to make a valuable presentation, a presentation that would make connections between the life of faith and the world of AIDS. But then a call came from the hospital: a woman was dying. Would Reverend Abrahamse come and minister to her? His reply was immediate; his priority was clear. He felt compelled — not just by the external phone call, but by an internal habit of the heart — to respond in love to this most profound human moment and need.

Between these two heavyweights of faith and of love, hope sometimes gets overshadowed. It shouldn't. Faith often looks back — for strength, courage, and reassurance. Love usually looks around — for opportunities to serve those who hurt, to encourage those who stumble, and gently to admonish those who fall. Hope typically looks forward — for visions of peace to pursue and ideals of justice to realize. Hope is the persistent "yes" in the face of the mantra of despair: no, no, no. No, you cannot make a difference. No, peace and justice cannot be realized. No, devastating powers such as poverty and deadly plagues such as AIDS will not yield to any human effort. Such is despair. Such, thought the medieval church at any rate, is sin.

But some have refused to pray the mantra of despair. Some have kept hope in the face of all odds. Some of those hopeful ones we know: Martin Luther King Jr. — hopeful in the face of racism's distortion of America. Nelson Mandela — hopeful in the face of apartheid's violence in South Africa. Mother Teresa — hopeful in the face of disease and indifference in India. But for every King, Mandella, and Mother Teresa there are a thousand others whose hope may have flicked but never died, who dared to pursue impossible dreams of justice and peace and wholeness.

Our gospel is too small if it does not embody all of the gifts that the Spirit of Christ bestows — especially the gifts of faith, love, and hope. Our gospel is too small if it seems remote from any corner of our lives or any corner of the universe. Let me illustrate. The prologue to the Gospel called John holds that the Word made flesh, Jesus the Christ, was a full participant in the creation of the whole universe. And certain epistles, such as Philippians and Colossians, affirm that Jesus the Christ saves not just people but the whole creation. How arrogant we sometimes are to think that God cares only for our species.

How will you portray and proclaim the good news, the gospel, to Mother Earth? Will you simply repeat, with pious regularity, the first article of the Apostles' Creed: I believe in God, the Father Almighty, creator of heaven and earth? Do you think that Mother Earth hears? Will you simply feel a twinge of pain, and think it is a love pang, as you watch the natural beauties of South Africa sink underneath layers of trash and waves of stench? Can Mother Earth here at Umphumulo see a community that cares *about* her enough to care *for* her? Will you — will we — simply feel powerless, not able to dare to hope that you — that we — could make a difference with respect to Mother Earth's crisis? Mother Earth must be anxious. If I were Mother Earth, I think that I'd have a panic attack about now.

Conclusion

If all this sounds even close to being the case, then I suggest that our gospel is too small. And I have bad news: we can do nothing to enlarge it. But I also have good news: faith, love, and hope are gifts and not achievements. They are God's good works, not ours. God is faithful, loving, and hopeful.

So ask the ever faithful, boundlessly loving, and perpetually hopeful God for increased measures of those gifts: faith, love, and hope. If the testimonies of scripture and the church are to be believed, God enjoys saying "yes" to our requests. And then watch and wait and work as God's gracious gifts begin to transform our small gospels into the sweeping gospel that God would delight to have portrayed and proclaimed throughout the whole universe.

Response:
Doubting faith

Kim Wilkens

And now faith, hope, and love abide, these three; and the greatest of
these is love.   — 1 Corinthians 13:13

I am so relieved that Paul identifies love as greater than faith and
hope. I may not be an optimist, but I don't often wake up dreading the
new day, so I think I do have hope. I may not always give it well or receive
it thankfully, but I think I recognize and value love. The least of these for
me is faith. Where it seems there should be faith, doubts plague my life.
Are we raising our child right? Am I making the right career choices?
Should I go to that party? Doubts leave me feeling confused, empty, anxious and alienated. I sometimes wonder if I'm the only one who feels this
way. I would really like some measure of predictability, some sign that
I'm on the right path and making the right choices.

I often wonder what Jesus was thinking when he implied that faith,
not proof, would be the basis of belief in God. Why not prove it once and
for all and be done with it? I've come to the conclusion that it's because
God wants us to make choices in our lives so that in the choosing we are
transformed. In this way, doubt can be a key ingredient in our faith-based
beliefs.

In a worship series recently, we explored some of the tension between
doubt and faith and how they interact each other. We studied lives affected
by different kinds of doubting faith. It turns out I am not alone. There are
other, far more famous doubters than me.

Doubting Thomas: The Skeptic
Doubting Thomas was having a crisis of faith after Jesus' crucifixion. Even after being with Jesus while he was alive and hearing firsthand
accounts of the resurrection, he still desired his own hands-on experience.

Modern society has put a premium on knowledge gained through scientific method (observable, empirical and measurable evidence). Clearly
faith is a leap in this environment. The skeptic is a logical person who
wants answers to questions. They want proof and they want it from the

source, not some substitute. The skeptic needs to be surrounded by love and patience and be given opportunities for firsthand experience with God.

Doubting Judas: The Suspicious

Doubting Judas was on board with his walk of faith with Jesus and thought he knew where it was headed. But things didn't seem to be going according to plan and he became disillusioned. He thought he could help get things back on the right track, but acting on his doubts had repercussions that he didn't anticipate.

We're in the midst of a cultural shift from modern to postmodern society. It is causing levels of change in society that make some uncomfortable and others impatient. Swirling around these changes are suspicion, disillusionment and injury. Dealing with doubt in this environment can be dangerous — open, authentic, transparent communication is key.

Doubting Peter: The Confused

Doubting Peter always seemed to be just one step behind. He really wanted to show his love by stepping out in faith, but sometimes he found himself in over his head. Often we feel like we're just a step behind others in our faith journey. We're afraid that we might be missing something, that we're just not quite getting it. We want to step out of the boat, but then find ourselves sinking. Community is the key here and not being afraid to make mistakes. This is how we gain experience and shape our faith.

Doubting Teresa: The dark night of the soul

Doubting Teresa showed great faithfulness in following a call to Calcutta and starting a ministry based on selfless giving. It may be that with great faith comes great doubt. Doubt challenges us to take our faith to the next level, but the trip is rocky. It may be helpful to understand that there are stages of doubt.[3]

- exile (stranger in a strange land)
- barely hanging on (why am I doing this?)
- feeling stranded (all alone)
- feeling helpless (letting go of ego)
- feeling at peace (transformed)

Once I had a better understanding of how doubt can play an important role in faith, I learned through reading Marcus Borg's *Heart of Christianity* that I had also been thinking about faith far too literally. Faith it turns out has four meanings.[4]

- Faith as *assensus* or faith as belief
- Faith as *fiducia* or faith as trust
- Faith as *fidelitas* or faith as faithfulness
- Faith as *visio* or faith as a way of seeing the whole

He summarizes faith this way, "The Christian life is about beloving God and all that God beloves. Faith is our love for God. Faith is the way of the heart."[5] With God, it seems everything always comes back to love.

Chapter Endnotes

1. The opening homily for a new academic year, presented in the chapel at Umphumulo Lutheran Theological Seminary located in KwaZulu-Natal Province, South Africa, on Friday, January 28, 2000.
2. See an earlier discussion of this matter in the background essay in ch. 8.
3. Dark Night of the Soul. *The Mystic.org*. Mystic World Fellowship. www.themystic. org/dark-night/.
4. Marcus Borg, *op. cit.*, 28-34.
5. *Ibid*, 41.

CHAPTER 20

THE CONFRONTING, COMFORTING JESUS

Background essay
Tom Wilkens

I was three years old; my brother, Jim, would have been nine. We had gone to Sunday school at our Baptist church home, as we did virtually every week. When the family gathered after the classes to go to the worship gathering, I noticed something rather strange: Jim was now wearing white pajamas. And when we went into the sanctuary, something else unusual happened: we walked directly to the front pew. I was very happy to be seated where I could see all the action up close.

At one point during the service the pastor, who I thought was my friend, disappeared for a few moments and his assistant temporarily took over leadership of worship. But then the pastor reappeared and to my great surprise he, too, was wearing white pajamas. He drew back some drapes in the front of the worship space and there, again to my utter amazement, was a huge bathtub filled with water. The pastor motioned to Jim to join him and they both got into the tub. By this time I was extremely excited. However, my parents, who were focused on Jim and the pastor, did not notice. That was a big mistake. The pastor then placed his hand over Jim's face and dunked him under the water. I could stand it no longer. I quickly slid from the pew and ran to the front, screaming "he's drowning my brother, he's drowning my brother!" Of course, by the time I got to the tub, also known as the baptistery, Jim was safely standing upright in the water again.

You will find frequent references to baptism in my writing, including the homily in this chapter. I find it somewhat ironic that my present denomination, which places so much emphasis on baptism and its renewing and healing efficacy, uses a procedure for baptism — sprinkling — that communicates so little. Even as a three-year-old child I got the message from the method used by the Baptists: baptism is a drowning and resuscitation, a dying and rising with Christ. I do not think that a three-year-old or even a thirty-year-old could get this message from ritual sprinkling. I often told my students that I was on a personal crusade to get the Lutherans to go back to the New Testament practice of baptism by immersion, though I knew it was a lost cause. The Baptists and related denominational groups have another thing right: in New Testament times baptism was for adults, not children. The Baptists do permit the innovation called the "age of accountability." My brother, Jim, could be baptized because he was deemed sufficiently mature to make his own decision about it. Lutherans, and before them the Roman Catholic and Eastern Orthodox bodies, had taken innovation a step further to allow and encourage infant baptism. The Eastern Orthodox still do it "right." They dunk the little ones.

Like Jesus himself, baptism comforts: it is a means of undeserved, God-initiated grace. It is there in our lives, if we trouble to recall, as a daily reminder of our dying to sin and rising to life in Christ. And it is more than a reminder: it is a reality and resource for gracious living. Luther called baptism our ordination into the common Christian vocation of love. Yet it is precisely because of this calling to love that baptism, like Jesus, also confronts: it jogs our memories about our failures to love, to serve, to pursue peace with justice. The confronting, comforting Jesus comes to us — among the many ways he can come — through our confronting, comforting baptisms.

One of my mother's favorite Bible verses, which she often quoted when she was around me as I was growing up, was Romans 12:3. Actually, she normally used just a portion of the verse and she paraphrased it so that it would not appear to be a frontal attack. "We should not think more highly of ourselves than we ought to think," she would say. That sentence sometimes seemed to come out of the blue, with little relation to the present immediate circumstances. In retrospect, I think that she understood me, my tendencies, and my needs with profound insight.

She knew that I was prone to think more highly of myself than I ought. She was offering me a gentle corrective, at times and in places when I might be more receptive than, for example, in the midst of a "melt down" or some other ego-tripping episode.

I do not remember whether she used this or other verses with my siblings. However, I do know that this thought, etched permanently in my memory, has served me well. Ego strength seems to be a nearly universal problem and, if the psychologists are correct, lack of such strength and a poor self-image are very widespread. These are not my issues. My issues have been the kind of pride that the ancient and medieval church identified as one of the seven deadly sins. I have needed to be alerted to this sort of unwarranted, ego-inflating, relation-destroying pride far more often than I would like to admit. And as the homily that follows makes clear, it remains a concern for me even now as I negotiate the slippery slope called aging. I suspect that I am not alone. *Simul iustus et peccator*: at once justified and sinner. I need the confrontation of law. I need the comfort of gospel. I need the whole word and the holistic sacraments.

The confronting, comforting Jesus[1]

Tom Wilkens

The text

Now some of the people of Jerusalem were saying, "Is not this the man whom they are trying to kill? And here he is, speaking openly, but they say nothing to him! Can it be that the authorities really know that this is the Messiah? Yet we know where this man is from; but when the Messiah comes, no one will know where he is from." Then Jesus cried out as he was teaching in the temple, "You know me, and you know where I am from. I have not come on my own. But the one who sent me is true, and you do not know him. I know him, because I am from him, and he sent me." Then they tried to arrest him, but no one laid hands on him, because his hour had not yet come. Yet many in the crowd believed in him and were saying, "When the Messiah comes, will he do more signs than this man has done?"   — John 7:25-31

Introduction

I have two problems this morning. I'm going to share both of them with you because I think that you will have similar problems when you are ministers of the gospel in the parishes of southern Africa.

My first problem is with the Bible reading, sometimes called a pericope. Pericopes are Bible passages assigned for reading during public worship on Sundays, for special festivals, and at other times in the church year. These lessons are designed to give the congregation a broad sampling of biblical literature over the course of the church year. It is a good idea, if they are well designed and if the texts are well chosen. A committee often does the selection and sometimes committees make strange decisions, such as leaving off integral verses at the beginning or at the end.[2] The text just read by my wife had an extra verse added to it, at my suggestion. You may need to make some decisions like that when you serve as worship leaders.

My second problem is that the lesson comes from the Gospel called John, these days sometimes called the Gospel of the Johannine community. I'm not a big fan of this Gospel. It seems to me that, upon a careful reading, the Johannine community that produced this Gospel was somewhat arrogant. They held their own understanding of Jesus as the Christ in high regard, but the understandings of Jesus in other Christian communities were apparently held in some contempt. That sounds harsh; it may be too harsh. And I certainly am in a minority. Most Christians, including Martin Luther, have loved and even favored this Gospel.

So what am I to do? What are you to do when the text or texts assigned for the day do not appeal to you as the basis for your sermon? I am tempted to run to the Gospel called Luke, which happens to be my favorite. But I should not and I will not. That is one of the advantages of having pericopes or assigned texts. They prevent the preacher from speaking only on her or his favorite texts or themes.

Exegesis

So let us briefly examine the text and its context. Our text is part of an extended story about Jesus in Jerusalem during a weeklong celebration called the Feast of Tabernacles. It was an autumn festival that focused on giving thanks for the harvest abundance. Each day of the Feast two very important events took place in the temple. First, water was poured over the altar of burnt offering — water, which had long been a symbol of cleansing and life in the Israelite community; water, which was to become such a central image in the Johannine community. Second, at the end of each day lamps were lit in the Women's Court of the Temple, producing so much light that it was said that all of Jerusalem was illuminated. Light also became a dominant image or motif in the fourth gospel.

Our particular text, only a small segment of the overall story, has Jesus causing a crisis for those around him — forcing them to question their own judgments, their traditions, and their leaders. Jesus, it turns out, could speak sharply and rebuke harshly. He evoked strong reactions, sometimes positive but often negative.

Hermeneutics

What does all of this have to do with me, the preacher of the day? And what does it have to do with you, the preachers of tomorrow? We all must, I think, proclaim Jesus both as a comfort and as a challenge. Jesus is the Living Water, offering cool comfort to road-weary pilgrims on their earthly way, offering a warm bath called baptism to those soiled by sin, offering a gentle rain to awaken the fertile potential of our parched lives. And Jesus is the Light from God, illuminating the world so that we stumble less and proceed further on an earth meant for light and not for darkness.

Jesus is a comfort for the afflicted. But in our text especially, Jesus is also an affliction for the comfortable. He was a challenge to one of the Messianic traditions, a tradition that held that Messiah would come unexpectedly and from an unknown place. The crowd knew, or thought they knew, where this Nazarene was from. They did not.

Jesus continues to challenge. He not only threatens religious self-confidence; he continues to function as a countercultural challenge. Jesus was a countercultural threat to apartheid. But don't relax just yet in post-apartheid South Africa. What aspects of your culture does Jesus challenge right now? What aspects of mine? What aspects of our global culture?

Conclusion

As proud as they may have been, the Johannine community nevertheless portrayed and proclaimed a Jesus who confronted and confused the proud and comforted the lowly. As proud as we may be of our Lutheran heritage and theology, we must nonetheless proclaim a Jesus who confronts the proud — sometimes even ourselves — and comforts the poor.

Anything less would be something less than the gospel: the good news of Jesus the Living Water and the Light from God, yet also a troubling, challenging, sometimes disorienting presence in our lives and in the world.

Even a troubling Jesus turns out, in the final analysis, to be good news. Part of the good news for me, a veteran of a lifelong battle with pride and arrogance, is that Jesus is not silent. Jesus does not walk away. He does me the saving favor of confronting me, thereby awakening in me an awareness of my need for his saving favor of comfort and acceptance. He then throws light on a world I now see needs serving. And he gives me an inexhaustible resource, the waters of baptism and through those waters the gift of himself, to sustain that service, irrigate it, and make it fruitful. But no credit to me. None to you. *Soli Deo gloria.* To God alone the glory for the rare gift of God's Son, the confronting and comforting Jesus.

Response:
A lesson in pride

Kim Wilkens

"At 11 a.m. on Tuesday, a prominent politician spoke to Americans about race as though they were adults."[3]
— Jon Stewart

I was a huge fan of C.S. Lewis' fiction before reading any of his Christian books. When I started exploring Christianity again, one of the first books that someone recommended was *Mere Christianity*. Now I must admit that there are a few sexist ideas in the book, but amazingly enough I was able to let that slide past (I mean, he was of a different age) and found the book really helpful. In fact, it led me to read more of C.S. Lewis as well as other Christian authors.

As I was thinking how to respond to this chapter about the confronting, comforting Jesus, the first idea that jumped out was dealing with pride. I remembered that C.S. Lewis called pride the greatest sin, so I went back and read that chapter to pull out some of his key ideas. I've tried to relate those ideas to a recent confrontation with my own pride.

Pride leads to every other vice: it is the complete anti-God state of mind.[4]

Is it any coincidence that in a week peppered with race relations rhetoric, the boy comes home from school singing the chorus to "Weird Al" Yankovic's "I'm White and Nerdy"[5]? Well he is and I am, heck our whole family's white and nerdy. What's wrong with that? On the surface, nothing, but if I let the label limit me and get me stuck then I think the possibility of problems are endless. So this week as I've viewed Barack Obama's former pastor Jeremiah Wright's most controversial comments on <u>YouTube</u> I haven't felt offended, I've felt convicted. As I listen to his detractors I wonder where they get off being so arrogant and self-righteous. Don't they see the mess we're in in America, the racial divide, the economic divide? Can't they understand the hurt and frustration?

There is no fault which makes a man more unpopular, and no fault which we are more unconscious of in ourselves. And the more we have it ourselves, the more we dislike it in others.[6]

Obama responded to the media hype with a speech titled, "A More Perfect Union." As I listened to it, I felt my support for him solidify. I also proudly claim the labels of liberal, anti-racist, and activist, but I'm finding there's a problem with those labels as well. Here's the crux of it: if I am so liberal and anti-racist and feel strongly about pursuing social justice, how come I can only count on one hand my peer to peer interaction with non-white people in any given week? I heard Robert Jensen, author of *The Heart of Whiteness: Confronting Race, Racism and White Privilege*, talking about race on NPR and something he said really struck me.

We are the most affluent country in the history of the world, we're the most powerful country in the history of the world, if we wanted to erase racialized gaps in wealth and well-being that exist, we could do it, but we simply choose not to. I think it's fair to call the United States a white supremacist society.[7]

Did he just say I'm part of the problem? Did part of my cultural upbringing contain subliminal racism training? What choices have I made and continue to make that shore up white supremacy instead of bridging the racial gap? Like Weird Al's parody, am I desperate for meaningful interaction with non-whites, but fail because I'm surrounded by my white stuff? What racial stereotypes am I still buying into? How are my ignorance, my self-righteousness, my pride continuing to oppress the very people I claim to support?

> The real test of being in the presence of God is that you either forget about yourself altogether or see yourself as a small, dirty object.[8]

You know, I really like being right and I hate admitting I'm wrong. I still feel that the sentiments of racial oppression expressed by Jeremiah Wright are right and that the desire expressed by Barack Obama to form a more perfect union is right. Does it matter if I'm right, if I'm part of the problem?

I'm white and nerdy and part of the problem; Lord, help me be part of the solution.

Chapter Endnotes

1. A homily for Morning Suffrages, presented at Umphumulo Lutheran Theological Seminary, KwaZulu-Natal Province, South Africa, on March 17, 2000.
2. For another example of this, see the homily in ch. 3, "The case of the missing punch line."
3. The Daily Show, *Barack's Wright Response*, March 18, 2008, www.thedailyshow.com; John Stewart.
4. C.S. Lewis, *Mere Christianity* (MacMillan, 1950), 121.
5. "Weird Al" Yankovic, White & Nerdy: *Straight Outta Lynwood* (Volcano, 2006).
6. *Ibid.*, 121.
7. Robert Jensen, "How Do Americans Talk About Race?" *Talk of the Nation*, March 20, 2008, www.npr.org/templates/story/story.php?storyID=88679503.
8. C.S. Lewis, *op. cit.*, 125.

Chapter 21

A Palm Sunday Homily Not Preached

Background essay

Tom Wilkens

I should have seen it coming. It happened shortly before the Easter break at Umphumulo Lutheran Theological Seminary. Almost since the beginning of the term in late January, student leaders had been asking for a face-to-face session with the whole faculty in order to air some of their concerns and grievances. The faculty adamantly, and I use the term advisedly, refused each request. Finally, the situation worsened precipitously. The students threatened a boycott of classes. The Rector told them that this was unacceptable and, if they persisted, he would shut down the Seminary. They persisted and he, in consultation with the Synod Bishop, closed the Seminary and sent the students home.

My first reaction was disbelief. How had this situation deteriorated so far and so fast? My second reaction was guilt: should I have acted? Could I have brokered a more helpful and healthful resolution to this conflict? I had determined in advance not to interject my views on internal matters such as this. I was, after all, in what was for me a new culture. I thought I would not be able to understand such situations sufficiently to make a positive difference. In fact, through ignorance and insensitivity I could easily make things worse rather than better. And yet it seemed so simple from my perspective: a short meeting might have resolved the matter before it got out of hand. The faculty did not need to take the students' request as a frontal assault on faculty authority.

Now some nine years later, I think it is just as well that I did not try to intervene. I may have been able to prevent this particular set of outcomes, but likely not. There was a long history being played out and there were social dynamics going on that would require much more understanding and expertise than I had.

Some very sad and negative consequences flowed from this drama. When the students were permitted to return shortly after Easter, it was on a provisional basis. Each of them had to go through a faculty examination process before they would be permanently reinstated. The half dozen or so student leaders who had organized the protest were apparently not sufficiently repentant. They failed the assessment and were denied reinstatement. They were sent home again, with no clear appeal procedure available to them. Thus the Lutheran churches in southern Africa had lost a part of their most promising leadership and positive future.

So what about the homily not preached? The Rector had earlier asked me to be the speaker of the day for the Palm Sunday service, complete with palm fronds and a community processional, to be held in the Seminary chapel. I had prepared the homily in what for me was the usual full manuscript rendering. But when Palm Sunday arrived there was no community left on campus: no audience to hear the proclamation and no participants to share the Eucharist. Not only had the students gone; so had most of the faculty. When I got back to the US, I transcribed this undelivered homily onto my computer and saved it on the hard disk. There it has been, in digital format, until we reviewed it for possible inclusion in this book. You, of course, must be the final judge as to whether or not it should ever have seen the light of day in print.

It becomes quite clear in the homily that I am not a big fan of Palm Sunday observances. There is typically, it seems to me at any rate, too much emphasis on the festive dimension of the day and not enough attention paid to the suffering to which it led. I favor a current trend in this matter initiated by our Roman Catholic sisters and brothers. Since the 1950s they have referred to the late Lenten segment of the church calendar as Passiontide and, since the 1970s, to the Sunday before Easter as Passion Sunday. I note with real satisfaction that the Sunday is now called Passion Sunday and only subtitled Palm Sunday in the new ELCA hymnal, *Evangelical Lutheran Worship*. The palms of Palm Sunday signaled a false start to what the week that followed actually brought: the passion of the Lord — anguish, betrayal, pain, and death.

214

A Palm Sunday homily not preached[1]

Tom Wilkens

The text

The next day the great crowd that had come to the festival heard that Jesus was coming to Jerusalem. So they took branches of palm trees and went out to meet him, shouting, "Hosanna! Blessed is the one who comes in the name of the Lord — the king of Israel!" Jesus found a young donkey and sat on it; as it is written: "Do not be afraid, daughter of Zion. Look, your king is coming, sitting on a donkey's colt!"

His disciples did not understand these things at first; but when Jesus was glorified, then they remembered that these things had been written of him and had been done to him. So the crowd that had been with him when he called Lazarus out of the tomb and raised him from the dead continued to testify. It was also because they heard that he had performed this sign that the crowd went to meet him. The Pharisees then said to one another, "You see, you can do nothing. Look, the world has gone after him!" — John 12:12-19

Exegesis and hermeneutics

Palm Sunday has rarely excited but often troubled me. When I was a child my family were members of congregations that did not follow the church calendar, although they did keep major holy days such as Christmas and Easter. Palm Sunday was observed but rarely prepared for: it seemed always to come as a surprise. I would find myself participating in a procession, carrying a palm frond into the sanctuary. After the procession I would learn, generally from the sermon, that I had played the part of a member of a crowd that deserved harsh criticism — criticism for not really understanding who Jesus was or what he was up to; criticism for being fickle and for turning against Jesus later on in the week. It bothered me.

Thereafter, in college, seminary, university and beyond, I was introduced to troubling discrepancies between John's account of Jesus' entry into Jerusalem and the accounts of Mark, Matthew, and Luke: little things like Jesus choosing his own riding animal in John but the disciples securing the animal for Jesus in the synoptic stories. And there were bigger things, such as differing perspectives, interpretations, and assessments of the event: from Mark's muted description to John's more elaborate portrayal.

What am I — what are we — to make of it today, the first Palm Sunday of the new millennium, the first Palm Sunday in Umphumulo for many of us? We have just reenacted a portion of Jesus' seemingly triumphal entry into Jerusalem. That day the Messiah came riding on an ass, a symbol of peace, and not on a horse, a symbol of military might. The Messiah came as a rising star, fresh from the stunning and miraculous resurrection of Lazarus, whose fans would reject him within the week. The Messiah came as a deeply longed-for and highly praised liberator, whose joyous procession led to a shameful crucifixion within five days.

I suspect that Palm Sunday is a trap: not just for Jesus two millennia ago, who finally would yield to the plotting of powerful enemies; and not just for the crowd two millennia ago, excited by the prospect of liberation from sickness, death, and oppression but unable to stay the course with a Messiah more like Gandhi than a general. Palm Sunday is also a trap for us today. We are tempted to think in terms of victory, of parades, of pageantry and celebration. But it is much too early. We must first recall the tragedy: the tragedy of sleepy disciples, of betrayal, of public humiliation, of personal pain, of death.

Palm Sunday, whatever it might mean for us and for the church, is not — I think — intended as a model or paradigm of church life and Christian discipleship. Palm Sunday, disconnected from the passion of Jesus, leads to what Martin Luther called a theology of glory or what some contemporary theologians call triumphalism. Palm Sunday is deceptive. It did not prefigure Jesus' future nor does it prefigure our own. Our theology, rooted in Luther's clear-eyed reading of the word of God, is a theology of the cross. It leads to life that is not surprised by suffering. It leads rather to life that is surprised by joy in the midst of suffering.

Palm Sunday, alone, has no sorrow. Palm Sunday, by itself and unattached to the rest of the Gospel narrative, is misleading. Palm Sunday is an event based on much misunderstanding and misinterpretation. Even Jesus' closest disciples did not comprehend the event at the time. As the Gospel lesson says in chapter 12, verse 16: "His disciples did not understand these things at first; but when Jesus was glorified, then they remembered that these things had been written of him and had been done to him."

There is a popular rock opera, composed in the 1970s, that depicts the disciples of Jesus as bumbling men who didn't have much of a clue as to what was going on. The rock opera is called "Jesus Christ, Superstar."[2] One of the best songs, as far as I'm concerned, is titled "What's the buzz? Tell me what's a-happening?" — sung by the inner circle of disciples. What's the buzz? Tell me what's a-happening? Not even Jesus' most intimate friends could figure out what was happening until after his arrest, trial, crucifixion, and resurrection. It is always — even today — difficult to figure Jesus out. Not only were the first disciples pretty well clueless about Jesus until the story had played itself out much further. It has always been a struggle for the church to get it right, for disciples of every generation to get beyond Palm Sunday.

So why observe it? Why mark Palm Sunday with such emphasis in the church year? I suggest to you that we ought to do it as a reminder of how often we get it wrong. Palm Sunday is an object lesson in what happens when the crown is thought to come before the cross or, even worse, without the cross. It is a reminder that being close to Jesus in space and time may have been no advantage at all. It is an encouragement to those of us who experience few triumphs in life that many — if not most — triumphs turn out not to be genuine at the end of the day. The comfort of the Lord comes not at points of shared victory but shared defeat.

God's surprising plot twist seems not to make sense. It turns our values and our expectations upside down. That seems to be God's way. Palm Sunday is not a triumph, at least not an enduring triumph. Palm Sunday is the calm before the storm, the eye of the hurricane before the winds deal their destruction and death.

The real triumph will be commemorated next Sunday, on Easter. It will not have the majesty or scope of Palm Sunday. The cast of thousands will be gone. It will be a story involving a few grieving women and some men still not over their confusion. Palm Sunday is a media event, a footnote to history raised to dizzying heights. Easter is the point of the story, the beginning of Jesus' rise to the right hand of the Father.

Yet this Jesus remains with us today, the Word incarnated in communities of love that share scarce resources; in baptism, which allows us to participate in Jesus' dying and rising; in the Eucharist, which provides relief from pain and guilt and rejection; and in the proclaimed and written word, which helps us to get past the distractions and see into the heart of God.

Palm Sunday is another one of God's surprises, but only for those who see it from the perspective of Easter through the lens of Good Friday. From another point of view, Palm Sunday is exactly what we want and expect: victory unmarked by defeat, joy unmarked by sorrow, liberation unmarked by struggle. But seen through Good Friday and Easter, Palm Sunday stands as a helpful warning against leaping to conclusions, against the dangers of not penetrating beneath surface appearances, against the false value of prizes won without sacrifice. The lessons of Jesus' life are not always easily understood and not always easily accepted once we grasp them. Even the lesson of his entry into Jerusalem may not be immediately evident or embraced.

But it is a lesson worth learning, worth incorporating into our lives. Beware of popular acclaim: it may be coming from a fickle and uninformed public. Be on the alert with respect to honors or titles that cost those who grant them very little: they are worth just that — very little. Think twice before joining the mindless crowd: you may get carried away even after you have come to your senses.

The church, too, can get caught up in the Palm Sunday syndrome. It can order its worship life along lines of pomp and ceremony rather than poverty of spirit and compassion. It can be motivated by self-serving ends, as no doubt many people were in the original Palm Sunday procession.

Yet Jesus rarely criticized the crowds of ordinary people. He knew first-hand about the lives of quiet desperation that most people endured in his day. But he did hold to close account those who should have known better: people with wealth or power or education. That means Jesus holds every adult in this assembly accountable. We are educated in the things of God. The very name of this institution says it: theological. We have no excuse for being easily misled or confused about God's story. Our grasp of Palm Sunday should be sure, our gaze upon it short. It is a strange preliminary to the main event: the death and resurrection of our Lord. Don't dwell too long on this day, Palm Sunday. Begin as soon as possible the journey through Good Friday to Easter.

Response:
Unpredictable

Kim Wilkens

I'm not sure how to communicate the *angst* of being a postmodern daughter of God to you. If you grew up in the modern culture, hearing about postmodernism may sound to you like it did to pastor and author, Bobby Brewer — "the most ridiculous and ludicrous worldview I had ever encountered. However, I quickly learned that postmodernism is a reaction to the most profound spiritual and philosophical crisis of our time."[3] Maybe you grew up like me with some church background, but then had a long period of being de-churched or more likely you are among the completely un-churched crowd. You may not see how church or Christianity could be relevant to your life.

Mike Breen, another author and pastor, used an earthquake analogy to describe the level of change we are experiencing in this postmodern era at a church conference I attended in 2006. The subject of the conference was postmodernism and I think some of the attendees got it, some didn't, and some just need help with translation.

Let me give this earthquake analogy a shot. Imagine that you have just survived a major earthquake. Everything around you has changed. The landscape is no longer recognizable. The landmarks you took for granted are gone. You are wandering around in shock. You happen to walk by a church. You see that there are people inside. The church building does not look stable. You go to warn the people that the earthquake has probably damaged the building and that they should get out. They don't seem to understand you. They urge you to come inside. "It's not safe," you say, "this building could collapse at any time." They just don't get it. They seem to be in denial that an earthquake even happened. You ask them if they know where you can find temporary shelter. All they can offer you is a map of the world as it was before the earthquake. You walk away bewildered.

That's me and my spiritual journey in a nutshell. I've been shaken up by the world's culture and its aftershocks like 9/11 and Katrina. I'm often bewildered by the response of the church to the changing landscape. I believe the emerging church movement is on the right path to address the fault lines that have developed between the world and Christianity.

You probably won't find a single, agreed-upon definition of the emerging church movement (which, if you find that frustrating, kind of puts you in the modern camp), but you will find common characteristics that are valued, such as authenticity, missional living, social action, conversational, narrative, relationship-building, indigenous, messy, open, and fluid. Instead of trying to define the movement, let me give you an example of a worship service I experienced at an emerging church in Minneapolis called Solomon's Porch.

Their current setting is an old church. They have taken out all the pews and altar and replaced them with sofas and comfy chairs, all oriented toward the center of the room. During the worship service I went to, I sang songs written and played by members, I participated in a small group discussion, I shared a communion meal with my neighbors, and I listened to a member share a story about her spiritual journey. Everything about the space and service is indigenous, created by the community for worshiping God. The setting is very relaxed and the combination of space and people encourage you to just hang out. Relationship building, creativity, participation, and authenticity are highly valued and encouraged.

From this experience I learned that worship should not be experienced as a spectator and that every church has its own unique combination of gifts. There is no formula for the perfect worship experience; instead a meaningful experience will come out of the community's involvement and their willingness to let the Holy Spirit work amongst them.

Did you catch that? There's the key to church health, a willingness to let the Holy Spirit work. To be open to the Holy Spirit is a life-long process with highs and lows, successes and failures. We expect that sometimes things will get messy and unpredictable. Kelly Fryer in her book, *Daring to be Church Again*, presents a formula:

People + Holy Spirit = A Recipe for Trouble[4]

In a workshop with Tony Jones, author of *Postmodern Youth Ministry* and member of Solomon's Porch, I learned why the modern church might have more issues with "trouble" than the emerging church. The culture that we are emerging from has been deeply influenced by foundationalism. This is the philosophy of Descartes — I think, therefore I am. As I understand it, this is a system of beliefs that relies on a foundation. For instance, fundamentalist Christians believe that the Bible is the inerrant word of God. Their belief system is based on this foundation. You will find a foundation in many forms of Christianity including liberal, universalist, liberation, and more.

The problem with having a foundation, is that when it comes under fire based on new knowledge or differing opinions or whatever, it often has to be to be propped up. When cracks develop in the foundation, the whole belief structure becomes unstable.

Tony feels that people actually know things in a web that encompasses experience, belief, and faith and it continues to grow throughout our lifetime. The picture he drew looked kind of like a neural network. So instead of thinking of our system of beliefs as based on a foundation, we really ought to think of our system of beliefs as an interconnected network that we build on over time based on our experiences, the knowledge we acquire and the faith we exercise. "We're all interpretive by nature — we can't know anything objectively."[5]

Do these ideas make you uncomfortable? Then you probably have a more modern view of the world. Do these ideas spark your imagination: then you probably have a more postmodern view of the world. I've been thinking a lot about who you are. Who would, could or even should read this book? Here are my hopes, if you decide to read it. If you are a thoroughly modern Christian, I hope that you will understand more about the struggles you are encountering with your modern view in our current postmodern culture. If you are a postmodern Christian, I hope that you will understand more about the struggles you are encountering with your postmodern view and the mostly modern ministry resources and church structures in existence today.

We're all survivors of this postmodern earthquake. I hope that between my dad and myself, we can offer some forms of translation and lines of communication between the two cultures, so that we can get on with the rescue work.

Chapter Endnotes

1. A homily prepared for delivery on Palm Sunday 2000 at Umphumulo Lutheran Theological Seminary, KwaZulu-Natal Province, South Africa.
2. Music by Andrew Lloyd Webber; lyrics by Tim Rice. First produced in 1971.
3. Dr. Robert Brewer, Postmodernism: *What You Should Know and Do About It* (iUniverse, 2002), xiii.
4. Kelly A. Fryer, *op. cit.*, 89.
5. Tony Jones, *Emerging Youth Ministry Workshop* (Minneapolis: Solomon's Porch, 2006).

CHAPTER 22

SOME REFLECTIONS ON SUFFERING FROM ONE WHO HASN'T

Background essay

Tom Wilkens

We recently had a next-door neighbor who contracted and died from Lou Gehrig's disease, the second such neighbor we have had in the past twenty years. What are the odds of that happening, since there are only 30,000 cases in the whole world? Yet this statistical oddity is not the point I want to make. The point is that many people suffer terribly, very often through no fault of their own. The further point for this essay and the next homily is that, by contrast, I have suffered so little

As noted in an earlier background essay, even our son Nick has suffered a great deal more than I have. He has had to deal with OCD, obsessive-compulsive disorder. In his childhood and youth it went undiagnosed because we did not recognize the symptoms. When as a young adult he received a professional evaluation, he was at first misdiagnosed. But later his condition was correctly assessed and since then he has received appropriate treatment. This long-standing personal ordeal has, in the surprising logic of life, made him much more effective at what he now does as a marriage and family therapist, working within the context of his vocation as a diaconal minister at a Christian counseling center. I marvel at his resilience, his sensitivity, and his insight. He has paid an enormous price in pain for his unique capacity to help and to heal.

So what is a person like me doing trying to preach and write about suffering? Or what credentials do I have for organizing, as I once did, a symposium on suffering?[1] Not many, it turns out. However, if I cannot somehow address the subject of suffering, a dark reality for so many people in the world, then I proclaim a gospel much too small and far too irrelevant. I must struggle to find a way. Those who suffer much will discern whether or not I succeed in this endeavor.

The poetic dialogues of the book of Job, not the prose sections, make perhaps the best case in the biblical literature for a postmodern perspective. Those dialogues portray a profound personal crisis, a crisis of suffering and faith. They called into question much of the widely held and deeply rooted conventional wisdom of ancient Israelite religion and culture. Today they continue to challenge a great deal of the conventional wisdom of modern religion and culture.

Postmodernism shares much of the spirit of Job's unconventional wisdom. It calls into question the presuppositions of connectedness and consistency in moral and rational life that undergird modernism. Postmodernism senses an inadequacy — in actuality, a crisis — in modernism's holistic pursuit and perception of truth, of meaning, and of reality. In fact, postmodernists deny the viability of such broadly conceived quests: we must, they say, have more modest intellectual goals. We need to prepare ourselves simply to cope with chaos, not overcome it or even fully understand it. Postmodernism in Christian thought challenges our traditional ways of thinking about God and acting as church.

Christian postmodernists have little patience for things — ideas, institutions, rituals, practices, and the like — that do not work. Workability or usefulness seems to be an exceedingly important notion to them. There is a significant historical precedent for this: pragmatism. American pragmatism, reaching well back into the nineteenth century, argued the case for workability or utility — not theories or principles — as the main criterion for determining verities and values. Yet John Dewey (1859-1952), perhaps the greatest of the pragmatists, recognized both the need for and the axiomatic — that is, unproved and unprovable — nature of a standard outside of the pragmatic scheme and method for deciding about truth and worth. Measure everything in terms of utility, as useful means or instruments to other ends, he held, except for one thing: people.

Surely Dewey was right to declare that people should never be used as means to other ends, that people have intrinsic value, that the measure of functionality is people — not the other way around. And just as surely this was for him the fundamental article of a faith, not an arguable or demonstrable truth. It is thus the case, it seems to me, that postmodernism, with its tendency toward pragmatism, has room for faith and potential as a standpoint from which to rearticulate Christian theology and reconstruct Christian practice. Most postmodernists would deny that as a desirable or even a possible project. But not all.

Christian postmodernism is, in my view, a contemporary analog to the centuries-old phenomenon of Christian humanism. I wish this less corrosive and more hopeful expression of postmodernism, Christian postmodernism, well. I think Christian postmodernists are making valuable, if sometimes unwanted or unacknowledged or underappreciated, contributions both to the Christian community and to the larger human community. I arrived too late for the voyage, but I track it with keen interest — especially through our daughter. Silently and within, I weep as I watch Kim sail on her journey, on her uncharted pilgrimage of life and faith. My tears are quiet tears of joy, not of fear or sadness.

Some reflections on suffering from one who hasn't[2]

Tom Wilkens

The text

> How then can I answer him,
>> choosing my words with him?
> Though I am innocent, I cannot answer him;
>> I must appeal for mercy to my accuser.
> If I summoned him and he answered me,
>> I do not believe that he would listen to my voice.
> For he crushes me with a tempest,
>> and multiplies my wounds without cause;
> He will not let me get my breath,
>> but fills me with bitterness.
> If it is a contest of strength, he is the strong one!
>> If it is a matter of justice, who can summon him?

Though I am innocent, my own mouth would condemn me;
    though I am blameless, he would prove me perverse.
I am blameless; I do not know myself;
    I loathe my life.
It is all one; therefore I say,
    he destroys both the blameless and the wicked.
When disaster brings sudden death,
    he mocks at the calamity of the innocent.
For he is not a mortal, as I am, that I might answer him;
    that we should come to trial together.
There is no umpire between us,
    who might lay his hand on us both.
If he would take his rod away from me,
    and not let dread of him terrify me,
then would I speak without fear of him,
    for I know I am not what I am thought to be.

                      — Job 9:14-23, 32-35

Exegesis and hermeneutics

Several years ago, Rabbi Harold Kushner published a book titled *When Bad Things Happen to Good People*.[3] It quickly became a best-seller. The book clearly struck a deep chord with millions of people who wondered why they or persons they loved were suffering. Of course, the classic tale of really bad things happening to a really good person is the tale of Job.

The book of Job is complex, challenging, and sometimes even contradictory. For example: on the one hand, the book has a story, told in prose, wherein Job is portrayed as a patiently suffering hero — commended by God at the beginning of the story and restored by God at the end. On the other hand, the book contains many dialogues, written in poetry, in which Job expresses his anger, his despair, and even his insolence before God.

On another level, the book of Job denies the ethics of conventional wisdom: ethics assuming that innocent and thereby good people will prosper, and that evil and thereby guilty people will suffer. Job rejects this easy logic. Job — a good person and as innocent as they come — Job suffers crushing losses of material possessions, of family members, and of personal health. It seems that every generation must deal with innocent suffering. The issue is stubbornly persistent.

The Job of the poetic dialogues turns out not to be like his popular image: he is not steady or patient at all in the midst of his suffering. He wavers between aggressive anger at his fate and abject acceptance of his lot in life. He rails against God and then he shudders at what he has done. Job is not a person who takes kindly to simplistic advice given by comfortable people who offer him no comfort at all. He does not take well to the easy confidence of those whose faith has never been tested or shaken. Job is an injured, trapped, desperate yet amazingly rational animal. Job suffers, but he will not suffer fools. And Job's three friends are surely that: pompous fools parading as pious sages; shallow people who don't recognize the profound mystery in all evil and suffering, much less comprehend it. They have answers; however, they don't even understand the question.

In our text, Job reacts to the second of his so-called friends — in truth, the second of his accusers — a fellow by the name of Bildad. Bildad refuses to take seriously the possibility that a truly innocent person might suffer. Bildad believes that Job's suffering must surely indicate Job's guilt and need of repentance. Job responds to Bildad's accusations with a torrent of words, challenging both the conventional image of God as one committed to order in the universe and also the conventional idea that human life takes place in a world of moral order. Job holds that God is a God of chaos: unpredictable; unmanageable; playing a cosmic game whose rules — if they exist — are not enforced by any referee. "There is no umpire between us," Job complains, "who might lay his hand on us both." To put it into our jargon, there is no grand jury before which God can be subpoenaed and no trial jury by which God can be held to account as we are. God is out of control, which is by definition the case if God's power is sovereign: there is no controlling it.

I recall some years ago on the campus of Texas Lutheran a Jewish rabbi explaining that he thought Christians behave as though God is fragile, as though God might break or break down if confronted with our anger, as though God can't stand criticism or sustain an argument. Jews, he said, are always arguing with God, always registering complaints, always finding something to contend. God, the rabbi declared, can take it. He referred to Job as an example of this. He could also have mentioned Jacob, who wrestled with God, or even Moses, who often disputed matters with God. God is not delicate and easily damaged. God is resilient, according to Jewish teaching and practice. God can take the best punch that we humans can throw.

227

Is there anything here for us today or for our lives tomorrow? Frankly, there is not much here for me. I have suffered so little in my life. I have so little to be angry with God about, so little to complain about. My idea of a major crisis is to do without electricity or running water or phone service for a few days in places such as South Africa or Guyana or Honduras. Of course, as a visitor I can escape at the end of a temporary stay and leave the inconveniences of unreliable infrastructure behind. I've done it often in the past twenty years. But the locals must remain to deal with poverty, disease, violence, corruption, and environmental degradation on scales that beggar the imagination.

And so the lesson in the book of Job for me does not come from Job himself. It comes from his friends: I must take care not to be as superficial, as self-righteous, as unsympathetic as they were; not to be as confident and unquestioning of my theology as they were of theirs. Perhaps there are others in this community in similar circumstances.

But I know that this is not the case for all of you. Many of you have suffered or are suffering deeply. You may be motivated to complain, to speak out against God, to shake an angry fist in the face of God. It's okay. God will not break, even if we do.

Most of you know people who have suffered even more intensely than you have. Do not be a Bildad, peddling cheap wisdom to people experiencing costly pain. Let them rage. Permit them to cry. Allow them to despair. Provide for them a ministry of silent presence, not a ministry of glib proverbs or pious platitudes or even Bible verses quoted as magical prescriptions for what ails them. Provide quiet sympathy and empathy, not a loud defense of God. God needs no defense, least of all from you or me. Rather represent to them a God who will not retreat in the face of the protests of distraught sufferers, but will stay with them to whatever end they come.

Some time ago I saw a portion of a press conference given by British Prime Minister Tony Blair. Blair was reacting to the protests of British farmers and truckers about the shortage and high price of gasoline. The farmers and truckers were hurting. Yet in the face of their angry actions and shrill calls for relief, Prime Minister Blair defiantly stated that British public policy is never set in response to protest: it is set only in the context of relatively composed parliamentary debate. What Blair rejected God apparently accepts: protest as a mechanism for catching God's attention, for affecting God's behavior, for altering God's direction.[4] God seems to prefer the noisy clatter of marketplaces and motorways to the comparative calm of Whitehall or the White House. How odd of God.

Conclusion

The book of Job is a reminder to all of us that God fits into none of our categories, none of our ideas of what God should be like. Yet in the end, God turns out to exceed our wishes and expectations. In the end, God embraces and loves and, on one side of the grave or the other, restores us. The other side — the Easter side — of Jesus' grave is where the chaos of our world recedes a bit and the mystery of God unfolds a bit in some astonishing new ways. The suffering, crucified, and risen Christ is the clearest expression we have — the clearest expression we're going to get, if our tradition is to be believed — of the mind and the heart of God. It is enough.

The book of Job contains God's word about innocent suffering and the utter despair it can bring. But it is not God's last word. God's last word about undeserved suffering is the Word incarnate, Jesus the Christ. Take care, however: this gospel Word does not invalidate the disturbing, disorienting message of Job. The good news of Jesus offers the light of hope. And yet for many it is a distant light at the end of a long maze of pain intensified by the perplexity of unanswered questions. Jesus is less the answer to suffering than the question of suffering fully framed. It is enough.

Response:
Reflections on suffering from a hypochondriac

Kim Wilkens

Therefore do not worry about tomorrow, for tomorrow will worry about itself. Each day has enough trouble of its own.   — Matthew 6:34

I guess you could say I'm a recovering hypochondriac. I can't actually remember the last time my self-diagnosis was terminal. Growing up, I was lucky to have a mom who was a nurse and could calm my nerves.

Of course, I was unlucky anytime I ventured to read her medical books — I could have some alarming symptoms.

Here's the thing. I've always thought my life has been too easy, so I just keep waiting for the other shoe to drop. I've worried that some darkness out there is going to finally catch up and get me or mine. In my young adult life, I remember worrying way too much about pain, death, and disease. I found that keeping myself busy helped. I kept so busy, I was on the "fast track" at work, but my personal life was a disaster. The disconnect between work and home finally manifested itself in severe anxiety attacks. It took me many years to move through this period in my life, as I tried to regain control. But, trouble eventually caught up with me and I couldn't handle it.

I was 29 weeks pregnant and Tom was away on a business trip. I woke up with terrible cramps and eventually hauled myself out to the car and drove to the doctor's office in extreme anxiety and pain. Lucky for me the hospital was right next door as I was whisked away to the emergency room, having gone into pre-term labor. Here, finally, was the pain and suffering of my worst nightmares. But it turns out the pain and suffering were not the worst part; it was the total lack of control. As doctors and nurses worked me over, trying to get the contractions to stop, I finally had a glimpse of how out of control I was. In that crowded hospital room, I was utterly alone, overwhelmed, mad, scared, and totally freaked out. Somewhere in this jumble of emotion, I remember having a conversation with God, maybe the first one ever. I wasn't playing let's make a deal or begging for mercy; at that point I was just ready to hand over the reins. Please, God, take control because I don't know what to do.

Does this story have a happy ending? After a few days in the hospital, they finally got the contractions to stop and I was sent home to bed rest. Xander was born healthy and right on schedule, after twelve hours of labor, three hours of pushing, and an emergency C-section; but that's another story. As with most stories in my life, there is happiness, but there is also some trouble. I've learned that trouble is not punishment, it's not predictable, it's not meant to level the playing field of my life. Trouble is part of life, a reminder that I am not master of myself let alone the universe. Trouble insists that I ask for help and turn control over to God. In hindsight, trouble is often the fork in the road, a choice on life's highway.

I agree with my dad that, compared to the suffering of many on planet earth, my trouble seems puny. For me and many other Christian Americans, the lessons in Job are difficult to grasp because we just can't relate to or can hardly bear hearing what's been happening to Job. I think we can relate to the three friends that came to visit Job in the hope to sympathize with and comfort him.

> When they saw him from a distance, they could hardly recognize him; they began to weep aloud, and they tore their robes and sprinkled dust on their heads. Then they sat on the ground with him for seven days and seven nights. No one said a word to him, because they saw how great his suffering was. — Job 2:12-13, NIV

Their hearts are in the right place and they let Job vent for a while, but finally his friend Eliphaz interrupts. It seems he wants to shake Job out of his funk by launching into a lecture about how important Job is, how much people look up to him for support and guidance, and that he should view his suffering as some form of discipline from God. Job's response is filled with pain and loathing and this little zinger:

> Now you too have proved to be of no help; you see something dreadful and are afraid. — Job 6:21

I think the story of Job and his friends has some parallels to the church and its relationship to those who are enduring long-term suffering, such as the poor. As the church, we are more than willing to provide the poor short-term relief in the form of food, clothes, even shelter and short-term mission trips. But getting involved with the poor long-term is distressing because we want the poor to be able to pull themselves up by their bootstraps and persevere. Instead, when we get beyond the problems on the surface, we see something dreadful and are afraid. It knocks our preconceived notions, about how God interacts with the world and what God expects of us, out of whack.

For me, this is the hope of postmodern Christians and the emerging church. For the postmodern person, actions and inaction always speak louder than words. Knowing is gained through learning, experience, and connection with others. So postmodern Christians are drawn to living out their whole life following Jesus' example of being a servant of God. I think this kind of faith looks like meeting and helping people where they are, without strings attached.

As a privileged American and recovering hypochondriac, whose worst nightmares are still firmly lodged in her head, I pray that God gives me the strength to see the dreadful, move beyond the fear, and to help each and every day those who endure long-term suffering. God, please curb my frustrations, expectations, and quick-fix mentality that get in the way of being your hands, feet, eyes, ears, and arms.

Chapter Endnotes

1. "Suffering: Interfaith and Intercultural Interpretations of Job," the Krost Symposium for 1990, held at Texas Lutheran. The speakers included a Christian theologian from Europe, a Jewish rabbi from North America (referred to in the homily that follows), a Christian graduate student from Africa, and a Christian contemplative from South America. If I were to organize the symposium today, I would add a Muslim spokesperson from the Near East or Asia.
2. A homily presented initially at Umphumulo Lutheran Theological Seminary, South Africa, on April 5, 2000. Revised, expanded, and presented subsequently at Texas Lutheran University and at Christ Lutheran Church, Georgetown, Texas. The version printed here is the latest iteration.
3. Rabbi Harold Kushner, *When Bad Things Happen To Good People* (Schocken Press, 1981).
4. This is consistent with the notion that God's perfection includes change and that God's power, including the power for good, has limits. See the paper in ch. 6 ("Who, what, and where in the world is God?") and the homily in ch. 16 ("The last homily") for some additional thoughts on these matters. Such ideas are central to Rabbi Kushner's discussion of suffering in his book.

CHAPTER 23

SOUTH AFRICA: SUNRISE OR SUNSET?

Background essay

Tom Wilkens

"Where there is no vision, the people perish" (Proverbs 29:18; KJV). As evidence I cite the Democrats during the first half of the George W. Bush administration. I rest my case. Well, not really: please permit a brief elaboration. Without a vision infused with hope and not despair, shaped by justice and not by greed, the people — individually and collectively — will decline and fall. Potential disaster for lack of hope and justice lurks in every society, and our own is not exempt. But there seems, even today, to be a special urgency in South Africa.

The lecture that follows, the sixth and last of the writings growing out of our sojourn in South Africa, shows just how rich and instructive the experience was. To be sure, as the disclaimer early on in the lecture makes clear, I do not have the background and expertise to mine the full treasure from our time there. I offer, as it were, a small snapshot album and not a full-length documentary film.

I spoke of six crises in South Africa today: medical, economic, ecological, political, social, and ecclesiastical. I cannot rank order them; I doubt that anyone one can. However, I am convinced that they are all interrelated; that while for purposes of analysis I must treat them individually, in reality they are inextricably intertwined.

My analysis of each crisis is extremely succinct and thereby also excessively simple. I apologize for this, but I was not in a position to do much about it. My desire was that my listeners, and now you our readers, might be motivated to explore each issue a bit further: to pay attention to what South Africans such as Desmond Tutu and Nelson Mandella are saying and have written; to track the records of the World Bank and International Monetary Fund *vis á vis* the economy there; to find out how your church body might be involved with South Africa; to see what opportunities for medical or other types of volunteer service might be available to you in South Africa today; and to learn whether our government is addressing in humble and helpful ways the social and political problems with which South Africa is grappling or ignoring them because of other distractions or due to indifference.

In other words, if you have not done so already, think seriously about becoming a citizen of the world. It requires no naturalization, only education; no passport, only a port of entry into your mind and heart; and no loyalty oath, only a commitment to enlarge your sphere of caring. It will give you, among other things, a fresh standpoint from which to comprehend and appraise your own national citizenship.

But I must warn you: there are reports from many people who have done it that global citizenship has changed them, influencing their lives and priorities. I probably should wear a warning label; so should my wife and now our daughter. Yet we do not look back nostalgically to our more parochial days in the past. We have no regrets about our personal globalizations.

What I endorse here is the globalization of an individual's outlook, not the super-sizing of the systems and structures of society. With respect to the latter there are huge downsides to, for example, the globalization of the economies of the world, especially for the "have-nots" in many nations — including the US. It is also the case that globalizing one's point of view can have a downside, can sometimes be discomfiting and disheartening. Yet, as I indicate in the lecture that follows, there seem always to be glimmers of light and elements of hope. This makes holding global citizenship and having a global perspective both bearable and invigorating.

So how might global awareness affect one's behavior? Let me give just one modest example. It is a project that requires no international travel, relatively little time, and hardly any special skills. A few years ago our senior group began selling fairly traded coffee, tea, cocoa, and chocolate bars once a month in our local parish. Fair trade means that small growers in developing countries are paid fair prices for their products: prices that provide those small growers and their workers sufficient income to rise above the subsistence level and to stabilize their production operations; prices that are well above the commodity prices generally paid by large multi-national corporations.

Our mark-ups on these items when we retail them are small. We charge only enough to be able to provide, *gratis*, fair trade coffee and tea for all of the public functions and social occasions held in our congregation. We thus buy even more of the fair trade goods. Is it a feasible project? Yes. Will our effort save the world? No. But does it make a real difference, one grower and several families at a time? Yes. By and large, with development projects, small is both beautiful and effective. Over the years and across the globe, I have been privileged to see this with my own eyes.

South Africa: sunrise or sunset?[1]

Tom Wilkens

My wife, Betty, and I spent most of the first five months of the year 2000 in South Africa at Umphumulo Lutheran Theological Seminary, located in rural KwaZulu-Natal province about an hour-and-a-half's drive outside of Durban, under the auspices of my church's Division for Global Mission. I taught two courses in theology; Betty taught an English class and assisted in the library. We were warmly received wherever we went. Our experience was overwhelmingly positive. Nonetheless, a question began to emerge in our minds: Is South Africa at a sunrise or a sunset in its history? Has South Africa's dark night of apartheid and oppression ended with the dawn of a new day? Or is South Africa sinking into a new darkness after the brief light of political liberation and the fleeting promise of ethnic harmony, economic prosperity, and environmental integrity?

After a year of reflection, those questions still engage us. We continue to be concerned for the rainbow of people, the collage of cultures, and the diverse natural environments that make up the nation of South Africa.

How will it go for them? What follows is not rooted in scholarly expertise. It is rooted in our experience, in our ongoing interest in and concern for South Africa. That interest and concern is expressed in brief analyses of several of the crises facing South Africa today.

Medical crisis: the multi-faceted challenge of HIV/AIDS

The HIV/AIDS crisis throughout Africa has finally made it into the popular western media. *Time* magazine, for instance, ran a cover story about it just a few months ago.[2] Rates of infection vary greatly among the African nations. It appears that in South Africa the overall infection rate lies somewhere between 10% and 20%. The infection rate in the province where we lived, KwaZulu-Natal, is currently reported to be over 35% — the highest rate in South Africa. As an example of how out-of-control the disease is in that area, the professor teaching pastoral theology at the Seminary said that in the hospital where he had previously served as chaplain, the infection rate among new mothers was 100%.

That sad reality is compounded by the fact that most of the medications that could reduce the transmission of the infection from mother to newborn are not available to the mothers. Part of the reason for this is the expense: the overwhelming majority of these mothers live in poverty. In addition, South African President MBeki has accepted the very odd view that the connection between HIV and AIDS has not been proven. He distrusts western culture, including its scientific community, for some very understandable historical reasons. That distrust, however, translates into government inaction with respect to the AIDS crisis. To cite just one example, drug company offers of drastically reduced prices for medications have yet to be accepted by the South African government.

Of course, even drastically reduced medicine prices are still too much for most South Africans or for their government. In something of a catch-22 situation, the AIDS epidemic is placing an intolerable strain on an already overburdened and under-funded health care system.

There are some other cultural factors at work worsening the crisis. One is sexual promiscuity, practiced by a large segment of the male population, arising at least in part from the tearing apart of families forced upon much of the black population during apartheid. This situation has been aggravated by a commonly held belief, especially among Zulu males, that sex with a virgin will prevent them from contracting AIDS.

Rape of young girls is thus commonplace in many regions. And in a culture more male-centered than anything we've seen in the States for some generations, there is little remorse for such behavior and little condemnation of it.

In addition to medicine, education is clearly needed. Many NGOs — that is, non-governmental organizations — are trying to fill in the huge gap left by the government's inability to mount effective education campaigns with respect to HIV/AIDS. But even these efforts run into a very solid wall of denial. The majority of South Africans, even those with AIDS-related deaths in their families or their circle of friends, refuse to acknowledge its deadly and growing presence in their midst.

In other areas, some good things are indeed happening in the South African health care system. It is delivering basic health care to millions of its citizens, helped by such factors as a contingent of some 120 Cuban doctors reinforcing the system with high levels of training and skill which they take into rural areas such as Umphumulo — where two Cuban doctors worked in the neighboring hospital.

Economic crisis: high unemployment rate and low level of investment

South Africa has an economic crisis of sobering proportions. Some estimates place the unemployment rate as high as 50%. It is likely that this figure is realistic when one includes underemployment in the mix. We saw the human evidence, including the resultant poverty, in both rural and urban environments.

Economic hardship has been intensified for the poor majority because for several years South Africa has been trying to meet International Monetary Fund and World Bank guidelines in order to attract foreign investment. The impact of meeting those guidelines — which typically includes deep cuts in social services — has been widely felt. As usual, the brunt of the cost has been borne by the poor. Yet the intended payoff of increased foreign investment has not, for the most part, happened. More and better jobs have not materialized in numbers sufficient to make a significant difference.

Thus the promise of a better life has not been fulfilled for the vast majority of South Africans. Their nearly blood-free revolution and transition from apartheid to democracy seems in real danger of descending into a pit of violent hopelessness. And yet the promise remains: South Africa is rich in human resources, waiting to be utilized in humane and effective ways, and rich in natural resources, waiting to be tapped in safe and sustainable ways.

Ecological crisis: environmental exploitation and degradation

South Africa also has an ecological crisis. We saw a large-scale example of this crisis in KwaZulu-Natal Province: the clear-cutting of forests. Clear-cutting promotes, among other things, soil erosion. Even replanting, which they are doing, will not prevent soil erosion in the early years of new growth. Nor will replanting remedy all of the damage to soil nutrition levels or the negative impact on species diversity so important to environmental well-being. Clear-cutting does not contribute to a sustainable use of a most important ecosystem of resources: the forest.

South Africa does have an effective program for protecting big game species, a program reported to be the best in all of Africa. This is a very positive factor not only for South Africa but also for much of the rest of Africa, which looks to South Africa for leadership by example. And yet the people who now enjoy South Africa's wildlife and beauty tend to be the foreign tourists, not the South Africans themselves — especially not the black majority. Tourism is held to be so important to the South African economy by those in power that it takes precedence over such things as flood control and improvement of infrastructure for the South Africans.

Abundant and amazing natural beauty remains in South Africa. Yet Betty and I also saw a high incidence of non-biodegradable trash across much of the landscape. Modern culture generates much more of that kind of trash than traditional cultures have generated. Patterns of waste management and waste reduction appear not to have kept pace with changing patterns of consumption in South Africa. I do not say this out of a spirit of superiority. The US, much better positioned to deal with such matters, is nonetheless hardly a poster child for environmental health and integrity.

Political crisis: widespread corruption and lack of competence

Each of the crises previously mentioned — medical, economic, and ecological — has a political dimension. But the South African political system itself is also in crisis. The crisis stems from, among other sources, corruption and incompetence.

Corruption seems to be a common denominator among the problems facing developing nations. Corruption, expressing itself not only in the political arena but also in the economic sphere, makes progress difficult if not impossible. Even where corruption is acknowledged as a serious issue — in such places as Mexico and China — it has not been easy to diminish. From the federal to the local levels of government, South Africa has yet to find effective counter-measures. For instance, last year a murder took place in Umphumulo near the entrance to the parish church. The chief suspect is related to the chief of police. No arrest has been made, even though there were many eyewitnesses to the daylight shooting.

Another difficulty arises when newly empowered people are not altogether ready to exercise that power competently. Non-white South Africans — systematically excluded from quality education, opportunities for leadership training, and positions of leadership for so long — often are not fully prepared to discharge the responsibilities that they must undertake today. They are learning on the job. Meanwhile, their inexperience seems to be taking a heavy toll: questionable policies, lost opportunities, legislative malaise, and bureaucratic inefficiency. To cite just one example, South African police were trained to impose the harsh rules of apartheid, not to investigate crime. Their inexperience in criminal investigation is a serious deficiency in the South African justice system today.

The generation of leadership that might have made more of a difference on these issues — including people such as former president Nelson Mandela and Archbishop Desmond Tutu — is now passing from the scene. The succeeding generation seems neither as sure of its vision nor as capable of moving toward the fulfillment of the peoples' dreams. In their defense, it is surely the case that revolution is easier to motivate and lead than the comparatively dull work of nation-building. And there do exist significant examples of corruption-free and competent civil service and political leadership.

Social crisis: inadequate education, increasingly violent crime, and persistent ethnic tensions

The social crisis in South Africa is evident in many ways. I'll mention only three. *First*, there are critical problems in public education. In several provinces, school funding is woefully inadequate. Some elementary and secondary schools have been closed for a lack of staff and/or funds. The promise of universal public education remains unfulfilled, largely because it remains underfunded — that in turn leads to shortages of fully qualified teachers. The university system also seems to be in a state of disarray. University closings have not been uncommon, and university quality seems to have become more and more difficult to sustain.

Second, violent crime is on the rise. Three murders have occurred in the rural community of Umphumulo in the year since we left. A rise in thefts and robberies seems understandable, even if not acceptable, in a context of poverty and economic pessimism. What is not so easily understood is the rapid rise in the often-deadly violence that typically accompanies these crimes. It seems not enough for thieves and robbers to take money and goods; they also frequently finish their work by taking life. I still remember a friend of mine in Pietermaritzburg telling me that each time he leaves to go home in the afternoon after work he has no real assurance that he will make it and — what is worse — no real confidence that his wife will be alive and well if he arrives. I stand in awe of people like him, who could easily emigrate back to Germany and find work but choose instead to participate in the struggle for justice and peace in South Africa.

Third, South Africa continues to experience ethnic tensions. Apartheid, which imposed racist norms and promoted ethnic envy and hatred from the outside, has been displaced. But the racism and the tensions are not gone. I once told my students there that it appeared to me that what apartheid once imposed externally now seems to be internalized by the various ethnic groups and sustained from within. Perhaps apartheid didn't lose; perhaps it won. The majority of my students, with great sadness, agreed. Once more, I did not speak with an air of superiority. My own nation should be well past racism and ethnic tension. It is not.

Is there no relief from this litany of social ills? Yes, there is. There are individuals, groups, and movements attempting to address these and other social problems. That they are not yet fully solved is in the long run less important than the fact that there are ongoing efforts to deal with them.

Ecclesiastical crisis: the church in search of an agenda

Finally, I want to make a few comments about what I see as an ecclesiastical crisis in South Africa. The Lutheran churches in South Africa were originally mission churches, founded by Europeans — including Germans and Scandinavians — and more recently subsidized by European and American benefactor churches. Many of the churches of South Africa that were founded in similar fashion have managed to become self-governing; but some of them are still not self-supporting. It is not healthy to remain a client church generation after generation. All of this has led to, among other things, the founding of many indigenous religious groups.

But despite this, and to use the Lutherans as an example, many mainline church bodies in South Africa finally came to participate and cooperate in the struggle against apartheid. During the 1970s, important strategy conferences were held at places like Umphumulo Lutheran Seminary, whose remote location was ideal for such "subversive" gatherings. Now it appears that the Lutherans, and some of the other denominations in South Africa, have lost their way. They find it difficult to agree on an agenda. They find it hard to speak out, and especially to act, on the serious issues of justice facing South Africa today.

Umphumulo Seminary once had a sense of mission that emboldened it to confront not only the church but also the nation with a strong prophetic message. That era is over. Not only has the Seminary lost its battle for sufficient autonomy to be able to function in prophetic ways. It appears to have lost its battle for survival as an independent institution: it is going to be folded into Natal University at Pietermaritzburg and lose much of its identity.

Once again, however, there are points of light in the ecclesiastical darkness. There are young people studying for ministry who are convinced of the need for change and willing to work for it. And there are pastors being elected as bishops and other leaders who are aware of the church's inertia and are trying to push it into motion.

Conclusion

Will hope or despair prevail? Is dawn or dusk on the horizon in South Africa? If South Africans can retain some element of hope, they may well be able to overcome the long odds that seem stacked against them. If they finally lose hope and slip past pessimism into despair, then I believe that dusk is inevitable. I think that the old adage is true: a people without hope will surely die.

I read recently that the word for "crisis" in Chinese is the same as the word for "opportunity." South Africa is in crisis on many fronts. Still, for many South Africans it is not yet time for despair: crises present opportunities for positive change and transformation — even when the odds are unattractive and hope seems unwarranted.

Is South Africa at a sunrise or a sunset? I do not have a definitive answer to this question. What I find that I do have is hope. As Saint Paul made clear in First Corinthians, hope is not an achievement; it is a gift. South African people from all walks of life have shared their gift of hope with me. I am not optimistic, but I am hopeful. There is a difference. Hope is more enduring. If the flame of hope remains lit in South Africa, the darkness cannot overcome it. It is a big "if." The stakes are very high.

Response:
Taking the first step

Kim Wilkens

As a follower of Christ, I understand that pursuing mercy and justice is my God-given call. I know that there are serious problems locally and globally. I realize that just talking about the problems — hoping to motivate some action — is not the best way to go about solving problems. So how do I become a citizen of the world that my dad is advocating?

Does it actually require passports, jet lag, bumpy roads, foreign food, and translation? I don't think so. While a trip to a third-world country can certainly give you a crash course in raising your global awareness, there are other ways to learn. Certainly keeping up with current events is good, but I don't think that is critical. Hey, my idea of keeping current is watching the *Daily Show*. Gaining an understanding of what problems are facing the poor and oppressed around the world is important, but that's not quite enough either.

I like how Paul puts it in his letter to the Philippians:

> Finally, beloved, whatever is true, whatever is honorable, whatever is just, whatever is pure, whatever is pleasing, whatever is commend-

able, if there is any excellence and if there is anything worthy of praise, think about these things. Keep on doing the things that you have learned and received and heard and seen in me, and the God of peace will be with you. — Philippians 4:8f.

I think we need an attitude adjustment. First, we need to look and find where there is good, honorable, just, pure, pleasing, and excellent work being done in the world and think about that. Next, we need to do the things that we have learned, received, heard and seen from people doing this work. I think becoming a citizen of the world starts with our feet.

Here's what worked for me — start with one step and do it with others. At my church, we are blessed to have many opportunities to serve with and for others. My first step started with People and Congregations Engaged in Ministry (PACEM) where we've welcomed local homeless men and women into this house of God as honored guests. With PACEM there are so many different ways to serve and so many other people to serve with. Serving definitely took me out of my comfort zone, but knowing I didn't have to do it alone helped me through the fear. At PACEM, I learned from one of the guests about the serious lack of affordable housing in the area. I started to feel passionate about this issue.

A few months later Pastor John hooked me up with the coordinator of Interfaith Movement Promoting Action by Congregations Together (IMPACT) and before I knew it, I had taken another step. I attended the very first IMPACT meeting with 25 other people from Peace where we voted on what issues to address that year and affordable housing became one of the first issues. Since then I've taken a few more steps, some with confidence and others on legs of jelly, but always in the company of others, who help push away my fears and provide the example I need to take the next step.

Chapter Endnotes

1. A paper presented in a Senior University lecture series at Southwestern University in Georgetown, Texas, in June of 2001.
2. See Johanna McGeary, "Death stalks a continent," *Time* (February 19, 2001). A web version is still posted; use the article title to search for it.

CHAPTER 24

PRAISE THE LORD AND
PASS THE AMMUNITION

Background essay

Tom Wilkens

Betty and I landed one September day at the airport in St. Petersburg, Russia. A representative from Novasaratovka Theological Lutheran Seminary, where we would teach that fall term, met us in the arrival lounge. He then drove us to the Seminary and showed us to our living quarters in a large multi-purpose facility, a converted church building, where we started unpacking. Soon we heard a knock on our door and, when we opened it, saw a young man standing there. He introduced himself as a US seminarian about to begin his internship in a Russian congregation.

We knew about him and had anticipated that we would meet him. But we did not expect to encounter a young fellow with an ashen face and extremely troubled eyes. "Have you heard?" he asked softly, almost inaudibly. "Heard what?" we responded. Before he replied, he requested to come into our small space to sit for a moment. After gathering his composure, he told us about the attack on the Twin Towers in New York City. It had just happened. We all quickly went out into the wide hallway, which also served as a lounge. It had a television set and we began watching. At first there was a live feed from CNN, with reporters' comments and observations in English. But before long, Russian TV switched to its own voice-over coverage and our new friend, fluent in Russian, had to translate the commentary for us. This was our welcome to the world of 9/11.

It raises all sorts of questions for Americans. One of the underlying issues, the synthesizing of God and country, is a front-burner topic in the homily with a misleading title that follows. We do it and have done it for generations: after giving the mandatory lip-service to the ideal of the separation of church and state, we then embrace the actual blending of God and country. These days, to note an example of this synthesizing cited in the homily, we sing "God bless America" with increased frequency and with renewed religious *and* patriotic fervor. Should we do it? If so, why? If not, why not? These and other questions seem freshly pertinent in the aftermath of 9/11.

I once delivered a chapel talk titled "In praise of apathy." It explored, initially, the good things that can result from the dispassionate use of reason. But apathy falters when it becomes the fundamental axiom of life, as it was for the ancient Stoics. Saint Paul saw this and, while he borrowed a great deal from the Stoics, he clearly was a man of passionate faith.

Yet he clearly was also a man of giant intellect, committed to the use of reason in the service of faith. The temptation of many, if not most, American Christians today is to live as though faith and reason are divorced. If this is true, then typical American Christians might not do very much even though they understand — rationally — that over half the world lives in poverty. Their minds and hearts, the latter the deep seats of faith and the powerful motivators to action, are out of touch with one another.

My own temptation over the years has been different: a form of reductionism that shrinks Christianity to its rational dimension. This is as inhibiting to the actions of love as the divorce of reason and faith. I have been challenged to change, especially by developing-world Christians. I am a slow learner but a much more willing one in my latter years.

Postmodern Christians very frequently are severe critics of the modern church — with its high-maintenance structures and institutions, its traditional and sometimes opaque and lethargic liturgies, its huge heritage of doctrine not always rendered relevant to today's world, and its often anemic commitment to pursue justice and serve the world. Not surprisingly, they are in far more agreement with regard to what they find objectionable about the modern church than they are concerning what ought to succeed it. When they do attempt to envision or model new ways of being the church, they at times use the expression "Emerging Church" to describe their dreams or efforts. There are numerous forms and formats being tested: some congregations have been started from scratch in new settings[1] and other congregations are attempting to reinvent themselves in their existing locations.[2]

Within the Emerging Church there are ongoing discussions about and experiments with what are commonly called tent-making ministries. Even if there is a role for theologically educated and ecclesiastically trained leaders in the church, and there seems not to be full consensus on this matter,[3] perhaps those leaders should not be professional in the sense of drawing their livelihoods from church positions. Maybe they should make their livings at ordinary occupations and live out their ecclesiastical vocations as most of the rest of the laity do: as volunteers.

To be sure, this is not a new model for ministry or for ministerial leadership. The very expression, tent-making, comes from the life and ministry of Saint Paul. Yet some postmodern Christians see fresh potential for this type of ministry as one element in the evolution, the reformation, or even the revolution that needs to take place in the church today.

Christians in the developed world have this model of ministry as an option. Christians in many sectors of the developing world have it as a necessity; that is, as the only way to sustain a church body with some learned leadership. As I observe in the following homily, tent-making ministry is the rule and not the exception among Protestants in most of the republics of the former USSR. It turns out that what many Christians in the developing world often have little choice about, namely utilizing tent-making ministries, some of us in the developed world — who do have other viable alternatives — are seeking to emulate. Could it be that the church in the developing world is pioneering our future? If so, we likely should look more closely and carefully at their examples, and not just from a distance. We may need their tutorials, on their turf and not on ours. Then we can adopt and adapt what we learn to our developed-world context.

Praise the Lord and pass the ammunition[4]

Tom Wilkens

The text

> Now concerning love of the brothers and sisters, you do not need to have anyone write to you, for you yourselves have been taught by God to love one another; and indeed you do love all the brothers and sisters throughout Macedonia. But we urge you, beloved, to do so more and more, to aspire to live quietly, to mind your own affairs, and to work with your hands, as we directed you, so that you may behave properly toward outsiders and be dependent on no one.

— 1 Thessalonians 4:9-12

Introduction

"Praise the Lord and pass the ammunition, and we'll all stay free." If you remember those lyrics to an American song, you're really old. The song was very popular during World War II. I remember singing it often and enthusiastically as a kid in the lower grades of elementary school. It was meant to be — and proved to be — an inspiring synthesis of Christianity with Americanism. I had no notion why it made me feel so good to sing it, but it did.

I haven't heard the words and music to "Praise the Lord and pass the ammunition" for over half a century. But I understand that during my absence in Russia another old song became freshly popular: "God bless America." It was and is being sung to help heal the gaping wound left by the September 11 terrorist attack, and also to help galvanize our resolve to prosecute the war on terrorism. Healing for our pain and grief is not at issue here this morning. However, there *are* some questions that our western Christian tradition says need to be asked about the war on terrorism: is it a just war? And equally important, will it result in a just peace?

I'm no longer young; I'm far from the age of my innocence. I confess that I now have some serious misgivings about what appears to me, at any rate, to be the uncritical joining of God and country that the song "God bless America" embodies. I'll share those misgivings in a few moments, but first we have a biblical text to confront.

Exegesis and hermeneutics

First Thessalonians is the earliest of all the New Testament writings. It is a letter that had been sent to Christians in Thessalonica, the capital city of Macedonia. It had been composed by Saint Paul, who was thoroughly grounded in Judaism, to a congregation whose members apparently had little if any knowledge of that religion. And so Saint Paul used relatively little Jewish imagery and made relatively few references to Jewish scriptures in this letter.

He chose instead, particularly in the verses just read, to use the language of Greek philosophy, specifically of Greek ethics. It was not the language of the great schools of Plato or Aristotle. Rather it was the language of philosophies of life that were known even by ordinary people, philosophies called Epicureanism and Stoicism.

It should be noted that Saint Paul was always both careful and selective in the Epicurean and Stoic moral virtues that he extolled. He rejected some of them, such as the Stoic virtue of apathy, as being incompatible with Christian faith and life. Those that he adopted he also adapted to conform to the gospel of Jesus Christ.

The virtues that Saint Paul called upon the Thessalonican Christians to exhibit in their lives were thus not uniquely or exclusively Christian. The practice of loving ones sisters and brothers was an Epicurean virtue, expanded by the Thessalonians to include all of the Christian sisters and brothers in the Macedonian region — for which they were commended and encouraged by Saint Paul. His admonition "to aspire to live quietly" sounds very much like the Epicurean tenet about living in a way that would not draw attention. That was good advice at a time when being noticed as a Christian could get one into trouble with the authorities or with a mob.

Continuing with the moral exhortations in the text, Saint Paul's urging of the Thessalonians "to mind your own affairs" was in harmony with the Epicurean prohibition against participation in civic or public life. And his counsel of his readers "to work with your own hands," and thus to be economically dependent on no one, was consistent with the Stoic teaching about self-sufficiency.

Some of Saint Paul's moral instructions are as valid and relevant today as they were at the time he gave them nearly 2,000 years ago. This is certainly true of his affirmation of loving larger and larger circles of our brothers and sisters in the community of faith.

Yet some of his admonitions seem to be helpful only under certain conditions. For instance, to live quietly so as to escape attention was surely relevant to Christians living in the Soviet Union during the communist era. Thankfully, that recommendation has lost most of its relevance in today's Russia. However, in other Republics of the former Soviet Union, specifically some of those with dominant Muslim populations, simply being identified as a Christian can be dangerous. In those nations, it is still wise to keep a low profile.

On another matter, Saint Paul's own example of working for a living with his hands — he was a tentmaker — will be followed by most of my students at the seminary in Russia. When they become pastors, they will have to support themselves financially by working at other jobs. That's not the case for those of you in this assembly headed for professional ministry in American churches.

Finally, Saint Paul's advice not to get involved in civic or public affairs likely needs to be reevaluated by Christians who live today in democratic societies. Surely we have an obligation to get involved and to speak out on matters of peace and justice, of human rights and environmental sustainability. Perhaps there are some new virtues and values that we Christians need to embrace in our time.

We should not shrink from this task. The importance of the text from First Thessalonians lies not only in the specific guidance that Saint Paul gave. It lies also in his bold example of a thoughtful Christian who, after critical reflection and prayer, promoted certain cultural virtues and values that were found to be consistent with the gospel of Jesus Christ and helpful for the followers of Christ.

It is, however, a process fraught with difficulties and pitfalls. Sometimes the Christian community embraces unworthy cultural views and values, such as the inferiority of women or the superiority of one tribe, nation or race over another. Sometimes we too hastily and easily equate our individual, ecclesiastical or national desires with the will of God.

And so we return to my misgivings. An American colleague of mine at the Russian seminary commented that, in the aftermath of a military attack or defeat, Israel of old was typically called upon to engage in self-examination and repentance for national failures and sins. Since the seventeenth century, Americans have often referred to themselves as the

New Israel. In the aftermath of the unspeakable evil of the September 11 attack, is not a call for national self-examination and perhaps even repentance in order? Has such a call been issued? Or does our national commitment to revenge and our national conviction that we are innocent preclude any concession of national guilt? Have we missed an incredibly costly wakeup call?

We Americans have a long track record of synthesizing God and state. The linking of God's will and national purpose formed one of the basic rationales for the removal of Native Americans from their traditional homelands by the immigrant European population. The immigrants called it their Manifest Destiny: to explore and exploit and own the land "from the mountains, to the prairies, to the oceans white with foam." The natives had other names for it, including Trail of Tears. Thomas Jefferson wanted an American empire; it became a reality. The cost was small in monetary terms, but enormous in terms of human suffering, bad faith, and ill will.

The identity of God's will with national purpose comforted both North and South during the American Civil War. President Lincoln was one of the few leaders on either side of that war who didn't assume that God was on their side but rather agonized over whether or not his group — the North — was on the side of God. This is the issue that needs raising, the question that always needs asking.

Today the equation of God's will with national purpose not only shapes the policies of fundamentalist Islamic regimes but also informs some of the policy makers and many of the policy supporters in America. Such formulas, and the political and religious mathematics that generate them, require critical examination. Our own religious tradition, at its prophetic best, encourages skepticism in the face of such claims with respect to God and country. We're not very good at it; we must get better.

In light of our errors and excesses, we should try to be as careful and selective as Saint Paul was when it comes to embracing a culture and its values. May God give us the insight, guidance, and courage needed to continue this task of sorting out virtues and values in our time and place. May we be given the humility to understand how difficult it is to do that work well. And may we thus undertake this ethical task worthily, for the benefit of the whole body of Christ and also for the benefit of the whole world.

Conclusion

So what will it be: "Praise the Lord and pass the ammunition" or praise the Lord and pass the peace? I suspect that the Prince of Peace would prefer that we choose the latter. I suspect that he would have us choose peace not just by passing the peace with hugs in this sanctuary but also — using different means available to the diverse people of God — by waging a just peace out there in the world that we Christians confess belongs not to us but to the Prince. What do you think?

Response:
The language of peace

Kim Wilkens

My friends, what good would it do, if I came and spoke unknown languages to you and didn't explain what I meant? How would I help you, unless I told you what God had shown me or gave you some knowledge or prophecy or teaching? If all musical instruments sounded alike, how would you know the difference between a flute and a harp? If a bugle call isn't clear, how would you know to get ready for battle?

That's how it is when you speak unknown languages. If no one can understand what you are talking about, you will only be talking to the wind. There are many different languages in this world, and all of them make sense. But if I don't understand the language that someone is using, we will be like foreigners to each other. If you really want spiritual gifts, choose the ones that will be most helpful to the church.

— 1 Corinthians 14:6-12, CEV

As you have probably figured out by now, I am fascinated with language, translation, and communication — not in the sense of learning a new language, but in the sense of understanding the nuances of our own language within our culture. Someone recently asked me about the language of peace and how it is best expressed through social justice ministry. In particular, where was the language of peace more effective, in direct action or community-based organizing.

This whole idea of a language of peace is so intriguing to me. I think it's the language of Jesus, Gandhi, Martin Luther King Jr. and many other non-violent activists throughout history. In my very limited exposure to engaging in grassroots social justice ministry, it is often a most elusive language. For instance, my first inclination in dealing with someone who just doesn't seem to understand the problem or maybe has no desire to understand that there are problems, is to want to start bashing a few heads together. Of course, I realize that this is not a productive response, but I have a very hard time stepping back and trying to see things from their perspective or imagining how I can communicate to them in a language they can relate to.

It seems that our American society is hurtling toward a manifest destination of life, liberty and the pursuit of happiness based on our cultural upbringing and traditions. When flaws are exposed in this pursuit through public actions like protests against the war, immigration policies, health care inequities, conditions in Darfur, and the seemingly unending list of global injustices, these actions seem to become mere sound bites in a cacophony of media coverage bombarding us every day. They may distract a few to move off the path, but the rest of society keeps tumbling on by.

Certainly public actions can have great value in highlighting social injustices and so I see them as potential sparks that can ignite the passion needed to actually address an issue. What I wonder is how many of those sparks flicker and fade because either the commitment to see a solution through is not there or the spark is cloaked in a language so foreign to most people that they can't or won't understand it. In other words, the action takers are so steeped in their own language and so removed from society as a whole that communication is extremely hampered.

Obviously, where I feel called is to participate in grassroots, interfaith, community-based organizing. I feel this call in Jesus' desire for me to love my neighbor and my enemy and in Peter's brief courage to step out of the boat. The spark for me started with a mission trip to Honduras. The flame was fed through serving homeless people at my church. The Interfaith Movement Promoting Action by Congregations Together (IMPACT) offers me a concrete way to get involved in an organization pursuing root causes to social injustice in my community.

It seems important that this work start with local problems. I think that is how you build an organization that is committed to see things through long-term. However, I don't see it being limited to a local context. Already, we are able to use research and best practices from other communities facing similar issues and I can see the potential to collaborate with other communities tackling common problems.

I do worry that because of the nature of community-based organizations, we pursue issues that the collective body can get behind and these are often chosen because they are winnable, not necessarily comprehensive. Good communication is critical to engage the community at large and bring people into the community organization. The better the communication, the more significant the changes that can be pursued.

I think this is where we get back to that language of peace. Most everything I do as part of my ministry at church is related to communication and so 1 Corinthians 14:6-12 is also a guiding principle for me. It convicts me to not always rely on my native tongue to communicate. My introductory course to the language of peace has come through IMPACT, both in trying to communicate to my congregation and to the powers that be, why addressing the root causes of social injustice really matters, and how that is different from charity. I've only picked up a few phrases and I still hopelessly corrupt the language with my own accent. What I've learned about the language of peace so far is to try and listen first, speak out of love, and to live what you speak.

Chapter Endnotes

1. A congregation called Solomon's Porch in Minneapolis, where I have worshiped with one of my nieces, would be an example of this. See their web page at www.solomonsporch.com.
2. Kim's home congregation, Peace Lutheran in Charlottesville, VA exemplifies this. See their web page at www.plchurch.org. Further comments on both of these congregations appear in the homily in ch. 30.
3. See Kim's essays in chs. 7 and 21 for some further postmodern reflections on this issue.
4. A homily presented at Texas Lutheran University in February of 2002.

CHAPTER 25

A ROUGH GUIDE TO TRANSFORMATION OF CONSCIOUSNESS

Background essay

Tom Wilkens

The title of this chapter and of the paper following this background essay contains an allusion to a series of travel books called *Rough Guides*. It is meant to signal that I will treat the matter of transformation of consciousness roughly and not rigorously. There will be no equivalents to maps or mileage charts, though most travel guides include them. In my paper you will find few detailed instructions for achieving a transformation of consciousness, only broad suggestions. And you will find no fully comprehensive description of the destination, of what a transformed consciousness looks or feels like, only hints from my own journey and experience. What you may find is sufficient provocation to explore the subject further. I hope that you do.

How did I come to write about this particular topic? After all, it deals with an area where my competence has severe limits. It happened like this: I have a casual friend, a retired psychiatrist, who enjoys exploring the world far outside his field of professional expertise. For instance, in the retirement community where we both live he hosts a bi-weekly discussion group that centers its attention on philosophical questions. He and I meet and speak only infrequently, and then typically in hallway conversations outside of events we are both attending. At these times we exchange information about what we are each up to, intellectually.

It was on one of those occasions that my friend told me his group had been discussing the issue of the transformation of people: what that might consist of and how it might be achieved. He challenged me to write something and to share it with him. So I did. He was not terribly impressed with my paper. He said that if I ever wanted it published it would have to be "tightened" considerably, which is scholarly shorthand for making my case in a more linear, concise, and convincing manner. I think he was right.

I have worked with it a bit more, tightening it, but I would guess not as much as my friend was suggesting. In any event, if it has made it into this book it may be because I got a "loose" paper past the editor. If I did, you can determine whether it is better than the psychiatrist thought or here only because editors are human and can get tired and less demanding of material toward the end of a book.

Please note that my references to Buddhism in this essay have less to do with extensive knowledge of it, which I do not possess, and more to do with its strong and unique focus on the transformation of consciousness. What I do know about Buddhism suggests to me that, among the major Far Eastern religions, it has the most similarities — the most points of contact and thereby the most common ground for mutually beneficial dialogue — with Christianity.

This is especially the case with respect to Buddhism's anthropology: its understanding of humanity and of the human condition. I may not find its prescription adequate, but I find its diagnosis insightful. Buddhism's concern with suffering and its steadfast refusal to be distracted by easy answers or effortless avoidance techniques — especially the chemically-induced avoidance techniques so prevalent in Western cultures — keep it real and relevant, often more real and relevant than Christianity has been. There seems to be, in my mind still only roughly and not yet rigorously thought through, at least some convergence on these matters between Buddhist and Christian views.

A rough guide to transformation of consciousness[1]

Tom Wilkens

Introduction

I wrote something in a personal journal seventeen years ago that likely still applies to me today. Lest it seem that I am overly confident in the brief summary of my thoughts that follows, let me reproduce those words:

> One would think that at age fifty, with over thirty years of disciplined theological reflection behind me, I could respond more definitively — with more of an air of self-assurance — to fundamental questions. That was supposed to be one of the tradeoffs: a consolation prize of equanimity in return for the losses associated with aging. Perhaps only senility displaces perplexity.

My current take on myself is that I remain perplexed. The reader may detect the onset of senility. Whatever the case, I have four main and surely debatable points growing out of my experience and reflection with respect to the transformation of consciousness.

1. Transformation of consciousness entails both insight and integration, with community playing an essential role

The insights requisite to transformations of consciousness emerge from what western religious traditions have often called epiphanies: appearances or manifestations of the divine, of the ground and source of being, of ultimate reality. There may be disciplines that can increase the probability or incidence of epiphanies. However, my own impression is that disciplines such as meditation or contemplation serve not to prepare for or engender epiphanies but rather as ways to explicate them once they happen.

The same holds true for retreats and seminars. It is not that what they offer does not have great value. It is that they sometimes promise what they do not, perhaps cannot, deliver: namely, epiphanies. The most that I have been able to do to render an epiphany more probable is to place myself in established, not hastily created, communities discontinuous with my own — yet not so discontinuous as to render communication and understanding impossible. For me those have been communities of the poor in the developing world.

261

There has been an erosion of healthy community in the developed world that makes positive transformations of consciousness less and less likely, an erosion for which there is no quick fix. When developing-world people are inserted into our communities, their transformations are at times negative rather than positive. They adopt core values and adapt to core insights that may be inferior to those of their own indigenous cultures. For example, developing-world students may come to the developed world with a vision and a commitment to return home and serve; but often they remain here in response to the siren call of a consumer culture. When we are inserted into their communities, on the other hand, the transformations are often healthy and helpful: we gain insight into the limits and flaws of our own culture and lives.

Communities have always had the power to travel with the exile, the recluse, the solitary monk. Simeon the Stylite, the first of the "pillar ascetics," was not alone in the Syrian desert. He brought his community or, more properly, his communities of faith, language, etc. with him into the arid wasteland. He was not alone even when no pilgrims were there to watch and wonder.

Nor was Gautama Buddha alone, not even when he walked away from well-trod paths that did not assuage his dis-ease to a solitary setting under a Bo tree. The diverse Hindu community he was finally to reform to a breaking point sustained him in his pursuit, much as a parent perceived to fall dreadfully short nonetheless sustains a searching adolescent. Gautama's enlightenment focused on suffering and provided a fundamental insight into reality. It became pivotal in shaping an integrated approach to life that could confront, cope with, and perhaps even overcome the reality of suffering. The insights of the Four Noble Truths begin a process of transformation of consciousness that must be integrated into life by the Eightfold Path. I would note that for Gautama only the last two steps of the Eightfold Path involved meditation: they are the two final scenes from the last act, not the first, of the transformation of consciousness.

While there is much that I admire in and accept from Buddhism, there is a fundamental clash between Gautama's approach and that of my particular community of Christians — the Lutherans. For me, epiphanies with positive potential and their integration into a life changed and a consciousness thereby transformed are graces or gifts, not accomplishments or achievements. The insight that love is the ground of all, the great power that manifests itself in weakness, and the integration of love into life that transforms everything, including consciousness — all of this comes to me from the ground and source of all and is mediated through people and their work (that is, liturgy) in community. I do not attain these things; I receive them. To put it another way, transformation of consciousness is not a goal to be pursued; it is a by-product of being pursued by love or, for that matter, by pain or even pleasure.

2. The transformation of consciousness typically happens incrementally, not dramatically

I would regard Gautama as an exception to this principle, though in truth there were years of searching prior to his dramatic breakthrough enlightenment. I would regard Jesus as illustrating the rule. My reading of the Gospel accounts has Jesus growing in his awareness of who he was, of what his life should be about, and of his *Weltanschauung* — his interpreting matrix of consciousness. There is a marvelous story in the Gospel of Mark, chapter 7, about Jesus' encounter with a Syrophoenician woman. They embodied the historically abrasive relationship between their two respective communities. At the beginning of the story Jesus was the picture of conventional religiosity, to say nothing of conventional masculinity and ethnicity. At the end, and as the result of the woman's sassy tutelage, Jesus had a deeper insight into himself and his role in the world.[2] Such insights and transformations began early in his ministry and continued until his death. Jesus' perplexity with the world and his questioning of God did not end even as he was dying.

Thus I do not think that Jesus had a single breakthrough event in his life; I think that he struggled and had epiphanies and changed throughout his life. In this I am closer to Jesus than to Gautama.

3. The transformation of consciousness is not always positive: it sometimes leads to chaotic thoughts and destructive behaviors

As already observed, not all transformations of consciousness are healthful and helpful. I once gave a response to a public lecture given by a social scientist on the theme of chemical dependency. He had impeccable credentials, including the fact that he was himself a recovering alcoholic. In the course of my remarks, I observed that in my view addicts often see reality more clearly than those who are not addicted. It is precisely their glimpses of the dark, uncontrolled, and uncontrollable dimensions of reality that can lead to the disintegration of their lives. They have a firmer grip on, or should I say that they are more firmly gripped by, reality than I. And it may do them in. Insight does not necessarily lead to integration.

And yet, paradoxically, if I am not placed in a position that can threaten to undo me then I may never experience a positive transformation of consciousness. The transformations of consciousness of which I speak call for what the philosopher-theologian Paul Tillich termed "the courage to be" in the face of the threat of non-being.[3] The ancient Stoics knew this: theirs was a strategy — a battle plan, if you will — to overcome all challenges to apathy, all the legions of threats to their dispassionate integrity. Christianity had a hard sell in the Roman world so infused with Stoicism. It is a wonder that the Christians succeeded: they presented themselves as people who coped, not always successfully, with the darker side of personal, public, cosmic, and even God's reality. They did not promise, in this lifetime at any rate, heroic overcoming. Strands of Christianity today that continue this commitment to truth in advertising continue to promise only coping, not overcoming. Nor do they suggest that the hope of equanimity in the next life negates the need for ongoing transformation of consciousness and life on this side of the grave.

4. The positive transformation of consciousness requires guidance or mentoring

The Western mystical tradition got it both right and wrong. What it got right is that a positive transformation of consciousness requires guidance or mentoring. What it often got wrong is the notion that the guide must be an individual. Guidance can also come from community as it shares its collective wisdom and insight, often distilled and mediated through prose and poetry, through drama and dance, through music and visual art, through bonds of family and circles of friends.

Another Western quirk is that if books or plays and the like undertake the role of guidance, then more is always better: reading more books, attending more theater, absorbing more visual or musical art. I beg to differ. Martin Luther once observed that 200 books well read, reread, and reflected upon would lead to both deeper and broader wisdom than a thousand books hastily read and not permitted to confront, comfort, challenge or change a person effectively, and I agree. The dilettante is a poor candidate for a transformation of consciousness. My own candidacy may not be much better: I tend, in pride, to hold potential mentors and mentoring at bay.

Conclusion

These musings about the transformation of consciousness are more notable for what they omit than what they include. For instance, there are few definitions of terms: this rough guide provides no glossary. The elaboration of ideas and examples is spare: this rough guide makes no claim to completeness. But perhaps there is something here to spark a train of thought or to encourage a conversation, something to evoke a hesitant "yes" or an emphatic "no!" If one or more of those things happen, then the modest mission of this rough guide is accomplished: an itinerary is begun, or revisited, or continued in a direction previously unexplored.

Finally, when I do let my guard down, what insight, integration, and transformation of consciousness have I experienced in the developing world? The platitude "It is better to give than to receive" begins to become a principle incorporated into my life; begins to penetrate my understanding as an expression of the nature of reality at its base; begins to be discerned as an axiom that integrates and gives meaning and purpose to life but that, like all axioms, remains unproved and incapable of proof; begins to be experienced as a correcting or transforming resource when my life gets out of synch with reality and meaning and purpose. It is only a beginning; yet it is enough to sustain me, if only for a time, when I return to my home culture.

Why is it that I have returned repeatedly to the developing world for help? Let me end with another quote from the same personal journal cited at the beginning:

> I don't fully trust anyone who has not suffered profoundly, wrestled with the meaningfulness or pointlessness of suffering, and at least occasionally shaken an angry fist at God because of it. By these criteria, particularly the first, I myself am not to be trusted. And I don't. This is one factor, though not the only, that impels me to go back to Latin America this autumn. Even, perhaps especially, in my profession as a Christian theologian I don't trust myself. I need to check my intuitions, insights, and inferences against those of people who suffer, agonize, and protest. They are there: Christians who fight the good fight of faith not in an amphitheatre of stone but in the arena of social, political, and economic

structures. They are, frankly, wimpy warriors doing battle against the principalities and powers of this world.

They are also the most transparent, inspiring, and joyful people I have ever known.

Response:
Seeker sensitive

Kim Wilkens

I've been caught up with labels lately: conservative vs. liberal, modern vs. post-modern, churched vs. un-churched, believer vs. seeker. Labels carry a lot of baggage that don't necessarily apply, but that does not stop us from using them. They are such a convenient way of categorizing someone and thereby trying to understand them.

When I think about what it means to be a Christian, the labels I immediately stumble on are believer vs. seeker. If forced to pick between calling myself a believer or a seeker, I would have to say that I am a seeker. Belief for me is fleeting. It's like the wisp of a smoke ring hanging in the air and then melting away. I can see it for a moment, but then it's gone and there's only the memory of it. I think that's why I write, to make remembering easier.

Many churches are trying to reach seekers. My church is trying to reach seekers. Most churches call this ministry outreach or witnessing. As a seeker, it makes me cringe. When I think of witness, I think of evangelism and when I think of evangelism, I think of hypocritical tele-evangelists or roaming Jehovah's Witnesses. I'm actually hypersensitive when I read or participate in discussions about how, when, why, where churches should, could, would approach the "seekers." The way some people talk about it and write about it, seeking usually sounds like kind of a bad thing, a less than thing, as if someone seeking is in need of remedial intervention. So, I loved finding the *Wineskins for Discipleship* blog (discipleshipgroups.blogspot.com) that has re-characterized "seeker."

In their ministry, a seeker is no longer someone out there seeking a church; a target of ministry campaigns to bring them in and convert them to membership. A seeker is someone seeking the spiritual dimension of discipleship, whether it is an "un-churched" or "de-churched" person who is looking for answers by trying out churches or a "churched" person who finds they are lacking in this dimension of their faith journey. Seeking is actually a discipleship goal!

I can't speak for all seekers, but I can tell you what kind of "witnessing" I'm looking for:

Respect my journey. Walk with me on my journey. Engage me where I am. I think my dad provides a great example of this. He has known since my college days that I was disillusioned with Christianity. But he respected my journey, he didn't try to block my way or change my course; instead he provides unconditional love, support, and examples of Christlike behavior.

Please don't try to save my soul. My soul is not yours to save and I don't think you should really be worried about it. Jesus did not ask his followers to make "believers" out of all nations, he asked them to make disciples. I think one of my favorite hymns, "They'll Know We Are Christians By Our Love,"[4] provides a good outline for making disciples: pray for unity, work side by side, walk hand in hand, and be recognized as a Christian because of your love.

Let me be authentic. I question everything. If you know my son, it appears this may be hereditary. I need a safe environment to be authentic in, to raise my questions and doubts. I need to be comfortable showing my weaknesses, flaws, and spiritual struggles. Only then will I be able to grow.

Chapter Endnotes

1. A paper written in the winter of 2003. See also the homily in ch. 15, "Conformation classes I have taken and taught," for additional reflections on the notion of transformation.
2. See the background essay in ch. 3 for additional comments on this text.
3. Paul Tillich, *The Courage To Be*, *op. cit.*
4. Words and music by Peter Scholtes (F.E.L. Publications, Ltd., 1966).

Chapter 26

The Mothering Vocation of God

Background essay

Tom Wilkens

I did a doctorate in historical theology at the University of Aberdeen in Scotland between 1966 and 1968. In those two busy years, I focused most of my time on the research for and the writing of the dissertation. It was for me, at that point in my life, an experience of heaven on earth.

We made some good Scottish friends in Aberdeen. Two of them, John and Enid Scott, invited us in January of 1968 to the annual Robbie Burns' Night Supper in the city. It was a most festive occasion that included a ritual dear to every Scottish heart: the piping of the haggis. Haggis is a mixture of sheep's "pluck" (heart, liver, and lungs) minced with onions, oatmeal, and spices, stuffed into the sheep's stomach, and boiled. Once ready and — behind a bagpiper — after wending its way on a platter through the great hall to the head table, the haggis was then dramatically speared, apportioned, and served to all of the guests. Haggis turned out to be, like so many traditional ethnic foods, quite filling but not particularly tasty. Traditional foods were meant primarily to fill up the stomach, not to delight the palate.

I recall that the speaker of the evening had set for himself an impossible task. He tried to convince the audience that Burns had possessed a deep respect for women. Now Robert Burns was a truly great poet, no doubt the best that Scotland has ever produced. But he was also a womanizing rake with apparently no morning-after regrets. It is difficult to make a feminist silk purse out of a sexist sow's ear. Even I saw through the speaker's game.

I say "even I." It is not that I had a whole lot of awareness of or sensitivity to women's issues at this time. After all, I had attended a male-only seminary just a few years earlier and it had not occurred to me that the absence of women as classmates and professors was passing strange. Perhaps this undistinguished speech meant to honor a distinguished poet prompted the first small step in my coming to realize the long history of discrimination women have endured and to recognize a legitimate and in many instances urgent women's agenda.

Women's voices began to catch my ear and feminist issues started to form a larger part of my own agenda in the ensuing years. Much of my growing awareness of women's deeply rooted problems and growing support for efforts to solve them came initially from the writings of feminist theologians, from female colleagues, and from female students. But the greatest influence with respect to these concerns has turned out to be my wife, Betty.

Our marriage had begun in a context of traditional gender stereotypes. Among other things, those notions prevented me for some years from appreciating Betty's toughness of spirit, her realism, and her determination. I had the "certain things cannot be said or shared with her lest she cannot handle them" mindset. How wrong I was. How much more she has meant to me — and, I think, I have meant to her — since I began to outgrow that demeaning, paternalistic view.

If you were to ask her, she would tell you that even today I have not left behind all of the sexist baggage that men of my generation have habitually carried. At times unasked, she lets me know when I regress to patterns of sexism and paternalism that she finds objectionable. She gets on my case, quietly and with little dramatic flair. This is one of the vocations of a spouse. Whatever rough edges have been smoothed out in my life have come about primarily as the result of my relationship with Betty. She is my most effective confronter. Yet she is also my most reliable comforter. I am, in this matter as so many others, a work in progress. Her continual, typically unspoken question of me has to be this: are you making sufficient progress? Her continual affirmation has always been and remains today an unconditional love that accepts even an unsatisfactory answer. She is, to use an expression coined by Luther, the most significant "little Christ" in my life and world.

Peter Cartwright was the most famous of the nineteenth century circuit-riding preachers. These were people who served clusters of Christians in areas, typically on the American frontier, where they had few permanent pastors. Cartwright kept an extensive journal of his ministry. One interesting bit of information that comes from the journal is this: as a circuit rider he had preached around 14,000 sermons.

That statistic always amazed my students. It figures out to one sermon a day for over 38 years. They could scarcely believe it. I then told them that on some days he would have preached more than one sermon. I further suggested that he had not preached 14,000 different sermons: it was more probable that, as a circuit rider with ever-new audiences, he had preached fourteen sermons a thousand times each. This was an exaggeration, of course. But the truth is that most preachers — not just circuit riders — repeat sermons, especially after they move from one congregation to another.

The closest I have come to the circuit-riding model of preaching happened while we lived in Scotland. When the Scots discovered a Lutheran pastor in their midst, they invited me to preach in congregations of the Church of Scotland throughout the country. At that point, busy with my research and writing, I really did not have time for sermon preparation. I had brought a single homily along from my years in the parish; I preached it over and over again. I got pretty good at it by the end. I assume that Peter Cartwright did also.

You will find the seeds of the following homily contained in a section of "The last homily" (chapter 16), preached nearly five years earlier in a different setting. I have done this kind of thing a few times after my retirement. I no longer have the excuse of the pressure of time. But if I find that what I said "there and then" seems to need saying again "here and now," I spend my preparation time refining or — as I did with the next homily — expanding the message and taking into account the new context in which it will be presented. And I always revisit the biblical texts. The occasional use of "prepackaged" fare — of my own mixes, to be sure, and not someone else's — seems to me a better stewardship of my time and energy than always doing "scratch" sermon preparation.

271

The mothering vocation of God[1]

Tom Wilkens

The text

At that very hour some Pharisees came and said to him, "Get away from here, for Herod wants to kill you." He said to them, "Go and tell that fox for me, 'Listen, I am casting out demons and performing cures today and tomorrow, and on the third day I finish my work. Yet today, tomorrow, and the next day I must be on my way, because it is impossible for a prophet to be killed outside of Jerusalem.' Jerusalem, Jerusalem, the city that kills the prophets and stones those who are sent to it! How often have I desired to gather your children as a hen gathers her brood under her wings, and you were not willing! See, your house is left to you. And I tell you, you will not see me until the time comes when you say, 'Blessed is the one who comes in the name of the Lord.' "

— Luke 13:31—35

A prayer

Let us pray:

Mothering God, you gave me birth
in the bright morning of this world.
Creator, source of every breath,
you are my rain, my wind, my sun.

Mothering Christ, you took my form,
offering me your food of light,
grain of new life and grape of love,
your very body for my peace.

Mothering Spirit, nurt'ring one,
in arms of patience hold me close,
so that in faith I root and grow
until I flow'r, until I know.[2]
Amen.

Exegesis and hermeneutics

Mothering God. Mothering Christ. Mothering Spirit. During my relatively brief career as a parish pastor and my relatively lengthy career as a college professor, gender has been one of the most persistent and pervasive issues on both the sacred and the secular agendas. Gender: gender as a formative influence in human development; gender as an important factor in the social, political, economic, and religious spheres of life.

Gender as an issue seems almost omnipresent. It manifests itself in matters ranging from the roles of women in church and society to the male gender bias of our language in both liturgy and life. Gender as an issue discussed and debated has the power both to divide the human family and the family of God, and to unite sub-groups within both of those families. Gender has been a basis for prejudice or privilege for millennia. It has also been a source of strength for millions.

Most of us are, I'm sure, familiar with the specific gender problems that have been articulated in our culture over the past several decades: unequal pay for women; the glass ceiling over the work space of women; an inequitably high incidence of poverty among women; an unconscionably high incidence of physical violence directed toward women. The litany is long and familiar.

And men don't escape the problem. We have to deal with such things as what I sometimes call the John Wayne Syndrome: living up to a cultural gender expectation that real men don't cry or become emotional — except, perhaps, in destructive ways. Or the bias in custody disputes that somehow a woman's claim to the children is, simply by virtue of her gender, stronger than a man's.

These gender matters and others are global in scope. And in many cultures, especially those in the developing world, women in particular experience gender discrimination with an intensity not known in our own culture for decades. Yet in my observations and in the observations of those charged with studying these matters in more depth, many of the women on the receiving end of gender bias turn out to be stronger and more resourceful than their detractors.

For example, it is mostly the women in Russia who refuse to give up in the face of the chaos and corruption of their society. Many of the men of Russia are caught up in a crisis of self-confidence and hopelessness, aggravated by alcoholism, that has reduced the life expectancy of Russian males by nearly a decade since the breakup of the Soviet Union. Russian women, on the other hand, have held their own. Women are the weaker sex? Not in Russia.

Another example of gender strength and resourcefulness came to my attention recently in an e-mail I received from Pastor Judy McGuire, a missionary whom the mission team from Christ Lutheran recently met in Guyana. I have her permission to read the following excerpt:

> In the five churches where I help out, there hasn't been a Lutheran women's organization in years so I decided to begin the Lutheran Church Women in that area. When asked what the women would like to see happen or what their objectives would be, their reply in unison was, "Pastor, all we want is an in-depth Bible study. We don't want anything else. Can't we just have a Bible study?" Due to my "other" job, my time is minimal but we have in-depth Bible studies twice per month. We've begun by studying one woman in the Bible each time. During the second session, my eyes and ears were opened while studying Lydia, a head of household and businesswoman. When I asked whether any of them had been businesswomen, they nodded their heads "yes" and then started explaining.
>
> Ninety percent of them had been or are business women out of necessity — growing crops and selling them in the market, sewing for others, selling newspapers — whatever they could find to do in order to sustain their children and themselves. The majority have had or presently have husbands who were/are drinkers and abusers, leaving the responsibility of caring for the children and keeping home and soul together to the women. The Bible study turned into a Bible study and therapy session. Usually an outsider would not hear any of this, but I suppose they've never had a woman with whom they could share their burdens. When the *door* tweaked open, they opened their *hearts* as well. One could think this is just a select group of women who share the same sorrows, but after questioning many others, I'm learning their stories are not unusual for women of about 35 years old and older. Praise God life is beginning to change for the younger generations.

What has all of this to do with our gospel text for today? Let me reread the verse 34 from the Lukan passage:

> Jerusalem, Jerusalem, the city that kills the prophets and stones those who are sent to it! How often have I desired to gather your children as a hen gathers her brood under her wings, and you were not willing!

We have in this text one of the very few female gender metaphors used to describe Jesus and his ministry: Jesus as a hen mothering her chicks. Luke, more than any other gospel, portrays a Jesus devoid of much of the male gender-bias of his day. Luke's take on Jesus is that Jesus took women, their contributions, and their needs seriously — an

274

unusual thing for a man of his time to do.[3] Yet the church, in succeeding generations, decided against traveling this new road of the affirmation of women. Fewer and fewer women found themselves accepted in leadership roles. Few female-gender metaphors for God emerged in Christian discourse. Women and their work were placed on pedestals, not to honor them but to marginalize them.

Let me be more specific with respect to our situation here at Christ Lutheran. We are looking for new pastoral leadership. How would we respond if the call committee placed a woman's name before us? Would the gender question come to the fore? Would we vote on the basis of the qualities and experience of the candidate or on the basis of gender? Would we embrace the idea of a woman's pastoral leadership or would we rationalize that the timing is somehow not right? Does that issue, timing, ever arise with a male candidate?

I belong to what appears to be a growing segment in both church and society which holds that these gender issues are important, that gender problems remain significant and not fully resolved today. But within this segment there is little agreement as to strategies or tactics to deal with gender bias. For example, some would like to de-gender our theology — our God-talk — and our liturgy. On this matter I find myself agreeing with the German systematic theologian Wolfhart Pannenberg, who holds that de-gendering is not really a good idea. There is, he argues, too much essential and irreplaceable content in the notion of God as father in our tradition to lay that notion aside. The problem, it seems to me, is not with male-gender metaphors for God. The problem is with male-biased communities of faith neglecting to nurture and be nurtured also by female-gender metaphors for God.

Therefore, maybe bringing more gender balance into our God-talk is the answer. One approach to this that has gained some support is to focus on the Third Person of the Trinity — the Holy Spirit — as a promising point from which to expand our appreciation for the feminine side of God. This focus is augmented at times by an emphasis on God as Wisdom (*Sophia* in Greek), the nominal embodiment of God as feminine, perhaps even of God as Goddess.

However, I prefer the approach taken by the poem that I used as a prayer at the beginning of this sermon. The words are based on writings by a woman named Julian of Norwich, a medieval mystic whose contemplative life focused on the mystery of divine love. The hymn is traditional in that it is Trinitarian. It is non-traditional in that it declares a feminine side to each Person of the Trinity: mothering God, mothering Christ, mothering Spirit. I suspect that for Julian of Norwich God was bi-genderal.

For myself, I suspect that God — like all good single parents — fulfills both the fathering and the mothering vocations. As God's children, however, we tend only to recognize and respond to God's fathering role. We may, for instance, do little better in our generation than did Jerusalem of old in reacting to Jesus' mothering desire to gather us into intimate community — symbolized by a brood of chicks closely huddled under a mother hen's wings.

What do we gain by breaking out of a male-exclusive mindset with respect to God? We gain half of the world's population as potential theological mentors and spiritual guides, whose mentoring and guidance come out of the very depths of their identity and experience as women of God and of God as woman. As a man, I gain new perspective on God mediated through feminine identity and experience, but only if women agree to be my tutors and I agree to be tutored. Some women have agreed; sometimes I agree. Not always. The community of God's people needs more women as trusted and respected guides, more men and women under their guidance, more access to the mothering vocation of God.

Let us pray:

> *Come among us Mothering God, Mothering Christ, Mothering Spirit. As you gave birth to us as the Alpha, the fertile source and beginning of all, so also embrace us at last as the Omega, the welcoming goal and end of all. Come among us Birthing God, Feeding Christ, Nurturing Spirit. Amen.*

Response:
A rebel without a clue

Kim Wilkens

Rebellion permeates all aspects of human life. It originates from the subconscious will of mankind not to surrender to destructive forces. But rebelling is not the same as defining a cause that would improve the quality of human life, or formulating a constructive program of action. Marching in a parade is easier than blazing a trail through a forest or creating a new Jerusalem. Daumier's hero looks like many rebels in our midst. He is fighting against evil rather than for a well-defined cause. Like most of us, he is a rebel without a program.[4]

— René Dubos

I've always had a rebellious nature. I don't think it's riotous or boisterous; it's more driven and determined. My primary cause has been feminism. My earliest memory of this rebellion was at some extended family gathering, probably Thanksgiving or Christmas. At the end of the meal, I noticed the women go into the kitchen and the men go to the living room. That didn't seem right to me, so I announced that I was not going to the help in the kitchen, I'd hang out with the guys instead. And as I've heard my mother say to me on many occasions the response I got was, "Where do you get these ideas?"

Well, she's not completely blameless. Even though she did a majority of the domestic chores and actually claimed to enjoy cleaning — "it's therapeutic," she said — my mom also balanced being a stay-at-home mom with a part-time nursing career (working the late shift). She was on the cutting edge of childbirth education, bringing couples into our home for Lamaze training when other facilities were not available or more likely not ready to support this radical new approach to childbirth.

My feminist rebellion energized me to excel academically. It drove me into the male-dominated field of computer science. It pushed me up the corporate ladder. It alienated me from religion. Sue Monk Kidd in *The Dance of the Dissident Daughter* gives a very good description of what this alienation feels like:

> A girl, forming her identity also experiences herself missing from pronouns in scripture, hymns, and prayers. And most of all, as long as God "himself" is exclusively male, she will experience the otherness, the lessness, of herself; all the pious talk in the world about females being equal to males will fail to compute in the deeper places inside her.[5]

For several years, I was humming along quite nicely in my feminist cause, but then I had a child, left corporate America, turned forty and had a huge identity crisis. I had done well in a man's world, but now I found myself in the world of motherhood. How was I supposed to excel at something I had no training for? What was happening to my feminist agenda? I thought I was helping to pave the way for the women after me to be treated as equals, but instead I was just playing by the rules of corporate America and they no longer seemed adequate for my life. I felt like a rebel without a clue. I needed to redefine the rules for living my life.

First, I tried finding balance. I searched for the magical formula that would give me just the right balance between family-life, career-life, community-life, volunteer-life and church-life. It felt like a juggling act and when I would get too much of one and not enough of the others, I started feeling out of control and unbalanced. I would lose track of some of the balls. I would have to regroup and try to figure out the formula again. Usually the new formula worked for a time, it was fresh and it was fun and exhilarating! But I would end up in a cycle of trying to arrange the balls just so, putting them up in the air, and juggling them for a while until I started to lose some of them. This strategy for living wasn't working either.

Then I heard an interview on NPR with a soldier in Iraq. He said he had to compartmentalize his soldier-life and his home-life. He gave an example of a cell phone conversation with his wife: She's talking about her "bad" day with the kids and he's thinking about his "bad" day cleaning up dead bodies. Compartmentalization was necessary for him to focus on the task at hand or he might get shot. But the cost is high as it wreaks havoc on relationships because the whole person is never completely present.

It struck me that this is what I've been doing. I hadn't been thinking of it as compartmentalization, but as I was performing my juggling act, I was really assigning out pieces of myself to get the tasks done. When I was working on one task, another part of me was usually occupied with lists that need to be completed for other tasks. I was rarely wholly involved with the task or relationship or situation at hand.

My new cause is wholeness. "There is nothing more important than being fully where we are, in the plain ordinary events, day in and day out. I think women understand that we create change as we live out the experiences of our souls in the common acts of life."[6] Where I used to be like Martha, worried and distracted, I am trying to be more like Mary, taking time to learn about Jesus (Luke 10:38-42).

I find my new cause still has room for the frustration I feel toward gender issues found in many religious institutions. Instead of fighting against the male/female stereotypes that have kept me from moving forward in my faith, I feel that God wants me to walk humbly through these human failures and acknowledge them. I believe that God can reorient the whole world from one of inequality to one of equality and I believe God wants you and me to help.

Chapter Endnotes

1. A homily presented at Christ Lutheran Church, Georgetown, Texas on March 7, 2004.
2. See "The last homily" in ch. 16 for more background to this hymn, here used as a prayer.
3. It is significant, I believe, that the editors of the Lukan gospel do not include Mark's story of Jesus' confrontation with the Syrophoenician woman, though the Matthean gospel does. See the background essay in ch. 3 for an interpretation of the Markan version of the story.
4. René Dubos, *So Human an Animal: How We Are Shaped by Surroundings and Events* (Transaction Publishers, 1998), 6.
5. Sue Monk Kidd, *The Dance of the Dissident Daughter: A Woman's Journey from Christian Tradition to the Sacred Feminine* (HarperCollins Publishers, 1996), 29f.
6. *Ibid.*, 222.

CHAPTER 27

THE SYMPTOM IS CORRUPTION, BUT THE SYNDROME IS IDOLATRY

Background essay

Tom Wilkens

Our congregation in Georgetown, Texas, teams up with a congregation in Tulsa, Oklahoma, to send two service mission teams each year to the small South American country of Guyana. Betty participated in the annual medical project in October of 2003. I joined the annual construction project in February of 2004. Most often we have done international service activities together, but in this instance we went with different teams. The homily that follows was developed on the background of my experience in Guyana. However, that experience was itself influenced by the report that Betty had brought back from her time there.

Betty has more recently (January 2008) participated in her second service mission to Guyana. Guyanese Lutherans have also visited the Tulsa and Georgetown congregations, sharing their considerable resources of faith, hope, and love. Such interchanges are essential to healthy developed-world/developing-world relationships.

In fact, similar service efforts are being replicated by a large and growing number of congregations sending work groups to developing nations all over the globe. And these small efforts are, as I have said earlier, very effective in dealing with symptoms of need. But they are not enough. A more comprehensive approach is required.

Most people in this hemisphere are familiar with the story of the Good Samaritan. That narrative has all sorts of moral implications for the Christian life. However, the story takes place in a rural setting and not an in urban milieu. Some Christian ethicists and biblical theologians have argued that the account needs some fairly radical recontextualization if it is to register relevantly with urban Christians today.

In the story, a man is robbed, beaten, and left for dead. He presents obviously severe symptoms of suffering. The point of the story is that whenever we encounter a person with such marks of misery we need to respond generously, effectively, and over the long haul: This is what it means to be a good neighbor.

But we no longer live in a world where we encounter the symptoms of suffering only occasionally, as individual incidents resulting from particular and quite circumscribed sets of conditions. We live in a world where much suffering — especially things like hunger, disease, and political oppression — results from pervasive underlying conditions: namely, unjust structures in society that are distorted and manipulated to the detriment of billions of people. The symptoms have become overwhelming, necessitating structural change and not just more palliative relief.

Thus there are two main strategies for dealing with human hurt and need. *First*, there is the strategy of alleviating the symptoms of distress directly. Clearly this is an obligation of the people of God in the world, spelled out in no uncertain terms in the biblical literature and carried forward through the centuries by both Jews and Christians until our own day. We are to love our neighbors — especially our suffering neighbors — as ourselves: in practical, down-to-earth ways with practical, down-to-earth effect.

The *second* strategy — also modeled in the Bible, though less frequently so — the second strategy has to do with changing the systems and structures of society in order to reduce the symptoms of suffering. One example of this is the phenomenon mentioned in the Hebrew scriptures called the Year of Jubilee. Years of Jubilee were to be observed once every half-century: All land was to be returned to its ancestral owners and all Israelite slaves were to be freed. It was a countrywide plan designed to redistribute land — the source of wealth — more equitably and to restore freedom to the enslaved. It was a formula meant to level the playing field of life.

In sum: The goal of the first strategy is to relieve the symptoms of human misery. The goal of the second is, by changing unjust economic and social conditions, to reduce those symptoms. Today we could also add unjust political structures to the second strategy's agenda. A leading sociologist of religion once called the first strategy "Christian welfare" and the second "Christian action."[1] Using more biblical language, we might describe them as the "priestly call to care" and the "prophetic call to change" models.

What are the positives of the first strategy, of providing symptom-oriented service to those in need? There are many; let me mention just three. First, we have both biblical and historical warrants for this kind of activity by the people of God. From the offering of what could at times be life-saving hospitality to friends and strangers alike in the Hebrew scriptures to the New Testament story of the Good Samaritan mentioned above, we have a responsibility spelled out unambiguously: to help; to assist; to cooperate in the repair of those who are broken, such as battered women and children; to participate in the reclamation of those who have been shunted aside, such as the homeless. We do have a priestly call to care, a Christian obligation that turns out to be an opportunity: to attend to the welfare of those who — in whatever way — aren't making it.

Second, these efforts — even the smallest of them — make real differences in the real lives of people. Never underestimate the power of a gesture, of a kind word spoken, of a bit of time or talent or treasure shared.

Third, virtually all provisions of service are widely appreciated and applauded. Reputations of the service providers do not suffer. And, with rare exceptions, their lives are neither endangered nor diminished. In truth, such lives are typically enriched and fulfilled in ways that surprise and amaze.

Those are some of the positives of working to relieve the symptoms of suffering. But there are also some negatives. How, for instance, can we dispense much-needed welfare without patronizing the recipients or rendering them chronically dependent on that welfare? It is not easily accomplished. However, the most disheartening downside, the most troublesome and persistent problem is this: we can never do enough. As stated earlier, no matter how much we give of ourselves and our possessions, the symptoms seem to multiply much faster than the resources we have for dealing with them. Is this, then, how it ends: we win a million small skirmishes and yet still lose the war?

Surely Jesus saw this serious problem in his day. He came from one of the least prosperous regions of Palestine. He knew firsthand about the omnipresence of poverty and of the poor. He no doubt understood that, for all the good it accomplished, his healing ministry did not eradicate disease. There is an additional strategy that also needs to be in place. Let me say a few words next about this other way: an approach that elicits many more raised eyebrows, disquieting concerns, and even outspoken criticisms. This second, alternative strategy seeks to transform the very structures of our society.

The social, economic, and political systems that surround, sustain, and sometimes diminish us did not drop from heaven. These are human constructs. We are responsible not only for the good they make possible but also for the evil they sometimes cause. We need to take ownership, not as uncritical propagandists but as critical people willing to change the systems when they become unfair and unjust, when they fail to provide for basic human needs, and when they dampen the flame of hope.

How do we do this? We can, for example, connect with organizations that promote what we hold to be sound public policies. Some might join the Sierra Club, to work for laws that will result in healthier, more sustainable ecosystems. Others might join Lutherans for Life, a group concerned for the unborn. Or we could participate in a public demonstration — a march, if you will — for or against some practice or policy that we care about deeply. We could, in other words, take part in efforts designed to change the very systems and structures of society.

What are the positives of this second strategy? Let me mention just two. *First*, peace, justice, and community well-being are social issues, not just individual matters. They require more than generous personal responses; they require wise systemic change, especially if we wish to reduce the incidence of the symptoms of suffering.

Second, this action agenda for systemic change also has biblical warrant, such as the Year of Jubilee mentioned before. More generally, the prophets of old issued clarion calls for justice and peace. And they held those in authority accountable. These days, in a democracy, that's us. We must quit complaining about "them" and start fixing what is wrong with our local, statewide, and national systems and structures — systems and structures that all too often favor the "haves" at the expense of the "have-nots."

However, there are some negatives, some problem areas here. In America, we have a special challenge with respect to the relationship of church and state. How can the church engage in advocacy on behalf of the poor without becoming embroiled in partisan politics? By the way, if as a church we do engage in partisan politics, we will lose some rights and privileges, including the privilege of tax exemption. Will there ever come a time when our obligation to justice or to peace will demand that we give up that privilege?

If it all seems a bit extreme, consider this: one of the major-party candidates for president this past year was an African-American. Whether or not you concur with his views and whether or not you voted for him in the fall election, I think we can all agree that his nomination and election represent a watershed in American social and political history. These developments are inconceivable apart from the Civil Rights movement, led by the black church and its leaders. That movement would not and could not have achieved the civil rights and voting rights legislative victories without civil disobedience. They — including Rosa Parks and Martin Luther King Jr. — they had to break the law in order to change the law. Most white Christians were too uncomfortable with that tactic to participate. It is, however, interesting to note that in the New Testament era, when the line between religious and civil matters was not always sharply drawn, the disciples and Jesus engaged in two acts of disobedience: the disciples broke the law about Sabbath rest by picking grain and Jesus broke it by healing on the Sabbath day.[2]

Will it come to that for us, for you or for me: breaking the law or becoming martyred? Likely not, though at least some of us should be prepared, as an old Sunday school song put it, to dare to be a Daniel — or a Rosa Parks or a Martin Luther King Jr. — if that is what it takes to pursue justice and to press for peace in a distorted and troubled world. Is public action for systemic change my calling? Is it yours? If not, will we at least support those who do respond? Will we lend our good names and our considerable resources to the cause of peace with justice? I would hope that the answer is a clear, immediate, and compelling "Yes!" And I suspect that Jesus has the same hope and expectation.

I should think that we are not dealing here with an either/or dilemma: that either the Christian welfare people have it right or the Christian action camp is correct. We are dealing rather with a both/and situation. We need to continue to relieve symptoms of suffering by feeding the hungry child, treating the diseased mother, and housing the homeless family. And we must continue our development efforts, such as teaching improved agricultural techniques and training health care workers and educators. However, this good work must be augmented by opposing unjust systems and by challenging policies that lead not to peace but to war, not to enough for all but to more than enough for only a few. Not everyone is good at both of these strategies; some of us are better at addressing symptoms, others at assessing and transforming structures. But we all need to be mutually supportive — not critical of one another, not dismissive of the strategy that other folks might be pursuing. Too often this has not been the case.

Does all of this — or any of this — make sense? Does all of this — or any of this — fall within the scope of God's will and purpose? And where does Jesus fit into the picture? Jesus has high yet not impossible expectations of us all: that we will use our energy and our creativity to move the whole of humanity — from the neighbor down the street to the neighbor around the globe — toward well-being, justice, and peace. The good news — the gospel — not only proclaims forgiveness. It also promises a life of meaning and purpose through working with and for the world, both the world of people and the world of nature.

This gospel life is not about selfishness, but about selflessness; not about acquiring, but about distributing; not about keeping more and keeping score, but about uncalculating liberality and service; not about protecting our own status, but about raising the status of others, particularly those of "low estate." It sounds a bit scary; it appears to be somewhat countercultural; it may challenge some long-held views and values. Nonetheless, followers of Jesus discover that — compared with the competitive pressures of the world to succeed, to be tough, to look good, to be cool 24/7, to craft a worthwhile goal for life and then to calculate a trajectory for reaching it — compared with all that, Jesus' yoke of cooperative service is easy and his burden of mutual support is light.

To live the gospel life, we not only need good hearts, recreated by God; we also need good heads, renewed and transformed by God. We need to discern when and where and how to apply the strategies of alleviating the symptoms of suffering *and* of changing systems when they produce or increase suffering. May we be granted those good hearts and good minds. May we be given not only convictions, but also the courage of our convictions: to accompany those in pain and in need as they take their journeys toward healing and wholeness. May our pilgrimages be shaped by the gospel of life, not by a culture of death.

The symptom is corruption, but the syndrome is idolatry[3]

Tom Wilkens

Introduction

Last April, *Time* magazine published another one of its occasional special issues. It was called "The *Time* 100," and its subtitle was "The lives and ideas of the world's most influential people." As I scanned the issue, one article in particular intrigued me. It was titled "Bjorn Lomborg: Green contrarian." It caught my eye because the article's author wrote that the Danish scientist "just might be the Martin Luther of the environmental movement."[4] As I read on, it was not Lomborg's specific ideas about the environment but his general notion about the underlying causes of global problems that held my interest. According to Lomborg, corruption — in politics, in business, in most all of the systems and structures of society — corruption is one of ten major obstacles to solving global issues.

Though I do not have Lomborg's credentials, I would have to agree with his conclusion. Corruption seems omnipresent in the modern world. It is present in our developed world. It is present also in the developing world, where it appears to have even more devastating effects. Let me illustrate with an experience from Guyana, where I spent some time on a volunteer construction mission last February.

My first job on the construction site was to be the assistant to Robin, a young Guyanese licensed electrician who was also donating his labor. As we worked together, I learned some of Robin's story. He had been trying to build an electrical contracting business in Guyana. He'd made several bids on commercial and governmental projects. But even when he made the low bid, he didn't get the job. Why? Because he refused to pay the expected bribes. So he backed off, and Guyana lost another potential small businessperson and employer — which Guyana desperately needs.

I could tell that Robin was somewhat depressed about the whole matter. What I did not realize is how far he would go to relieve his depression. A few months after I left Guyana, I got an e-mail that reported that Robin had emigrated to Canada. Robin has joined a decades-long brain drain that has depleted Guyana of the majority of its educated people.[5] Score yet another victory for corruption, another defeat for hope.

The text

It turns out, of course, that corruption is not a modern invention. Let's take another look at the text read a moment ago:

> Hear this, you that trample on the needy,
>   and bring ruin to the poor of the land,
> saying, "When will the new moon be over
>   so that we may sell grain;
> and the sabbath,
>   so that we may offer wheat for sale?
> We will make the ephah small and the shekel great,
>   and practice deceit with false balances,
> buying the poor for silver
>   and the needy for a pair of sandals,
>   and selling the sweepings of the wheat."
>
> The Lord has sworn by the pride of Jacob:
> Surely I will never forget any of their deeds.
> Shall not the land tremble on this account,
>   and everyone mourn who lives in it,
> and all of it rise like the Nile,
>   and be tossed about and sink again, like the Nile of Egypt?
>   — Amos 8:4-7

Exegesis

First, a few brief exegetical comments: the "new moon" in the text refers to a monthly religious festival day when business was suspended. That practice apparently frustrated the commercial community, which saw it as a lost opportunity for profit. The term "ephah" refers to a dry measure of volume, roughly half a bushel. And the "shekel" was a standard unit of weight, approximately 15 grams. What was going on here was that the powerless poor were being ripped off by the powerful rich. It still happens with dismal regularity. I remember a few years ago listening to the frustration expressed by some Mexican peasants about the practice, apparently widespread in the bakeries in impoverished villages and neighborhoods, of merchants placing their thumbs on the scales while weighing out tortillas — the staff of life for Mexico's poor.

Hermeneutics

Amos the prophet spoke about the same reality as Lomborg the political scientist: corruption. In Amos' diagnosis, corruption is symptomatic of the syndrome called idolatry. Addressing the *symptom* — corruption — requires human vigilance and patience and an understanding of the chronic nature of corruption. It also helps to have a legal system relatively unscathed by corruption, something that developing-world countries do not typically enjoy.

Addressing the *syndrome* of idolatry, on the other hand, requires more drastic action. It requires the transforming power identified by Buddhists as enlightenment, by Christians as grace. It requires a transplant: a new heart, a new and right spirit.

There is little grace in Amos; the prophet didn't even bother to speculate about what might transpire if Israel would be transformed by repentance. His diagnosis is grim: Israel is obsessed by greed and compelled by corruption. His prognosis is grimmer still: Israel will be destroyed. Period. No negotiation. No more chances. The few words of hope toward the end of the book of Amos speak not of the avoidance of destruction but of the restoration of Israel *after* its ruination.

We are partners in a global economy where lust for wealth often energizes the entrepreneur and corruption frequently overwhelms the pursuer of economic justice. We are participants in a fractured and fractious yet nonetheless global society — where lust for power thrives and corruption disheartens the peacemaker and the nation-builder. These are the bleak realities outside of the comfortable corridors of academe.

I recall a class discussion here at Texas Lutheran some years ago. We were talking about end-of-life issues, issues such as finishing life strong and dying well. One student offered the opinion that he wanted to come to the end of his life without any regrets. He thought that he could die happy and well if he had no regrets about missed opportunities or misused time and talent. I wished him luck, but did not offer much hope. Lives without regrets do not happen often, if ever.

But there may be a way to reduce regret — learn, as early as you can, the lesson about God and mammon. The lesson is this: We cannot serve both God and gain. Don't wait until the end of your career to discover that you got it wrong. Let me repeat. Don't wait until the end of your career to discover that you got it wrong: that gain — power, prestige, popularity, prosperity, a Porsche — that gain is how you score and win the game of life. It is not gain; it is God. It is not win at any price, by any tactic. It isn't even win some, lose some. It is lose it all and, by the grace of God — I say that not as a vague and pious platitude but as a focused and incarnated principle — by the grace of God, gain God. If you ask me — or Robin, or Amos, or Jesus — we are beyond reform or repair; we need remanufacture. We need, to use a metaphor both biological and biblical, a rebirth. That rebirth is mediated by baptism, maintained by regular confession and absolution of sin, and manifested in changing lives — not perfect lives, but continuously reorienting lives.

Amos won't let us stop at the personal or individual level. Amos was concerned also about larger collective and corporate realities. In the social, political, and economic spheres we have another term in the modern world for the requisite transformation: revolution. The genius of the American revolution is that it took into account the need for constant vigilance against greed and corruption, against unjust manipulations of the law and its administration, and, though perhaps to a somewhat lesser extent, against unconscionable concentrations of wealth and power in fewer and fewer hands. These days we likely need less singing of "God Bless America" and more supplications that God would help us find a more just and peaceful way in the world. It will mean shedding American idols and seeking the just and generous Lord of the globe and of the universe.

The symptom is corruption, but the syndrome is idolatry. The symptom is disabling, but the syndrome is fatal. Where in this world of corporate greed and preemptive war and prisoner abuse is the call for personal and national confession and repentance? Where is the recognition of personal and public need for renewal? Christianity is not a serum that immunizes us from individual or corporate evil; it is a faith that helps us to cope with the darker dimensions of our reality. When the symptom is corruption and the syndrome is idolatry, the only solution is resurrection from the dead: from dead values and from deadly deeds.

Conclusion

There was a speaker from El Salvador, Jon Sobrino, here for a Krost Symposium some twenty years ago. Sobrino opened his address with these words: "I come to you from a culture of death." For the remainder of his presentation, you could have heard a pin drop among the audience of some 900 people. El Salvador was at that time the hunting ground of death squads, who sought out and murdered — by the thousands — those who spoke out on behalf of the poor and the oppressed. They even murdered the Archbishop, Óscar Romero.

I suspect that today we — you and I — belong to a culture of death. Not just the cultures of Islamic fundamentalism or ethnic-cleansing tribalism, but our own culture — increasingly focused on war, not peace; on acquiring, not sharing; on rage, not reconciliation. And yet often we are too distracted, too amused, too self-absorbed to notice. I suspect that, like Israel and the Israelites confronted by Amos, we are beyond repair or reform. But we are not beyond resurrection by God, a God who regularly has had to deal with toxic cultures that are in defiance and dying people who are in denial.

Response: This I believe

Kim Wilkens

"I hear that you refuse to worship my gods and the gold statue I have set up. Now I am going to give you one more chance. If you bow down and worship the statue when you hear the music, everything will be all right. But if you don't, you will at once be thrown into a flaming furnace. No god can save you from me." — Daniel 3:14-15; CEV

I've been doing a Bible study on the book of Daniel. One of the first lessons you encounter with Daniel has to do with the fiery furnace. I can remember the story from Sunday school as a child and now as it did then, it always prompts the question: Would I, like Daniel's three friends, be prepared to face the fiery furnace instead of bowing down to a false god? Beth Moore puts it this way: "I don't have to wonder what I'd do if placed in the position to die in order for one of my children to live. No discussion. No need to pray about it. It's done."[6] I agree that's a no-brainer. She goes on to ask if I've predetermined that same loyalty to Christ. I honestly don't think I know. I'm afraid that I do bow down to the false gods of my own Babylonian culture without much conscious thought. It's ingrained in me.

Maybe the question is difficult to answer because my beliefs have really never been put to such a test and probably never will be. I don't live in a culture where I could literally die for my beliefs. But I do live in a culture that could suck the life out of me for them and so I worry about what I believe. Beliefs are important. They define who we think we are and how we think about the world around us. But are there truly beliefs worth dying for, worth killing for, worth siding with the poor, the lost, and the lonely for? It seems to me that belief does more to divide and conquer than it does to bring us together to address the corruption and idolatry surrounding us. I like the way John Mayer describes the futility of fighting over beliefs in his song called "Belief."[7]

So if belief isn't what we should be fighting for, what is? What is worth standing up for instead of bowing down? I think it's based on the relationships we build and the love we share. Archbishop Óscar Romero didn't die for his beliefs; he died because he was in relationship with his community in El Salvador. Because of his love for his community and for his God, he stood up and spoke out against injustice.

We're trying something new in Charlottesville, Virginia. It's called IMPACT (Interfaith Movement Promoting Action by Congregations Together), a grassroots initiative bringing a diverse group of congregations together to live out our religious traditions' call for justice. So far there are 25 local congregations involved that range in size from 20 to 1,500 people, including Protestants, Catholics, Unitarian Universalists, Jews, and Muslims. While the concept of grassroots interfaith organizations that address social justice issues is not new in this country, it is

292

certainly new to Charlottesville and Albemarle County. I'm not sure any of us knew what to expect from this first year.

It has been a tremendous learning experience for me. As a member of IMPACT, I've been part of a community that determined what social justice issues to focus on, researched the core issues associated with the injustice, and identified solutions to address some of those issues. We met with public officials to explain our findings and express our desire for change. Before this experience, it was easy for me to believe that a particular party or a particular political figure was the "root of all evil." But more often than not during these meetings, what I discovered were blind spots and ignorance and a desire to come on board with the solutions if it was the will of the people. We started building relationships based on addressing social justice issues within our congregations, within our research groups and with our public officials. Because of those relationships over 1,300 people packed the high school auditorium at the first Nehemiah Action meeting, where we presented proposed solutions and many of our public officials were willing to sit up front and respond to the will of the people.

This was clearly not business as usual and there are still some politicians who don't understand why this organization can't work within the established processes. There are still some congregations that won't participate in this organization because of their belief that they shouldn't work with non-Christians. I don't understand that. It makes belief sound dangerous to me. It is so much easier for me to state what I don't believe. I don't believe in discrimination based on religious beliefs or political association or sexual orientation or gender or race or age. I don't believe in war. I don't believe in oppression. I don't believe in genocide or ethnic cleansing or poverty.

So, what do I believe? I believe in evolution. I believe in miracles. I believe in doubts. I believe in love. I believe that when I can somehow ignore what the world thinks is important and practice having an attitude that is "the same as that of Christ Jesus," I may then, on very rare occasions, briefly understand what Daniel's friends understood and I will stand up instead of bowing down.

Why do I find it so hard to write it down? As a Christian, there's usually an expectation that certain beliefs are non-negotiable. These are called articles of faith or creed and they usually define what it means to be Christian. I've always had a difficult time with them. Does that make me a heretic? As an American, I am called to stand up for my country and believe in our unalienable rights of life, liberty, and the pursuit of happiness. But at what cost to human rights and the environment around the world? Does questioning our public policies make me un-American?

Chapter Endnotes

1. See Peter Berger's classic critical analysis, *The Noise of Solemn Assemblies: Christian Commitment and the Religious Establishment in America* (Doubleday and Company, 1961), for a more thorough analysis of these categories.
2. See Matthew 12 and synoptic parallels.
3. A homily presented at Texas Lutheran University, on September 20, 2004.
4. Matt Ridley, "Bjorn Lomborg: Green contrarian," *Time* (April 26, 2004), 106.
5. Since its independence Guyana has lost over one-half of its entire population, mostly due to emigration. From a population of 1.5 million in 1966, its population in the 2007 census was only 770,000. It is projected to decline to 440,000 by 2020.
6. Beth Moore, *Daniel: Lives of Integrity, Words of Prophecy*, (LifeWay Press, 2007), 61.
7. John Mayer, *Belief* from the album *Continuum* (Aware Records LLC, 2006).

CHAPTER 28

GOD DOES NOT PULL WEEDS

Background essay

Tom Wilkens

Because I prepare fully articulated versions of my remarks in writing, my style of sermon delivery is sometimes called "manuscript preaching." I stand in good company. Even Jonathan Edwards, that most exceptional and effective colonial preacher — and arguably the leading American intellectual of his day — read his homilies from manuscripts in, as it happens, a high, thin, reed-like voice. There were no chancel-prancing theatrics or pulpit-thumping histrionics from him; nor do I indulge in them.

There is another expression that I think also describes my homiletical style: "stealth preaching." I often open a homily with a commonplace observation or a homespun yarn that poses no threat at all to the listeners. Then, once they are at ease, I strike a loud note or sound a discordant chord. The following homily illustrates this stealth technique. It begins with some innocuous lawn and garden comments, but it quickly moves on to a discussion of American civil religion that is meant to raise some serious issues and questions — even some hackles. Later on in the homily I remark on the hot-button topic of homosexuality.

Who would have anticipated this transition from the opening comments on yard maintenance? It is not that the introduction is disconnected from the main body; it is simply a bit misleading with respect to where the homily is going. Like a stealth airplane, it escapes most listeners' radar detection; the target is not immediately clear.

I want to write a few final words about my family, in this instance my siblings. I have a sister named Sue, nearly nine years younger than I, who is talented in so many ways. Trained as a teacher, she has become skilled in home design and decor. She is also a paradigm of equanimity, grace, and hospitality. Sue has been sorely tested in her personal life, especially by a difficult and contentious divorce that sparked deeply resentful, grudge-holding anger. Yet she has emerged with more tolerance, more of a forgiving spirit, and more strength and ability than ever to serve as a stable anchor for her children and grandchildren. Our lives are never fully under our control. Sue found, unexpectedly, that she had to plot a new course. I have been impressed with how well she has handled it. She herself calls the experience her graduate program in forgiveness.

I have previously referred to my brother Jim's baptism.[1] Jim is the bright one of our litter of four siblings. His mind is — and always has been — razor sharp. At one point during his career as a research chemist, and unknown to his employer, he did a law degree in night school. He served as the law review editor during his final year of the program. It must have been quite a juggling act to keep family, law school, and work all in motion during those years. Not long after passing the bar exam he began his second career, as a patent lawyer — first for the chemical company where he had done research and subsequently for The Ohio State University. Jim plotted this new course for his professional life by choice, not out of necessity. It registered with me as a remarkable accomplishment.

However, it is my oldest brother Frank who, among the siblings, has had the greatest impact on my life. It started early. When I was nearing my ninth birthday, our recently widowed maternal grandmother came to live with us. I lost my bedroom and moved in with Frank, who, though I was a potential "weed" in his "garden," never gave me any indication at all that this was an imposition for him. Because he was seven years older than I, when he gave brotherly advice and warnings — about such things as smoking — I listened. And he and Jim often included me in activities with their friends, which even at the time I recognized as a huge plus in my life.

It did not end there. Frank's generosity made my graduate program in Scotland financially feasible. Afterward he turned what was supposed to have been a loan into a gift. "Not to worry," he said. "I don't need it. Go have another kid." Our son, Nick, is deeply and permanently indebted. In the latter years, Frank and his wife, Maureen, have been incredibly generous with his sister and brothers. In short, very little of the life and service that I have shared in these essays, homilies, and papers would have been possible apart from him. I only hope that the imprint I am leaving can have something of the positive influence his mark on life has had and continues to have.

I have never asked him, but I doubt that Frank has ever thought consciously about being a role model — whether as a caring brother, a helpful son to our father and mother and stepson to our stepmother, or finally as the generous patriarch of our family. He just did it. One of his stock, self-effacing comments when he is confronted about an act of his kindness is this: "I must have been raised right." He was, of course; we all were. "Train children in the right way, and when old, they will not stray" (Proverbs 22:6). Sometimes this is the case, but not always. People well brought up do go badly astray occasionally. That we four siblings have not is to me another manifestation of grace at work in our lives.

God does not pull weeds[2]

Tom Wilkens

The text

He put before them another parable: "The kingdom of heaven may be compared to someone who sowed good seed in his field; but while everybody was asleep, an enemy came and sowed weeds among the wheat, and then went away. So when the plants came up and bore grain, then the weeds appeared as well. And the slaves of the householder came and said to him, 'Master, did you not sow good seed in your field? Where, then, did these weeds come from?' He answered, 'An enemy has done this.' The slaves said to him, 'Then do you want us to go and gather them?' But he replied, 'No; for in gathering the weeds you would uproot the wheat along with them. Let both of them grow together until the harvest; and at harvest time I will tell the reapers, Collect the weeds first and bind them in bundles to be burned, but gather the wheat into my barn.' "

Then he left the crowds and went into the house. And his disciples approached him, saying, "Explain to us the parable of the weeds of the field." He answered, "The one who sows the good seed is the Son of Man; the field is the world, and the good seed are the children of the kingdom; the weeds are the children of the evil one, and the enemy who sowed them is the devil; the harvest is the end of the age, and the reapers are angels. Just as the weeds are collected and burned up with fire, so will it be at the end of the age. The Son of Man will send his angels, and they will collect out of his kingdom all causes of sin and all evildoers, and they will throw them into the furnace of fire, where there will be weeping and gnashing of teeth. Then the righteous will shine like the sun in the kingdom of their Father. Let anyone with ears listen!"

— Matthew 13:24-30, 36-43

Introduction

In our family, my wife, Betty, has the green thumb. She is the one who plants and tends the flowers. She selects the shrubs and trees, and chooses where to place them. She does all of this very well, as one might expect that a former farm girl would. Our yard has a pleasing design and often exhibits a whole palette of colors.

My own contributions are minimal. I used to be the lawn person. I fertilized, watered, mowed, and trimmed. However, my success with the grass paled in comparison with Betty's success with the flowers and shrubbery. I was not very good at it and it showed. One of the ways it showed was that I was always changing the fertilizing sequences and buying different sprinklers, as though each year's new techniques and technologies might have enough magic to compensate for my own gardening shortcomings. They didn't. And so now, finally, we contract out our lawn care.

What does all of this have to do with this morning's sermon? More than you might think. You see, as a Lutheran clergyperson I usually develop sermons on the basis of biblical texts. But most of the biblical literature was written at a time when the majority of God's people were engaged in some form of agriculture. Thus the language, the imagery, and the settings for many stories and teachings have a decidedly farming or ranching flavor. Because of my non-farm background, I have to work extra hard and long to try to understand much of the Bible.

So please bear with me and be prepared to forgive comments that reveal my agricultural ignorance. The text that I have studied in preparation for this sermon is a familiar one, the parable of the weeds, from the gospel of Matthew.

300

Exegesis and hermeneutics

I have learned a great deal about texts from the so-called synoptic gospels — the gospels of Matthew, Mark, and Luke, which give us a synopsis or overview of the ministry and meaning of Jesus — from my long-time colleague and biblical scholar, Dr. Norman Beck. Dr. Beck continues to serve as a professor of theology at Texas Lutheran University. However, he is also a former farm boy and therefore can be trusted more than I with the interpretation of an agricultural story. He has made some observations about this text that I find both persuasive and helpful.[3]

First, who is the evil enemy in this parable? The answer is provided by Jesus' own explanation: the enemy is the devil. Yet we misread the text if we then conclude that this devil is some easily identifiable spiritual power, often envisioned in the popular imagination wearing a red costume and carrying a black pitchfork. The devil is no threat as a childish caricature, a cartoon character, or a special effect in a movie or video game. But the devil truly is a threat when he becomes incarnate, when children of the evil one appear in the earth garden. For many early Christians, the Roman emperor was a child of the evil one and zealous advocates of Roman civil religion were the grandchildren. The advocates of Roman civil religion sometimes infiltrated Christian congregations and informed on the members to state officials. That betrayal could cost those early Christians their reputations, their careers, their property, their freedom, and even their lives.

Christians in the Roman Empire thus lived with a well-founded fear of persecution for nearly 300 years, years in which their religion had no legal standing. Charges against them ranged from disloyalty to cannibalism: disloyalty because early Christians had given Jesus the title of "Lord," the same title that the Roman emperor claimed for himself; and cannibalism because Christians claimed to eat and drink the body and blood of the Lord Jesus.

I used the expression "civil religion." Just what is civil religion? It is religion that binds together people within a political entity. For instance, much of the Hebrew scripture was written when the religion of the Israelites was in many respects a civil religion — when God was referred to in terms of a particular political province, Israel. However, to conceive of God simply as the deity of your own tribal or national group is a very narrow way of thinking about God. And that way of thinking about God fails completely if the political entity is destroyed, as Israel was destroyed by the Babylonians some 600 years before the time of Jesus.

When many Israelites — including most of the leadership — were carried off into Babylonian exile, they made an unwelcome discovery. They discovered that the God of their civil religion had proved to be too small. They *could* have given up on God. They *could* have walked away from their religious heritage. Many did, but a remnant did not. Instead, that remnant took a courageous leap of faith that permitted them to begin to think about God in larger ways, in terms of a God of all peoples and even of the entire universe.

This is not an easy leap of faith to take: not for exiled Israelites; not for insecure Christians. When push came to shove, some early Christians chose Roman civil religion. Under pressure, they chose parochial and uncritical patriotism rather than catholic and critical Christianity. It's understandable, even if not commendable.

Push doesn't always come to shove; but if it does, you may have to make a similar choice. We have a lively civil religion in America. It is expressed on national holidays during Memorial Day and Veterans' Day ceremonies, practiced at scout meeting and service club opening rituals, voiced in the creed-like pledge of allegiance to the flag, and sensed at sacred sites such as the Tomb of the Unknown Soldier. It becomes especially evident and influential during times of national crisis, when presidents ask for our prayers and for divine providence. American civil religion also has a presence in Christian congregations, symbolized by the American flag standing in many church sanctuaries and by the patriotic songs printed in most American hymnals.

Though modern American civil religion differs from ancient Roman civil religion in important ways, there have been some hauntingly similar scenarios — such as an FBI agent infiltrating a Presbyterian congregation in Tucson, Arizona, and informing on the membership during the 1980s. Those Christians gave sanctuary to Central American refugees who were fleeing from roving death squads and bloody civil conflicts in their homelands. "Giving sanctuary to these people is an illegal and unpatriotic act," our government said. "Stop it." "Giving sanctuary to them is a moral imperative," replied the Arizona Presbyterians. "We won't stop." And so yet another confrontation between state and church was joined. In this case, push did come to shove; a dozen church members were arrested, charged, tried, and convicted.[4]

This episode may sound like an occasion for a witch-hunt, a call to identify and then exclude persons of divided loyalty and questionable faith from the Christian community. However, the second major point of our text is exactly the opposite: witch hunts and weed removals are *not* God's intention for the people of God's kingdom. In truth, if this text and sermon have a central theme or need a title, it is this: God does not pull weeds.

God does not pull weeds. That can be very frustrating. The Christian community surely would be a more pleasant place to live and grow if only God would pull out the weeds of hypocritical or compromising or otherwise objectionable people. But God doesn't: God does not pull weeds.

It gets worse; *we* are not authorized to pull weeds, either. Apparently we will have weed-like people in our midst until the end of time. And we are told to tolerate it. This is *not* a comforting image. It is the image of an uncultivated field that, while it may have a certain natural beauty — weeds, after all, often display some magnificent blooms — this natural beauty comes at a very high price of efficiency and productivity.

God does not pull weeds. And in the community of faith, God asks us not to pull weeds. I'm not at all sure that, as a city-dweller, I can fully appreciate what a powerful attack on common sense, life experience, and economic well-being those statements would represent to a farmer. Yet it appears that, in the church at any rate, there is no technique of cultivation or technology of weed killing that is not also a deadly threat to the faithful. Therefore, there should be no more attempts to weed out undesirables by witch hunt or inquisition; no more cutting down by insult or innuendo; no more exclusion based on prejudice or suspicion.

We can and should debate about behaviors. Some acts should be commended, others questioned, and still others contested. Ethics is a legitimate and necessary endeavor, a way of thinking critically about both personal and social conduct. Christians need to do ethics.

In addition, we can and should discriminate among beliefs. Some beliefs stand up to critical examination and to the tests of time, tradition, and — most crucially — biblical witness. Others do not. Thus theology is also a legitimate and necessary undertaking. Christians need to do theology.

But we cannot — as Martin Luther understood in his time and we should in our own — we cannot judge the heart, the inner being, the validity of another person's faith in God. This brings a profound and for some a troubling dimension to the idea of inclusivity in the church. The church is to be an open and inviting community — not gated; not a private club for the acceptably pious, the sufficiently orthodox, and the suitably heterosexual.

Conclusion

God does not pull weeds. God calls us to lay aside our preference for the security of a safe and sanitized environment. Instead, God summons us to accept the risk of faith lived out in a more dangerous and toxic environment where sin and evil are present. They *are* present, even in the church; however, they will not prevail. We are invited to have that hope and to take courage from it. Some lines from a familiar hymn sum it up well:

> This is my Father's world;
> oh let me not forget
> that, though the wrong
> seems oft so strong,
> God is the ruler yet.[5]

God rules, but God does not coerce or compel. God does not pull weeds. Nor should we — not in the community called family and not in the community of faith called church. A slightly altered version of the poet Robert Frost's definition of home serves, I think, as a good description of family: family is the place where, if you go there, they have to take you in. This should hold true not only for human families but also for God's family, the church. We must say to the world — the *whole* world — that if you show up, we'll take you in. And we must mean it. At the end of the day, judgment is God's business and not ours. Therefore, no litmus tests of color or ethnicity or political correctness or sexual orientation allowed, because they never get to the heart of the matter. The heart of the matter is the gospel, the good news of God's outrageously costly and generous love; the great news of our Lord Jesus' indiscriminately wide and deep and embracing love for all: the whole of the universe, the whole of humanity, the whole — warts and all — of you and me.

Let us pray:

Come down, O love divine. Seek thou this soul of mine and visit it with thine own ardor glowing. Let me not waste my time and energy pulling weeds, but rather help me to focus my time and energy on sharing the water and all of the other resources of life. Implant in me a life-shaping and vocation-motivating hope for a more loving church and a more just society. And in the end, let me be remembered not for what I feared or condemned or excluded, but for whom I embraced and affirmed and loved. Come down, O love divine. Seek thou this soul of mine and visit it with thine own ardor glowing. Amen.

Response: Worry

Kim Wilkens

I'm a recovering worrywart. I used to worry about everything. My worst worries were about either contracting a deadly disease or being a victim of a violent crime. So maybe I was also a hypochondriac who watched too many murder mysteries. However, if anyone deserves to worry, it seems to me that women have a long list of possibilities to consider. The violence and degradation committed against women in the world is shocking. One of Amnesty International's campaigns this year is "Stop Violence Against Women."[6] Of course, I'm very lucky because I live in the United States where I have legal rights and opportunity for education and employment, but some days when I read another statistic or hear another example of abuse against women, hope dies for me.

I don't think losing hope or worrying is the reaction God is looking for toward the evil in the world. If God does not pull weeds, then apparently we're stuck with evil and I think it's much closer to home than we'd like to admit. In Mark 7:15, Jesus said, "Listen to me, all of you, and understand: There is nothing outside a person that by going in can defile, but the things that come out are what defile." He was addressing Jewish critics who saw him and his disciples eating "unclean" food. I think Jesus was also reminding us that evil resides in us, that it is part of our make-up. We cannot blame outside influences for the existence of this evil. What outside influences can do is make it very hard for us to overcome our resident evil. Outside influences give us plenty of opportunity to feel justified in our evil intentions, where we can hide them under the guise of retribution, security, or righteous indignation.

But what can we do to keep this evil in check? Frankly, not much without God's help. We have been given a path to follow in Jesus and his life. We have been given words of wisdom to consider. It requires a tremendous attitude adjustment from the expectations of society. Instead of being encouraged to live in a "don't worry, be happy" world, we're instructed, "Do not fret" (Psalm 37:8). That seems like a weak response to evil, but I think it means that we shouldn't let the evil, out in the world, feed our resident evil or it will lead to our undoing.

Look up worry in the dictionary and you'll find this definition: "to torment oneself with or suffer from disturbing thoughts."[7] Maybe we can't pull the weeds, but we women can surely stop tormenting ourselves and act instead. Jean Shinoda Bolen, author of *Urgent Message from Mother*, sums up this action in her subtitle: *Gather the Women, Save the World.*[8] This was the same call in the original Mother's Day Proclamation.

> Arise then ... women of this day! Arise, all women who have hearts! Whether your baptism be of water or of tears! Say firmly: "We will not have questions answered by irrelevant agencies, our husbands will not come to us, reeking with carnage, for caresses and applause. Our sons shall not be taken from us to unlearn all that we have been able to teach them of charity, mercy, and patience. We, the women of one country, will be too tender of those of another country to allow our sons to be trained to injure theirs."
> — Julia Ward Howe, Boston, 1870

There are actions that need to be taken that are rooted in speaking truth to power. Many are outlined in *Urgent Message from Mother* in what the author calls antidotes to the "poison of patriarchy."[9] Some days you are going to feel overwhelmed, nothing you do will seem to help and you won't be able to find a sister for comfort. When I feel like this, I often turn to music to help me move past the hopelessness and worry. One of my favorite songs that provides the balm I need in this situation is "Come to Jesus"[10] by Mindy Smith.

Chapter Endnotes

1. See the background essay in ch. 20.
2. A homily presented initially on the 9th Sunday after Pentecost, 1993, at Faith Lutheran Church, Seguin, Texas. Redacted and presented subsequently on the 9th Sunday after Pentecost, 2005, at Christ Lutheran Church, Georgetown, Texas.
3. See Norman Beck, *Anti-Roman Cryptograms in the New Testament: Symbolic Messages of Hope and Liberation, op. cit.* See also *Scripture Notes, Series A*, (CSS Publishing, 1983).
4. The sanctuary movement in the US is experiencing a resurgence today, this time largely with respect to illegal immigrants from Mexico.
5. "This Is My Father's World" words by Maltbie D. Babcock, 1858-1901. Lyrics in the public domain.
6. For more information see the website www.amnestyusa.org/stopviolence.
7. Worry. Dictionary.com. *Dictionary.com Unabridged (v 1.1)*. Random House, Inc.
8. Jean Shinoda Bolen, *Urgent Message From Mother: Gather the Women, Save the World* (Conari Press, 2005).
9. *Ibid.*, 100.
10. Mindy Smith, "Come to Jesus: One Moment More" (Vanguard Records, 2004).

CHAPTER 29

TO ERR IS HUMAN,
TO FORGIVE DIVINE

Background essay

Tom Wilkens

Kim and I have focused on some of the countercultural themes in Christianity. In a sense, my whole life has been countercultural. While many in my generation have been traveling from left to right politically and theologically, my journey has been from right to left. I began life in a solidly conservative Republican family soon to reside in a solidly Republican state — though at a time, it should be noted, when the term conservative did not so typically signify mean-spirited or self-serving. I come toward life's close as a liberal Democrat, actually uncomfortable with my own party's recent tentativeness about the liberal agenda and causes. I began life in a context of Christian fundamentalism, though not nearly as shrill and hostile as today's version. I come toward its close as a theological liberal, with some tendencies in the direction of more revolutionary thinking.

It has been a fascinating journey, a fascinating life. I could never have anticipated the script I have been living; I surely could never have written it in advance. And the journey continues: a visit to the Baltic countries, with teaching English as a foreign language in a Lithuanian summer language institute as its centerpiece. And a service mission to Honduras with Kim that included an interesting role reversal: I was her assistant as she upgraded the computer technology in a school and a church office in Tegucigalpa, the capital city.[1]

It has also been a life punctuated by forgiveness — forgiveness liberally mediated to me by family and friends, and by people across the globe. I am very human; I have often erred. I do not sin less as a liberal, though I may sin differently. Yet I have experienced the divine at work, again and again, through the forbearance and acceptance people have shown me. And of course, this places upon me an even stronger obligation to forgive and forget the slights and sins of others.

Recently there was a sobering reminder as to just how committed some people are to a lifestyle grounded in forgiveness. It came from the schoolhouse at Nickel Mines, Pennsylvania. Can one even imagine the Amish anguish at the murder of those schoolchildren? Yet, as a newspaper columnist so graphically put it, before the blood was even dry on the schoolhouse floor, the Amish community sent words of forgiveness to the family of the shooter. Say what you will about other facets of the Amish way of life, they have incorporated the very core of the Christian way into their way: forgive and forget. I am shamed into silence before this astonishing living model of divine discipleship.

I have received many interesting comments in response to the following homily, preached on several occasions in several locations. The comments have ranged from "I am going to spend this afternoon mending some personal fences and relationships" to "I had not realized the social and even political significance of forgiveness." Those are the kinds of remarks that sustain preachers, that pull us back into the pulpit with renewed enthusiasm for sharing a message that we hope will be helpful. If you are active in a parish or synagogue, I encourage you to give similar feedback to your pastor, priest, or rabbi. Go beyond the perfunctory "I enjoyed your sermon" or "Nice job this morning." Share a remark with some specificity, with a pointed indication of how the homily spoke to you. On the other hand, do not hesitate to indicate disagreement, to argue for a different point of view or interpretation. We preachers need that sort of feedback also.

To err is human, to forgive divine
or
Holy housekeeping, Batman!
Do I really need to clean out my grudges?[2]

Tom Wilkens

The title of this sermon — To err is human, to forgive divine — comes from a work penned by Alexander Pope, an eighteenth century English Enlightenment poet, essayist, and critic. It is somewhat ironic that he should have written these words because often he was himself a bitterly quarrelsome and unforgiving man. Nonetheless, his theology was right on: humans do err; humans who forgive do exhibit a divine quality. Alexander Pope was Roman Catholic at a time when Catholics were being harshly persecuted in England. There was much to forgive.

Pope was no mere child of the Enlightenment; he was one of its co-creators. This champion of human reason was also a champion of the poor, the ever-present and always vulnerable poor — especially the extremely destitute whose poverty was dehumanizing. I sometimes wonder why it is that critical rationalists so often "get it" about the need to be aggressive public advocates for the poor at home and abroad while uncritical religionists so often don't get it. But that's another story.

This morning I want us to consider two verses from the gospel of Matthew:

> Then Peter came and said to him, "Lord, if another member of the church sins against me, how often should I forgive? As many as seven times?" Jesus said to him, "Not seven times, but, I tell you, seventy-seven times." — Matthew 18:21-22

In the Hebraic tradition, the number seven symbolized completeness. The number 77 in this text clearly indicated no end, no limit to the obligation to forgive. Are we looking at an implausible dream and an impossible moral obligation? Or are we dealing with one of the most important bases for human community, from the spheres of family and neighborhood to the realms of nation and global village? I think, or at least I hope, that it is the latter.

Now in Matthew's gospel, our brief text is followed by the familiar parable of the unforgiving servant. However, I want to look at our text in light of what comes before, especially Matthew 18:15-17. Jesus was speaking:

> "If another member of the church sins against you, go and point out the fault when the two of you are alone. If the member listens to you, you have regained that one. But if you are not listened to, take one or two others along with you, so that every word may be confirmed by the evidence of two or three witnesses. If the member refuses to listen to them, tell it to the church; and if the offender refuses to listen even to the church, let such a one be to you as a Gentile and a tax collector."

I used to think that this passage dealt with discipline in the church that would occasionally lead to the sad necessity of excluding people from the fellowship. I no longer think this is the case. In Jesus' own ministry, Gentiles and tax collectors — stereotypical outsiders and wrongdoers — were not objects of contempt and separation but subjects of love and inclusion. Offenders may well be candidates for the sanctions of law and other embodiments of morality, but they are not candidates for exclusion from the body of Christ and from the proclamation of the gospel. Rather, they are nominees for more intensive gospel activity and for more extensive forgiveness once the word of God elicits a confession of sin.

What does forgiveness have to do with the local communities to which we belong: communities such as neighborhood or city; such as workplace or school; such as service club or congregation? Forgiveness is a lubricant for relationships within those communities, allowing them to function without generating destructive heat and distracting noise. To use another metaphor, forgiveness enriches the communal soil in which people can flourish.

Forgiveness is also a requirement for national communities and for the global community. South Africa, for example, has been trying a new approach to nationhood. Rather than cleansing the country of its former white oppressors, the non-whites — at the instigation of leaders such as Desmond Tutu and Nelson Mandela — have been promoting forgiveness through a countrywide commission for reconciliation. The new leadership believed that apart from forgiveness there can be no community and thus, ultimately, no nation. There is, I suspect, a lesson here for us.

of the printed word has caused us to believe we can be far more objective and rational creatures than we really are.

George Lakoff, Professor of Cognitive Science and Linguistics at UC Berkeley and author of *The Political Mind* said some amazing things about how the brain works in an interview with Diane Rehm: things like; "people mostly think their thoughts are conscious, however 98% are unconscious" and "we think reason is dispassionate, however reason requires emotion."[6]

So, it seems to me that once we open up a Bible and read from it, we've already gone beyond it because we've brought our unconscious thoughts and passion to it. Does this make the Bible irrelevant? I don't think so. I agree with Marcus Borg "to be Christian is to be centered in the God of the Bible. This is not a mark of Christian exclusion, but of Christian identity."[7] He goes on to say that "the point is not to believe in the Bible — but to see our lives with God through it."[8] We live these lives in community and so it is with our community of faith that we pray, listen, learn, study, teach, struggle, admonish, encourage, and try to live our lives in God's way. This way has been recorded for us in the Bible by our predecessors and continues to be lived out, beyond the Bible in Christian lives today. The medium is the message and we, the people, are the medium for God's message.

Chapter Endnotes

1. See ch. 6.
2. A homily presented at Christ Lutheran Church, Georgetown, Texas, on June 3, 2007.
3. For further reading see Nathan P. Frambach's *Emerging Ministry: Being Church Today* (Augsburg Fortress, 2007). Frambach is Associate Professor of Youth, Culture, and Mission at Wartburg Theological Seminary in Dubuque, Iowa. Another excellent work is Marcus Borg's *The Heart of Christianity: Recovering a Life of Faith, op. cit.* Borg is Hundere Distinguished Professor of Religion and Culture at Oregon State University. A former Lutheran, now an Episcopalian, he is one of the most widely read Christian authors of our time. He uses the term "emerging" in a broader theological and historical sense than Kim and I do, but much of what he says is both consistent with and an elaboration of some of the issues and ideas about which we have been writing.
4. Shane Hipps, *The Hidden Power of Electronic Culture* (Zondervan, 2006), 39.
5. *Ibid.*, 53.
6. The Diane Rehm Show, Monday June 2, 2008; George Lakoff, *The Political Mind* (Penguin Group USA, 2008).
7. Marcus Borg, *op. cit.*, 43.
8. *Ibid.*, 57.

AFTERWORD

Kim has asked for respect for her journey of faith with a more loving church that will listen to the ways she expresses her faith. We are all challenged to offer the type of community in our churches that encourages honest dialogue and acceptance of the person with unconditional love. Allowing for differences in how we perceive faith will open ways of being transformed into what it means to be a Christian in the here and now. The community of faith can be about building relationships, nurturing discipleship, and taking risks. Asking better questions might be a better path in growing faith than relying on answers that have served the past but not the present and future. Questions help us move from what others believe to what I believe. God does provide answers in many powerful ways as we more fully serve the needs of others. The epiphanies, assurances that God is with us, can come in the least expected places as Tom so often realized when he was with the poor in the developing world.

May the reading of this book be a blessing to you in your faith journey. If you would like to be in contact with Kim on her blog, where she develops strategy for ministry and keeps in touch with others in the Emerging Church movement, go online at:

kimxtom.blogspot.com

You may contact Tom by this e-mail address in order to continue the dialogue with him:

tomwilkens@suddenlink.net

Betty Wilkens